The
Canine Hiker's Bible

DOUG GELBERT

illustrations by
ANDREW CHESWORTH

Cruden Bay Books

MONTCHANIN, DELAWARE

There's always a new trail to look forward to...

THE CANINE HIKER'S BIBLE

Cruden Bay Books
PO Box 467
Montchanin, DE 19710

International Standard Book Number   0-9644427-5-2

Manufactured in the United States of America

Table of Contents

PREPARING TO GO   **7**
 HIKING WITH YOUR DOG   8
 OUTFITTING YOUR DOG FOR A HIKE   9
 ON THE ROAD WITH YOUR DOG   11

ON THE TRAIL   **13**
 A CANINE HIKER'S WATCH LIST   14
 OTHER ANIMALS ON THE TRAIL   15
 CANINE HIKING IN THE DESERT   17
 CANINE HIKING AT ALTITUDE   19
 LOW IMPACT HIKING WITH YOUR DOG   21
 THE CASE FOR LEASHES   22

**RULES FOR DOGS IN 100 OF THE MOST
POPULAR NATIONAL PARK SERVICE LANDS**   **25**

**RULES FOR DOGS ON STATE PARK
AND PROVINCIAL PARK LANDS**   **35**

DESTINATIONS   **41**
 ATLANTIC CANADA   42
 NEW ENGLAND   48
 MIDDLE ATLANTIC   63
 SOUTH   74
 MID-SOUTH   81
 MIDWEST   89
 ROCKY MOUNTAINS   102
 SOUTHWEST   111
 SIERRAS   118
 PACIFIC COAST   127

EXPLORING HISTORY WITH YOUR DOG   **137**

TAKING YOUR DOG TO THE BIG CITY   **149**

FIVE TOWNS YOUR DOG WILL LOVE   **185**

YOUR DOG AT THE BEACH   **193**
 DOGS ON ATLANTIC OCEAN BEACHES   194
 DOGS ON GULF OF MEXICO BEACHES   218
 DOGS ON PACIFIC OCEAN BEACHES   223
 DOGS ON GREAT LAKES BEACHES   237

INDEX   **251**

Hiking With Your Dog

So you want to start hiking with your dog? Hiking with your dog alongside can be a fascinating way to explore the outdoors from a canine perspective. These are some things to consider before you start:

🐾 Dog's Health

Hiking can be a wonderful preventative for any number of physical and behavioral disorders. One in every three dogs is overweight and running up trails and leaping through streams is great exercise to help keep pounds off. Hiking can also relieve boredom in a dog's routine and calm dogs prone to destructive habits. And best of all, hiking with your dog strengthens the overall owner/dog bond.

🐾 Breed of Dog

All dogs enjoy the new scents and sights of a trail. But some dogs are better suited to hiking than others. If you don't as yet have a hiking companion, select a breed that matches your interests. Do you look forward to an entire afternoon's hiking? You'll need a dog bred to keep up with such a pace, such as a retriever or a spaniel. Is a half-hour enough walking for you? It may not be for an energetic dog like a border collie. If you already have a hiking friend, tailor your plans to his abilities.

🐾 Conditioning

Just like humans, dogs need to be acclimated to the task at hand. An inactive dog cannot be expected to bounce from the easy chair in the den to complete a 3-hour hike. You must also be physically able to restrain your dog if confronted with distractions on the trail (like a scampering squirrel or a pack of joggers). Have your dog checked by a veterinarian before significantly increasing your dog's activity level.

"Dogs are our link to paradise...to sit with a dog on a hillside on a glorious afternoon is to be back in Eden, where doing nothing was not boring - it was peace."
- Milan Kundera

Outfitting Your Dog For A Hike

The basics for taking your dog on a hike:

▶ **Collar**.　　It should not be so loose as to come off but you should be able to slide your flat hand under the collar.

▶ **Identification Tags**.　　Get one with your veterinarian's phone number on it as well.

▶ **Bandanna**.　　Can help distinguish him from game in hunting season.

▶ **Leash**.　　Leather lasts forever but if there's water in your future, consider quick-drying nylon.

▶ **Water**.　　Carry 8 ounces for every hour of hiking.

🐾　*I want my dog to help carry water, snacks and other supplies on the trail. Where do I start?*

To select an appropriate dog pack. Measure your dog's girth around the rib cage to determine the best pack size. A dog pack should fit securely without hindering the dog's ability to walk normally.

🐾　*Will my dog wear a pack?*

Wearing a dog pack is no more obtrusive than wearing a collar, although some dogs will take to a pack easier than others. Introduce the pack by draping a towel over your dog's back in the house and then having your dog wear an empty pack on short walks. Progressively add some crumpled newspaper and then bits of clothing. Fill the pack with treats and reward your dog from the stash. Soon your dog will associate the dog pack with an outdoor adventure and will eagerly look forward to wearing it.

How much weight can I put into a dog pack?

Many dog packs are sold by weight recommendations. A healthy, well-conditioned dog can comfortably carry 25% to 33% of its body weight. Breeds prone to back problems or hip dysplasia should not wear dog packs. Consult your veterinarian before stuffing the pouches with gear.

How does a dog wear a pack?

The pack, typically with cargo pouches on either side, should ride as close to the shoulders as possible without limiting movement. The straps that hold the dog pack in place should be situated where they will not cause chafing.

What are good things to put in a dog pack?

Low density items such as food and poop bags are good choices. Ice cold bottles of water can cool your dog down on hot days. Don't put anything in a dog pack that can break. Dogs will bang the pack on rocks and trees as they wiggle through tight spots in the trail. Dogs also like to lie down in creeks and other wet spots so seal items in plastic bags. A good use for dog packs on day hikes is trail maintenance - your dog can pack out trash left by inconsiderate visitors before you.

Are dog booties a good idea?

Dog booties can be an asset, especially for the occasional canine hiker whose paw pads have not become toughened. Many of the trails involve rocky terrain. In some places, broken glass abounds. Hiking boots for dogs are designed to prevent pads from cracking while trotting across rough surfaces. Used in winter, dog booties provide warmth and keep ice balls from forming between toe pads when hiking through snow.

What should a doggie first aid kit include?

Even when taking short hikes it is a good idea to have some basics available for emergencies:

- 4" square gauze pads
- cling type bandaging tapes
- topical wound disinfectant cream
- tweezers
- petroleum jelly
- veterinarian's phone number

On The Road With Your Dog
by Robyn Peters
Owner & Publisher, DOGGONE NEWSLETTER

Before you get on the trail, you need to get to the trail...

🐾 Preparing the dog's duffel
- *Record of vaccinations*   (often required by kennels and campgrounds)
- *Poop bags*
- *Comb and brush*   (helps keep dog's coat clean and remove burrs)
- *Towel and shampoo*
- *Blanket and favorite toy that smells like home*
- *Zip-lock bags*   (they come in handy for lots of things)

🐾 Food nibbles to take along (for car and trail)
- *Raw nuts and seeds*
- *Bits of firm fruits (apples, pears) and vegetables (carrots, celery)*
- *Unsalted, unbuttered popcorn*

🐾 Border Crossings
Always, always, always check with both the United States Customs Department and the Customs Departments of Canada and Mexico to find out up-to-date restrictions and requirements regarding pets. These change frequently. Generally speaking, to travel across the US/Canadian border, doggie papers documenting shot records are the only requirements. For Mexico, check with the area where you plan to cross. There can be differences with each Custom's gate. Papers will be required though.

"What counts is not necessarily the size of the dog in the fight but the size of fight in the dog."
- Dwight D. Eisenhower

❧   Car sickness

Signs of motion sickness can include vomiting or excessive drooling. Before resorting to medication, try cracking a window for circulating fresh air. Add a small amount of Gatorade to your dog's water. Carry a small piece of powdered ginger for those dogs that get carsick. Put the ginger on your finger and stick it in your dog's mouth and rub it on his lips. It is an old anti-nausea snake-oil treatment and astronauts have used it for motion sickness.

What appears to be chronic motion sickness may only be anxiety. Before embarking on a long trip with a dog not used to the car, take short pleasure trips to the pet store or park. Teach your dog that rides in the car are FUN!

*Not all dogs are cool and calm characters
when riding in a car.*

Robyn Peters resides in Boulder, Colorado on the side of a mountain. In addition to publishing the DOGGONE NEWSLETTER, a 16-page bimonthly publication about fun places to go and cool things to do with your dog, she is the author of HAVE DOG, WILL TRAVEL, a handy little reference guide containing everything you need to know while traveling with your pooch. You can find Robyn on the Web at www.doggonefun.com.

On The Trail...

A Canine Hiker's Watch List

🐾   Weather

Hot humid summers do not do dogs any favors. With no sweat glands and only panting available to disperse body heat, dogs are much more susceptible to heat stroke than we are. Unusually rapid panting and/or a bright red tongue are signs of heat exhaustion in your pet. Always carry enough water for your hike. Even days that don't seem too warm can cause discomfort in dark-coated dogs if the sun is shining brightly. In cold weather, short-coated breeds may require additional attention, or even a hike-hardy coat.

🐾   Trail Hazards

There are many types of grass seeds and plant seeds that attach to animal fur for a ride as part of their seed dispersal mechanism. Some of these can be very hazardous to your dog if they go up a nose, grab on to the hair between the toes and work their way into a leg. Be sure to thoroughly check your dog after a hike for these seeds and burrs. Dogs won't get poison ivy but they can transfer it to you. Stinging nettle is a nuisance plant that lurks on the side of many trails and the slightest brush will deliver troublesome needles into a dog's coat. Some trails are littered with small pieces of broken glass that can slice a dog's paws. Nasty thorns can also blanket trails that we in shoes may never notice.

🐾   Old Mine Shafts

In the West, the public lands are often peppered with abandoned mines. Dogs have fallen down uncovered shafts, many of which are not marked, so be careful when straying from established recreation areas.

🐾   Water

Surface water, including fast-flowing streams, is likely to be infested with a microscopic protozoa called *Giardia*, waiting to wreak havoc on your dog's intestinal system. The most common symptom is potentially crippling diarrhea. Algae, pollutants and contaminants can all be in streams, ponds and puddles. If possible, carry fresh water for your dog on the trail - your dog can even learn to drink happily from a squirt bottle.

Other Animals On The Trail

🐾   Black Bears

Black bears inhabit wooded mountains across the continent. Although black bears rarely attack people, they demand your respect, especially since bears do not like dogs. There are things to do to reduce your chances of encountering a bear on the trail. Among these are to avoid food sources such as berry patches and carcass remains. Also hike in groups; go slowly, especially on downhills and around blind corners; make noise occasionally (not by wearing useless "bear bells" sold to tourists - the annoying tinkling of these little bells carries little distance and is rarely heard except by passing hikers) and STAY ALERT!

Should you see a black bear on the trail, keep your dog leashed closely and give the bear plenty of room to move on. If you cannot avoid an encounter, do not run. A bear can outrun you and running from a black bear may stimulate its instinct to chase. Stand and face the animal, establishing eye contact without staring. If a black bear approaches, speak quietly and walk backwards. Unfortunately, black bear behavior is quite variable. Should a bear become aggressive, try to demonstrate that you are a danger to it. Make yourself appear larger, raise your arms, make noise and, if necessary, throw rocks and branches. Less common, less predictable and far more dangerous are grizzly bears. These animals are cinnamon-colored, although black bears can also be similarly hued, and found mostly in the northern Rocky Mountains. Again, your best tactic for dealing with a grizzly bear is avoidance - bang a stick loudly on a rock every now and then to alert bears you are in the area.

🐾   Big Cats

Mountain lions, cougars and other big cats are extremely shy and are rarely seen by canine hikers. Mountain lions are fearful of humans but dogs don't frighten them. Still, they might view smaller dogs as prey - one more reason to always keep your dog close on the trail. They are nocturnal animals but if you see one, maintain eye contact, try to make loud noises and attempt to make yourself appear as large as possible.

❧   Rattlesnakes

Rattlesnakes are found in every state in America, not just the rocky desert. Timber rattlers predominate in the east and the vipers in the Midwest are most likely to be the Prairie Rattlesnake, found at elevations under 5000 feet. It is not a particularly aggressive animal but you should treat any rattlesnake with respect and keep your distance. A rattler's colors may vary but they are recognized by the namesake rattle on the tail and a diamond-shaped head. Unless cornered or teased by humans, a rattlesnake will crawl away and avoid striking. Avoid placing your hand in rocky areas and crevasses and hiking in areas where the ground cover (weed or grass) prevents you from seeing the ground. These are all places where snakes are are likely to hang out. If you hear a nearby rattle, stop immediately and hold your dog back. Identify where the snake is and slowly back away. If you or your dog is bitten, do not panic but get to a hospital or veterinarian with as little physical movement as possible. In many cases the rattlesnake might give "dry bites" where no poison is injected, but you should always check with a doctor after a bite even if you feel fine. Keep in mind that snakes fill an important function in the ecosystem; without them we would drown in mice and other rodents, so there is no reason to harm them. If you anticipate hiking extensively in remote areas there are professional snake-avoidance trainers who can train your dog or horse to stay away from rattlenakes.

❧   Porcupines

Porcupines are easy for a curious dog to catch and that makes them among the most dangerous animals you may meet because an embedded quill is not only painful but can cause infection if not properly removed.

❧   Ticks

All ticks are nasty but the deer tick - no bigger than a pin head - carries with it the spectre of lyme disease. Lyme disease attacks a dog's joints and makes walking painful. The tick needs to be embedded in the skin to transmit lyme disease. It takes 4-6 hours for a tick to become embedded and another 24-48 hours to transmit lyme disease bacteria. When hiking, walk in the middle of trails away from tall grass and bushes. If your walk includes fields, consider long sleeves and long pants tucked into high socks. Wear a hat - ticks like hair. By checking your dog - and yourself - thoroughly after each hike you can help avoid lyme disease. Ticks tend to congregate on your dog's ears, between the toes and around the neck and head.

Canine Hiking In The Desert

by Jessica Powers
Author, A BARK IN THE PARK: THE 45 BEST PLACES TO HIKE WITH YOUR DOG
IN THE EL PASO-LAS CRUCES REGION

Canine hiking in the American southwest means hiking in a desert environment. If you are unused to hiking in general, or used to hiking in mountainous regions or cool climates, you can easily find yourself in trouble unless you heed some simple common-sense precautions.

❧   Avoid hiking in June or July

The optimum hiking period is August through May. If you must hike in June and July, stick to the early morning or evening. Daytime heat is blistering, and it is dangerous to be out in direct sun exercising for long hours. Even if *you* can stand the heat, chances are your dog can not. Although desert heat is dry, most of these hikes provide few, if any, trees for shade and little or no water for swimming or drinking. Hiking in this kind of heat may not only give your dog heat stroke, but she may burn the pads on her paws on the hot sand or scorching cement-like dirt.

❧   Bring plenty of water, no matter how cold it seems when you set out

The desert is dry, dry, dry, and it is unlikely you will encounter water anywhere along your route. A good rule is to carry one gallon of water for every hour you plan to hike. It is always better in the desert to bring more water than you need. If you have a big dog who drinks more than his share, get him a pack so he can carry his own water.

❧   Be prepared for varying temperatures

The desert is an land of extremes. In the winter, the temperature can dip well below freezing at night, even reaching single-digit temperatures, and then climb to 60 or 70 degrees Farenheit during the day. Summer temperatures can drop to 50 degrees at night, seeming quite cool, and then reach over 100 degrees during the day.

❧   Wear sunscreen and a hat

Always, always.

🐾   **Avoid arroyos, ditches, and washes when it is raining**

Flash floods occur in the desert after significant rainfall. Water cascades down from the mountains; arroyos that have been dry for years can fill to the brim within seconds. Though flash floods are rare, they occur without warning. *Please take this caution seriously.* Hiking in arroyos is perfectly safe when it is not raining, but forego canine hiking plans if it is, especially if you see thunderclouds and rain in nearby mountain ranges. Every year a sad story shows up in the news in the Southwest of people who have died in a flash flood. Desert areas receive less than 10 inches of rainfall annually, most of it falling during the month of August, when the yearly monsoons hit.

🐾   **Keep an eye out for scorpions, centipedes and black widow spiders**

Some folks will be scared of hiking in the desert with a dog because they are afraid of venomous snakes and insects. In all my years of desert hiking the only snakes, scorpions, or spiders I ever encountered were in my own backyard.

🐾   **Hunting minerals or removing plant species from federally owned land or state parks is prohibited**

Although cacti may seem prolific out in the desert, many species are endangered, and thus, protected in their natural environment. Do not remove them. The penalties can be rightly severe if you are caught.

The desert can be tough going for a dog.

Canine Hiking At Altitude

Some of the most rewarding hikes with your dog will be in the mountains. Oft times you can reach a memorable destination with an elevation gain of less than 1,000 feet, other times a hike will take you on an ascent of more than 3,000 feet (about the equivalent of climbing the Empire State Building three times). Either way, plan ahead for canine hiking in the hills...

Learn to pace youself

There is a truism in hiking that you get tired going up the mountain, but you get hurt going down. In other words, don't go so fast going up that you will be exhausted and don't go so fast coming down that you will fall. The descent is also hard on your knees and a walking stick can help relieve the pressure on your legs on the mountain slopes.

Pay attention to the effects of altitude

Regardless of your physical condition, it is common to begin feeling the effects of low air pressure at altitude at about 10,000 feet; even lower for other hikers. As you take in less and less oxygen you can begin to feel nausea, dizziness, headaches or heart palpitations. Never go higher should you encounter any of these symptoms. Take a rest and if the symptoms go away, continue on. If they persist for more than a few minutes, turn back. You are most at risk for altitude sickness if you climb too quickly.

Rest often

A mountain climb is not a race and not a place for pride. Rest often - for both you and your dog. And resting is not just an option on the way up.

Drink plenty of water, before and during your climb

Always have plenty of drinking water on hand for you and your dog. Climbing burns alot of calories and you will work up quite a sweat, even as the temperature drops. Proper hydration also lessens your chances of suffering altitude sickness.

🐾   Be careful of mountain streams

The water in rushing mountain streams is often ice cold and after a quick swim your dog is likely to emerge into cold air. Pack a towel for your dog on mountain hikes to keep your dog dry.

🐾   Protect yourself from the sun

Above the treeline the rays of the sun intensify on a mountaintop. Take along the sunscreen even if the temperatures are bone-chilling. Sunglasses will not only help with the bright sunshine but also with snowblindness.

🐾   A word about canine hiking in canyons

For canine hikers, remember that canyons are simply mountains in reverse. The big difference obviously is that you *finish* with the climb, when you may already be tired from the hike to the canyon floor.

Dogs sometimes dream of hiking up mountains just like we do.

Low Impact Hiking With Your Dog

Every time you hike with your dog on the trail you are an ambassador for all dog owners. Some people you meet won't believe in your right to take a dog on the trail. Be friendly to all and make the best impression you can by practicing low impact hiking with your dog:

- Pack out everything you pack in.

- Do not leave dog scat on the trail; if you haven't brought plastic bags for poop removal bury it away from the trail and topical water sources.

- Hike only where dogs are allowed.

- Stay on the trail.

- Do not allow your dog to chase wildlife.

- Step off the trail and wait with your dog while horses and other hikers pass.

- Do not allow your dog to bark - people are enjoying the trail for serenity.

- Have as much fun on your hike as your dog does.

"The greatest pleasure of a dog is that you may make a fool of yourself with him, and not only will he not scold you, but will make a fool of himself too."
- Samuel Butler

The Case For Leashes
by Dave Musikoff
CALIFORNIA CANINE HIKERS

If you have done any amount of hiking with a dog (or dogs), you have surely been aware of the occasional dirty look from other trail-users, if not direct negative comments concerning your furry friend. The sad fact is that we who choose to hike with dogs have a very serious image problem — one that we had better solve ourselves before it gets solved for us.

As a life-long dog-lover, I used to find this anti-dog attitude impossible to understand. But in talking to other trail-users over the past few years, and seeing first-hand some of the problems that dogs can cause, I have come to the conclusion that this hostility has its roots primarily in the fact that so many canine hikers turn their dogs loose the moment they get on the trail.

Unfortunately, loose dogs have been known to chase wildlife (and sometimes catch it, with disastrous results to one or both parties), trip other hikers, spook horses and pack-animals, frighten children, and, all too often, get into fights with other dogs. Loose dogs routinely get injured in a variety of ways, and, more often than many people would care to admit, they get lost — sometimes permanently.

The obvious and simple answer to all of this is to keep our dogs leashed. A leashed dog cannot harass humans or other animals because he is attached to his human and has to go pretty much where you go. He is far less likely, therefore, to become lost or injured, and he is less likely to eat something that will make him sick, or to lift his leg on a fellow hiker's trousers or steal a sandwich at lunchtime. Being leashed, other trail-users can see ahead of time that our dogs do not present a danger to them or to their children or dogs.

"But," you say, "my dog is very well-behaved and friendly, and he always comes right back when I call him!" Great! Good for you! But, can you honestly say, with absolute, 100% certainty, what your dog would do if her or she was loose and was suddenly confronted at close range by a skunk or a deer or a rattlesnake?

How about a bear? What about a string of pack-mules or twenty or thirty screeching, running cub scouts? What if a nearby hunter fired his gun? How does your dog react to thunder? Besides, how are other trail-users supposed to know that your dog is friendly? Take your word for it?

In Perfect World we could turn our dogs loose all the time, to run and romp and chase. No rules, no restrictions of any kind. They'd love it! But like it or not we live in a world of limitations, restrictions, and compromises, and we all need to do whatever we can reasonably do to make sure that our dogs are not seen by others as an annoyance or a danger (real or imagined). We bear the responsibility for their safety and for making sure they behave whenever we take them out in public.

Nobody is suggesting you have to use a standard six-foot leash; there are long leads, used for tracking and obedience training, that come in lengths from ten to twenty feet. These, as well as the German-made "Flexi-leads," which are spring-loaded and can extend from eight to about 25 feet, are ideal for hiking, and offer the dog more freedom to romp and explore while giving the owner instant control when it is required. These items should be available in any well-equipped pet shop or from mail-order catalogs.

Hiking with a dog is a privilege. Our dogs have absolutely no inherent "right" to be on a trail or anywhere else, and if we want to continue to be able to hike in the company of dogs, we must act more responsibly. Otherwise, the dreaded "No Dogs Allowed" signs we see all too often will continue to spread. It is already done in far too many places, and the trend is continuing. This hasn't come about because the authorities are dog haters. It is because dog owners have not acted responsibly and have allowed their dogs to be seen as a bother and a danger to others.

Who knows; maybe if we all strive to keep our dogs under control and show others that dogs can be good citizens on the trail, they will eventually be welcome in more places, and on more organized outings, rather than fewer.

Rules for Dogs in 100 of the Most Popular National Park Service Lands...

1. *Blue Ridge Parkway*   (21,646,864 visits in 2002)
Dogs are allowed on most trails and in all 9 campgrounds.

2. *Golden Gate National Recreation Area*   (13,806,766)
Dogs are welcome on most of the nearly two dozen parcels of Federal land. No dogs are permitted in Tennessee Valley, China Beach, Muir Woods, Alcatraz and the Phleger Estate.

3. *Great Smoky Mountains National Park* (9,215,806)
Dogs are prohibited from all park trails except the 2-mile trail from Park Headquarters to Gatlinburg and the 2-mile trail between Cherokee and the Oconaluftee Visitor Center. Dogs are allowed in the picnic areas and campgrounds.

4. *Gateway National Recreation Area*   (8,955,609)
At Sandy Hook dogs are allowed on the beach from Labor Day to March 15 and throughout other areas of the park at any time; no dogs are allowed on Jacob Riis Park from Memorial Day weekend through Labor Day weekend and no dogs are allowed at the Breezy Point Tip from March 15 through August.

5. *Lake Mead National Recreation Area*   (7,627,906)
Dogs are allowed on trails but not on the beaches.

6. *Delaware Water Gap National Recreation Area*   (5,248,958)
Dogs are welcome on trails and most locations within the recreation area. No dogs are allowed at Milford Beach, Hidden Lake Beach, Smithfield Beach or on the mowed areas at Kittatinny Point Visitor Center, Bushkill Visitor Center, Watergate Recreation Site or Hialeah Picnic Area.

7. *Gulf Islands National Seashore*   (4,572,364)
Dogs are not permitted on the beaches or in the picnic pavilions.

8. *Cape Cod National Seashore*   (4,431,059)
Dogs are prohibited from nature trails, shorebird nesting areas and all lifeguard-protected beaches. In addition to non-protected beaches, canine hikers can use seashore fire roads and the West and Sunset horse trails in the Province Lands. Dogs are welcome at the seashore fresh water ponds from October 16 through May 14.

9. *Grand Canyon National Park*   (3,936,823)
Dogs are allowed on trails throughout developed areas of the South Rim but never below the rim. On the North Rim, dogs are allowed only on the bridle trails that connects the lodge with the North Kaibab Trail.

10. *Olympic National Park*   (3,654,022)
Dogs are not permitted on park trails or meadows. Dogs are not allowed on any beaches except Rialto Beach north to Ellen Creek and on the Kalaloch beach strip between the Hoh and Quinault Indian reservation. Dogs are allowed in the campgrounds.

11. *Cape Hatteras National Seashore*   *(3,651,066)*

Dogs are allowed throughout the park except on designated swimming beaches.

12. *Chesapeake & Ohio Canal National Historical Park*   *(3,477,090)*

Dogs are allowed along the towpath and on most trails. No dogs are permitted on the boardwalk trails on the Olmsted Island Bridges and on the Billy Goat "A" Trail around Bear Island.

13. *Colonial National Historical Park*   *(3,320,873)*

Dogs are allowed to walk the battlefield at Yorktown and play on the beach at Cape Henry.

14. *Yosemite National Park*   *(3,305,631)*

Dogs are not allowed on any park trail or in any picnic area. Dogs are permitted anywhere on the Yosemite Valley floor between the Happy Isles Nature Center or Mirror Lake parking lot and the Pohona bridge. Dogs are not permitted on any slope above the Valley floor. Several campgrounds allow dogs.

15. *Cuyahoga Valley National Park*   *(3,191,359)*

Dogs are allowed on all park lands.

16. *Rocky Mountain National Park*   *(3,005,524)*

Dogs are not allowed on any park trail. Dogs are allowed in parking areas, picnic areas and campgrounds.

17. *Yellowstone National Park*   *(2,969,868)*

Dogs are not allowed on trails or boardwalks. Dogs are permitted within 100 feet of roads, parking areas and campgrounds.

18. *Chattahoochee River National Recreation Area*   *(2,712,783)*

Dogs are permitted across park lands.

19. *Grand Teton National Park*   *(2,606,492)*

Dogs are not allowed on park trails; dogs can walk on roads and road shoulders, parking lots, picnic areas and campgrounds.

20. *Acadia National Park*   *(2,550,586)*

Dogs are allowed everywhere in the park except Sand Beach, Echo Lake Beach, the Isle au Haut campground and the "ladder" trails.

21. *Zion National Park*   *(2,510,627)*

Dogs are allowed on only one trail: the Pa'rus Trail. Dogs are allowed in campgrounds and along roadways.

22. Point Reyes National Seashore   (2,254,465)

Dogs are not permitted on trails or in campgrounds. Dogs are allowed on the south end of Limantour Beach, Point Reyes Beach North and Point Reyes Beach South.

23. Mount Rushmore National Memorial   (2,159,189)

Dogs are not allowed anywhere in the park except in the pet exercise area at the end of the upper parking ramp

24. Glen Canyon National Recreation Area   (2,127,265)

Dogs are allowed in the park.

25. Assateague Island National Seashore   (2,107,032)

In Maryland, dogs are allowed on the beach and in campgrounds, but not on the trails. In Virginia, dogs are not allowed in the park - even in a car.

26. Rock Creek Park   (2,099,504)

Dogs are allowed on trails throughout the park

27. Mammoth Cave National Park   (1,898,817)

Dogs are allowed on the above-ground trails in the park.

28. Glacier National Park   (1,864,822)

Dogs are not allowed on park trails but can stay in drive-in campgrounds and visit picnic areas.

29. Indiana Dunes National Lakeshore   (1,834,435)

Dogs are allowed on most park trails.

30. Gettysburg National Military Park   (1,829,790)

Dogs are permitted outside park buildings.

31. Chickasaw National Recreation Area   (1,511,522)

Dogs are allowed on park trails except on paths leading into the Environmental Study Area (east of the Travertine Nature Center).

32. Hot Springs National Park   (1,438,043)

Dogs are allowed on the trails and other areas outside buildings in the park.

33. Sequoia & Kings Canyon National Park   (1,418,512)

Dogs are not allowed on park trails; dogs can visit the picnic areas and campgrounds.

34. Mount Rainier National Park   (1,267,044)

Dogs are allowed on no trails except a small portion of the Pacific Crest Trail near the park's eastern boundary.

35. *Valley Forge National Historical Park*   *(1,190,893)*
Dogs are allowed on all park trails.

36. *Sleeping Bear Dunes National Lakeshore*   *(1,190,748)*
Dogs are allowed on most park trails but cannot make the Dune Climb. Dogs are not allowed on North or South Manitou Island.

37. *Joshua Tree National Park*   *(1,174,142)*
Dogs are not allowed on the trails but can be in the campgrounds.

38. *Vicksburg National Military Park*   *(1,067,130)*
Dogs are allowed in the park.

39. *Lake Meredith National Recreation Area*   *(1,043,380)*
Dogs are permitted throughout the park.

40. *Canaveral National Seashore*   *(1,042,090)*
Dogs are not allowed on the beach or beyond the parking lots.

41. *Amistad National Recreation Area*   *(952,096)*
Dogs are allowed on trails and in most areas of the park.

42. *Everglades National Park*   *(940,482)*
Dogs are allowed in parking lots and campgrounds but not on trails.

43. *Cumberland Gap National Historical Park*   *(928,596)*
Dogs are allowed on park trails.

44. *Badlands National Park*   *(906,868)*
Dogs are allowed only in developed areas such as campgrounds, parking areas and along roads - not on any trails.

45. *Big South Fork National Recreation Area*   *(901,419)*
Dogs are allowed on most park trails.

46. *Bryce National Park*   *(899,408)*
Dogs are not allowed on park trails; dogs can visit the picnic areas and campgrounds.

47. *Curecanti National Recreation Area*   *(892,408)*
Dogs are allowed on the trails.

48. *Chickamauga & Chattanooga National Military Park*   *(845,037)*
Dogs are allowed in the park.

49. Manassas National Battlefield   (790,086)
Dogs are allowed throughout the park.

50. Fire Island National Seashore   (779,241)
Dogs are prohibited from swimming beaches and other posted areas.

51. Canyon de Chelly National Monument   (764,186)
Dogs are allowed on overlook trails but not below the rim.

52. Arches National Park   (761,861)
Dogs are not allowed on any hiking trails but are permitted in campgrounds.

53. Guilford Courthouse National Military Park   (757,267)
Dogs are allowed on park trails.

54. Whiskeytown National Recreation Area   (704,747)
Dogs are allowed on most park trails.

55. Wind Cave National Park   (696,402)
Two trails allow dogs within the park: the Elk Mountain Nature Trail takes off around the campground and the Prairie Valley Trail near the Visitor Center.

56. Cape Lookout National Seashore   (643,507)
Dogs are permitted in the park year-round.

57. Saguaro National Park   (642,457)
Dogs are not allowed on unpaved trails.

58. Petrified Forest National Park   (575,650)
Dogs are not allowed on unpaved trails in the park.

59. Cedar Breaks National Monument   (558,454)
Dogs are not allowed on park trails.

60. Padre Island National Seashore   (534,484)
Dogs are allowed anywhere except on the deck at Malaquite Beach and in front of the Visitor Center at the swimming beach.

61. Capitol Reef National Park   (516,379)
Dogs are not allowed on any park trails.

62. White Sands National Monument   (509,480)
Dogs are allowed on trails throughout the park.

63. Carlsbad Caverns National Park   (472,670)
Dogs are not permitted on park trails above or below ground.

64. Theodore Roosevelt National Park   (471,210)
Dogs are prohibited on all park trails.

65. Santa Monica Mountains National Recreation Area   (468,977)
Dogs are allowed on many park trails; dogs are not permitted on trails that run into state park land.

66. Fredericksburg & Spotsylvania National Military Park   (455,826)
Dogs are not allowed in most areas of the park.

67. Crater Lake National Park   (455,648)
Dogs are not allowed on park trails but are permitted in the picnic areas.

68. Catoctin Mountain Park   (453,302)
Dogs are allowed on park trails.

69. Pictured Rocks National Lakeshore   (428,390)
Dogs are welcome in designated developed areas and on most primary front country trails but not in the backcountry or selected posted lakeshore trails.

70. Little Bighorn Battlefield National Memorial   (418,755)
Dogs are allowed to explore the park.

71. Mesa Verde National Park   (411,399)
Dogs are not allowed on park trails.

72. Devil's Tower National Monument   (407,688)
Dogs are not allowed on park trails.

73. Redwoods National Park   (398,973)
Dogs are not allowed on any trails but are allowed at Crescent and Gold Bluffs beaches. Dogs are permitted in picnic areas, campgrounds and at the Freshwater Lagoon Spit.

74. North Cascades National Park   (390,277)
Dogs are not allowed on park trails.

75. Lassen Volcanic National Park   (387,480)
Dogs are not allowed on park trails.

76. Morristown National Historical Park   (384,303)
Dogs are permitted to hike on park trails.

77. Canyonlands National Park *(366,861)*

Dogs are banned from all trails.

78. Big Bend National Park *(322,329)*

Dogs are not allowed on trails, off roads, or on the Rio Grande River. Dogs can stay in campgrounds.

79. Antietam National Battlefield *(313,201)*

Dogs are not allowed on trails across the park.

80. Harpers Ferry National Historical Park *(310,489)*

Dogs are allowed on park trails in Maryland, Virginia and West Virginia.

81. Bandelier National Monument *(300,760)*

Dogs are not allowed on park trails but can stay in campgrounds.

82. Dinosaur National Monument *(299,622)*

Dogs are allowed on most of the park trails.

83. Organ Pipe Cactus National Monument *(295,080)*

Dogs are allowed on two trails: the Palo Verde Trail and the Campground Perimeter Trail. Dogs are allowed in the campground.

84. San Juan Island National Historical Park *(276,018)*

Dogs are allowed on park trails and mutt mitts are provided at trailheads.

85. Kings Mountain National Military Park *(265,673)*

Dogs are allowed on park trails.

86. Fort Donelson National Battlefield *(237,063)*

Dogs are allowed on park trails.

87. Great Sand Dunes National Monument *(235,535)*

Dogs are welcome outdoors anywhere in the park.

88. Voyageurs National Park *(233,825)*

Dogs are not allowed on any park trails but can stay in campgrounds on the four main lakes. Dogs can also visit picnic areas and boat launch ramps.

89. Guadalupe Mountains National Park *(216,095)*

Dogs are allowed only on the trail between the campground and the Visitor Center and the Pinery Trail at the Visitor Center. Dogs are also permitted in the campgrounds.

90. Cowpens National Battlefield   (213,629)
Dogs are allowed on park trails.

91. Craters of the Moon National Memorial   (182,789)
Dogs are not allowed off the pavement onto trails.

92. Petersburg National Battlefield   (176,311)
Dogs are allowed throughout the park.

93. Black Canyon of the Gunnison National Park   (174,346)
Dogs are allowed on overlook trails, some of which are nearly a mile, but are not permitted below the rim. Dogs are also prohibited from the Warner Nature Trail.

94. Apostle Islands National Lakeshore   (172,871)
Dogs are allowed on the islands.

95. Pinnacles National Monument   (165,011)
Dogs are allowed only on roads and in parking and picnic areas.

96. Saratoga National Historical Park   (148,490)
Dogs are permitted on trails throughout the park.

97. Jewel Cave National Monument   (131,481)
Dogs are allowed on above-ground trails in the park.

98. Lava Beds National Monument   (114,418)
Dogs are not allowed in the wilderness area.

99. Scotts Bluff National Monument (113,885)
Dogs are allowed on park trails.

100. Congaree Swamp National Monument   (110, 182)
Dogs are allowed to hike in the park but not on any boardwalk trails.

101 Shenandoah NP — (ok) EXCEPT for Fox Hollow, Stony Man, Limberlost, Old Rag Ridge, Old Rag Saddle, Dark Hollow falls, Story of the Forest, Bearfence Mtn, Frazier Discovery

"Happiness is dog-shaped."
- Chapman Pincher

Permits required for
Weakly Hollow
Whiteoak Canyon
Little Devil Stairs

Rules for Dogs on State Park and Provincial Park Lands...

Alabama

Dogs are allowed on most state park trails and campgrounds.

Alaska

Dogs are subject to restrictions in some state parks.

Arizona

Dogs are welcome in Arizona state parks but at Red Rock State Park pets are not allowed outside vehicles and pets are not allowed on the trails at Tonto Natural Bridge State Park.

Arkansas

Dogs are allowed on state park trails.

California

Assume dogs are not allowed on state park trails unless otherwise indicated.

Colorado

Dogs are permitted on Colorado state park trails except in Mueller State Park, Navajo State Park and Roxborough State Park.

Connecticut

Dogs are not permitted at Sherwood Island, Dinosaur State Park or Squantz Pond State Park. Dogs are not allowed in Connecticut state park campgrounds.

Delaware

Dogs are allowed on state park trails.

Florida

Dogs are excluded from the following places in Florida state parks: food service areas; designated camping areas; cabins; bathing and swimming areas including land and water portions; park buildings; playgrounds and other designated areas. Some parks permit dogs in campgrounds and proof of rabies vaccination will be required.

Georgia

Dogs are welcome at Georgia state parks and campgrounds; however, they are not allowed in or around historical sites, cottages, lodges, group camps, swimming areas or on Panela Mountain's trails.

Hawaii

Dogs are allowed on Hawaii state park trails unless specifically posted; dogs are not allowed on state beaches or in state campgrounds.

Idaho

Dogs are allowed on Idaho state park trails but not in beach areas or at Eagle Island and Harriman state parks and at Sandy Point Beach in Lucky Peak State Park.

Illinois
Dogs are welcome in Illinois state parks except in campground cabins.

Indiana
Dogs are allowed on Indiana state park trails and in campgrounds.

Iowa
Dogs are allowed on Iowa state park trails.

Kansas
Dogs are allowed on Kansas state park trails.

Kentucky
Dogs are allowed on Kentucky state park trails.

Louisiana
Dogs are allowed on Louisiana state park trails.

Maine
No dogs are allowed on state beaches or in the Sebago Lake State Park campground. Otherwise, dogs can hike Maine state park trails except in Baxter State Park, where they are strictly forbidden.

Maryland
Several of Maryland state parks restrict dogs to certain trails. The following parks do not allow dogs at all: Assateague, Calvert Cliffs, Cunningham Falls (except in the wildlands area), Fort Frederick, Greenbrier, Merkle Wildlife Sanctuary, the beach and trails at Point Lookout, Sandy Point, Smallwood and Swallow Falls (from Memorial Day to Labor Day).

Massachusetts
Dogs are not permitted in Walden Pond State Reservation or Boston Harbor Islands State Park and are restricted at Moore State Park, Plum Island State Reservation (from April 1 to October 1) and Sandy Point State Reservation.

Michigan
Dogs are allowed on most Michigan state park trails.

Minnesota
Dogs are welcome in Minnesota state parks when personally attended at all times.

Mississippi
Dogs are allowed on Mississippi state park trails.

Missouri
Dogs are allowed on Missouri state park trails.

Montana

Dogs are not allowed in Spring Meadow State Park or Wild Horse Island State Park.

Nebraska

Dogs are allowed on Nebraska state park trails.

Nevada

Dogs are allowed on Nevada state park trails.

New Hampshire

Dogs are not allowed in many New Hampshire state parks, restricted in others and never on state beaches.

New Jersey

Dogs are allowed on New Jersey state park trails but not in campgrounds.

New Mexico

Dogs are permitted in all New Mexico state parks except Living Desert State Park and Rio Grande Nature Center State Park.

New York

Dogs are not allowed in buildings, bathing areas, campgrounds, picnic areas and cross-country trails in New York state parks. Dogs are not allowed in the following state parks: Bayswater Point, Bethpage, Caleb Smith Preserve, Caumsett Historic Park, Clay Pits Pond Preserve, Connetquot River, High Tor, Jones Beach, Lake Taghkanic, Nisseqouque River, Orient Beach, Riverbank, Rockland Lake (May 1 to September 30), Watkins Glen (on the Gorge Trail), Wildwood, and Woodlawn (in summer).

North Carolina

Dogs are allowed on North Carolina state park trails.

North Dakota

Dogs are allowed on North Dakota state park trails.

Ohio

Dogs are allowed on Ohio state park trails but some parks charge a $1 pet fee.

Oklahoma

Dogs are allowed on Oklahoma state park trails.

Oregon

Dogs are allowed on Oregon state park trails.

Pennsylvania

Dogs are allowed on Pennsylvania state park trails.

Rhode Island

Dogs are allowed on Rhode Island state park trails but not in campgrounds.

South Carolina

Dogs are allowed on South Carolina state park trails.

South Dakota

Dogs are allowed on South Dakota state park trails.

Tennessee

Dogs are allowed on Tennessee state park trails.

Texas

Dogs are permitted on most Texas state park trails but check for specific park restrictions. Dogs are not allowed on trails or campgrounds in Big Bend Ranch State Park.

Utah

Dogs are allowed in all Utah state parks save the Rock Cliff Recreation Area at Jordanelle State Park.

Vermont

Dogs are allowed on Vermont state park trails but not on lake beaches or in any picnic area.

Virginia

Dogs are allowed on most Virginia state parks trails and in most campgrounds but not on any state beach.

Washington

Dogs are allowed on Washington state park trails.

West Virginia

Dogs are allowed on West Virginia state park trails.

Wisconsin

Several Wisconsin state parks are especially welcoming to dogs: Bong State Recreation Area main tains a dog training area. Chippewa Moraine State Recreation Area allows dogs off-leash except in the picnic area. Governor Dodge State Park has a pet swim area next to each swimming beach and designated pet picnic areas. Governor Nelson State Park has a pet beach. High Cliff State Park features two pet picnic areas. Kettle Moraine State Forest Northern Unit has pet picnic areas and training areas. Kohler-Andrae State Park has a dog beach. Lake Kegonsa State Park has a dog beach. Whitefish Dunes State Park allows dogs on the beach. Dogs are not permitted in Heritage Hill State Park, Copper Culture State Park and portions of Havenwoods StateForest.

Wyoming

Dogs are allowed on Wyoming state park trails.

CANADA

Alberta
Dogs are allowed on Alberta provincial park trails but not in swimming areas.

British Columbia
Dogs are not permitted on the trails in the following provincial parks: Cathedral and Garabaldi.

Labrador
Dogs are allowed on Labrador provincial park trails.

Manitoba
Dogs are allowed on Labrador provincial park trails unless posted otherwise.

New Brunswick
Dogs are allowed on most NewBrunswick provincial park trails.

Newfoundland
Dogs are allowed on Newfoundland provincial park trails.

Northwest Territories
Dogs are allowed on most Northwest Territories provincial park trails.

Nova Scotia
Dogs are allowed on Nova Scotia provincial park trails.

Ontario
Dogs are allowed on most Ontario provincial park trails.

Prince Edward Island
Dogs are allowed on Prince Edward Island provincial park trails.

Quebec
Dogs are not permitted in any Quebec provincial park.

Saskatchewan
Dogs are allowed on most Saskatchewan provincial park trails.

Yukon Territory
Dogs are allowed on Yukon Territory provincial park trails.

Destinations...

Maritime Provinces

Cape Breton Highlands National Park

The Park:

Stretching from coast-to-coast across the northern tip of Cape Breton Island, the national park embraces 366 square miles of highland wilderness and dramatic coastlines. Cape Breton Highlands is known for its scenic kinship with the coastal regions of Scotland. The Cabot Trail, one of the world's great driving roads, tickles the edges of the park from the eastern shore to the western sea and travels along the picturesque Margaree Valley in the south. When the Canadian government decided to establish the first national park in the Atlantic provinces, Cape Breton Highlands was a natural choice.

The Walks:

Canine hikers accustomed to the restrictive policies of American national parks will encounter a dog-friendly paradise at Cape Breton Highlands. Of the 26 marked and named hiking trails in the park only one, the *Skyline Trail*, is off-limits to dogs. (This trail, restricted due to heavy concentration of moose, is a flat two-mile walk to exposed headland cliffs and well-worth giving the dog a rest in the car in the normally cool weather). Some of the highlights include:

L'Acadien Trail. The marquee trail of the park's west side, the 6-mile loop climbs steadily beside the Robert Brook to an elevation over 1,000 feet to a windswept landscape of stunted trees and panoramic views of the Gulf of St. Lawrence coast to the west and the highlands to the east.

Bog. A chance to stop and experience the interior plateau of the park, this trail is a half-mile boardwalk around a nutrient-starved alpine bog where specialized plants, including several carniverous ones, have adapted to a hostile life.

Lone Shieling. This is a quiet half-mile descent into a 300-year old hardwood forest where more than 90% of the trees are vibrant sugar maples. Highlights include a replica of a Scottish sheep-crofter's hut and a rushing stream that makes an excellent doggie whirlpool.

Coastal. A short wooded hike leads to a generally deserted sandy beach for good Atlantic Ocean dog swimming (dogs are not allowed at the main swimming beach in Cape Breton Highlands National Park) and then heads along the coast for three miles. A good place to turn around on this linear trek is a large beach covered with smooth, egg-shaped cobbles.

Cape Breton Highlands National Park is home to the Highland Links, a masterpiece by legendary golf course designer Stanley Thompson. He called this 1939 creation his "mountains and ocean course" and is currently ranked the top golf course in Canada and the 69th top course in the world. Since it is in the national park, the same rules apply for the golf course as the hiking trails and your dog is welcome to join your foursome as you play.

Jack Pine. This 1.7-mile loop travels through a forest of pioneering jack pines that grow tenaciously on the hard rocky surface and pops out onto the rocky Atlantic coast with several dramatic blowholes at water's edge.

Franey. One of the star trails on Cape Breton, the Franey trail climbs 366 meters (almost 1200 feet) in 3 kilometers, ending on rocky summits with the best overlooks of the Atlantic Ocean, Middle Head and Ignonish Beach in the park. The descent is totally on an old access road and uninspiring in comparison to the climb.

Middle Head. An easy-walking 2.5-mile loop leads out into the Atlantic Ocean where spruce woodlands give way to grassy headlands. You'll get surf and mountain views on both sides of the loop.

Directions to Cape Breton Highlands National Park (Nova Scotia):

The park stretches from the Gulf of St. Lawrence on the west coast to the Atlantic Ocean on the east coast; entrances are along the Cabot Trail at Ignonish Beach (Atlantic) and Chéticamp (Gulf of St. Lawrence).

Phone: (902) 285-2273
Website: parkscanada.pch.gc.ca/pn-np/ns/cbreton/index_e.asp

Cape Chignecto Provincial Park

The Park:

Cape Chignecto juts like an arrowhead into the eastern side of the Bay of Fundy. Featuring sheer 600-foot cliffs and miles of broken shoreline, this wilderness has rarely been pierced by civilization. A lumbering community called Eatonville once supported 350 people here in the late 1800s but only traces of that settlement remain. Today, Cape Chignecto is Nova Scotia's largest provincial park and the only one operated by the local community.

The Walks:

Cape Chignecto Provincial Park is a canine hiker's paradise - save for a couple of picnic tables there are no other activities here. The centerpiece trail is the coastal footpath that travels west to Cape Chignecto from the Red Rocks Visitor Center and continues north along Chignecto Bay to Eatonville Harbor. Covering 30 miles through old growth forest, the cliff walks are broken at regular intervals by plunging ravines. A six-mile overland trail returns canine hikers to the starting point at Red Rocks.

For those unable to devote days to this spectacular clifftop trail, a variety of day hikes poke out from Red Rocks, ranging from a short stroll to the beach to steep 650-foot descents in canyons at McGahey Brook and Mill Brook. These trails are well-blazed by the local caretakers of the park. The waves for canine swimmers are particularly frisky on Advocate Bay beaches where the tides can rise at the rate of one foot per minute. Warning signs remind canine hikers to stay vigilant against being trapped against the cliffs.

Sidetrip: Cape Split (Route 358 west off Highway 1; the road deadends at the trailhead)

Across Advocate Bay from Cape Chignecto Provincial Park is Cape Split, a hook-shaped peninsula separating Minas Channel and the Bay of Fundy. From the trailhead at the end of the road at Scotts Cove this 5-mile walk on private land leads to the tip of the peninsula that has been ripped apart by the relentless tidal action in the bay. The hiking is easy, slightly uphill most of the way through dark, often wet woods, before emerging onto grassy, unprotected ledges high above the water. Careful navigation leads to the treacherous beach below.

Directions to Cape Chignecto Provincial Park (Nova Scotia):

The park is located in Advocate Harbor, Nova Scotia. Take Highway 2 to Route 209 West.

Phone: (902) 392-2085
Website: capechignecto.net/

Fundy National Park

The Park:

Fundy National Park was created to protect an 80-square mile swath of the Maritime Acadian Highlands. This is an area where the deep green forests of the Caledonia Highlands sweep across a rolling plateau to reach the highest tides in the world at the Bay of Fundy. You can watch the water level change as much as 40 feet between low and high tides.

The Walks:

Fundy National Park features 25 dog-friendly trails, most of which are quite sporty. The trails are broken out for canine hikers by the natural features they highlight: coastal trails, waterfall trails, river valleys, forest trails and lake trails. Only a handful are loop trails, although there are many combinations to be formed to create ambitious loops. The Fundy Circuit links seven hiking trails and covers 30 miles, including four campsites.

While the big attraction of Fundy is its great tides, most of the trails offer only sporadic views of the famous bay. Some of the best come on the *Matthews Head Trail*, a 4.5-kilometer loop that begins and ends in open meadow and in between dips into thick red spruce forests. Nearby is the eerie *Devil's Half Acre* loop. Its dark mossy crevasses, nooks and crannies are the park's best testament to the region's ultra-moist climate.

Away from the coast, fast-flowing streams have been busy cutting valleys and canyons through the plateau. Look for hardy climbs through hardwood and spruce forests here. Wooden steps have been added on several trails to help out. One, the *Dickson Falls Loop*, is completely built on boardwalk from the top of the falls into a valley cooled by cascading water.

Directions to Fundy National Park (New Brunswick:

The park is located in New Brunswick between Moncton and Saint John on Highway 114.
Phone: (506) 887-6000
Website: parkscanada.pch.gc.ca/pn-np/nb/fundy/index_E.asp

Several beaches are accessible from the trails to experience the phenomenal tides of the Bay of Fundy. The *Point Wolfe Beach Trail* is a short descent to a long beach (at low tide) where your dog can frolic in the receding (or oncoming) waves.

Kouchibouguac National Park

The Park:

The park was established in 1969 to protect a variety of distinct landscapes, mostly aquatic in nature. The park takes it name from the river native Mi'kmaqs called "river of long tides." Tidal water from the Northumberland Strait reaches several miles upstream through the flat woodlands. Kouchibouguac covers more than 90 square miles and features salt marshes, bogs and lagoons in addition to its rivers.

The Walks:

Hiking at Kouchibouguac takes place across ten mostly short (less than an hour) nature trails. Dogs are permitted on all trails save for the *Kellys Beach Boardwalk Trail*. For dogs itching to get a paw in the sand, take the *Osprey Trail* along the Kouchibouguac Lagoon or along the narrow Callanders Beach on the Saint Louis Lagoon. The walking is easy here and it is a simple matter to visit all the habitats in a single day; several of the nature trails feature self-guided interpretation stands. The longest hike in the park traces the journey of the Kouchibouguac River for its final seven miles before reaching the sea. Some of the best trails in the park are on water. Eight flat water rivers permeate the park's interior.

The *Alpine Bog Trail* leads to a 20-foot high

observation tower that is dog accessible. Do not allow your dog off the wooden boardwalk - moose and other animals have perished after being trapped in the mucky bog.

Sidetrip: Bouctouche Eco-Heritage Trail System (off Canada 11 in Bouctouche)

Here you can find ten miles of groomed paths through the town of Bouctouche and the Black and Bouctouche rivers. The trail begins at the Irving Eco-Centre, created to preserve a 7-mile

dune that stretches across the Bouctouche Bay. The dune is one of the few remaining sand dunes on the northeast coast of North America.

Directions to Kouchibouguac National Park (New Brunswick):

The park is located in New Brunswick on Highway 11 on the shores of the Northumberland Strait.

Phone: (435) 564-3633
Website: parkscanada.pch.gc.ca/pn-np/nb/kouchibouguac/index_E.asp

Prince Edward Island National Park

The Park:

Lucy Maud Montgomery introduced the world to the Cavendish region of Prince Edward Island in her much-beloved coming-of-age tale, *Anne of Green Gables*. Montgomery waxed rhapsodic over the Cavendish shoreline on the Gulf of St. Lawrence, calling the sandy beaches framed in red sandstone the prettiest in the world. Many visitors since the book's publication in 1908 have agreed with her.

Canada established Prince Edward Island National Park in 1937, preserving forever 25 miles of the island's north shore. In addition to protecting salt marshes, sandstone cliffs, dune-fringed beaches and Acadian woodlands, the park service oversees the original Green Gables House of Montgomery's childhood. She came here at the age of 21 months to live with her grandparents.

Further east, a separate section of the park was established on the western tip of Greenwich, a peninsula that separates St. Peters Bay from the Gulf of St. Lawrence. Here, a rare parabolic sand dune sweeps along the coast inundating forests and leaving blanched, skeletal remains in its wake.

The Walks:

There are 11 trails at Prince Edward Island National Park, ten of which welcome dogs. Dogs can also visit park beaches but must wait until the off-season starts on October 15. All of the hiking on these trails is easy going - the elevation in the park tops out at 160 feet.

The longest of the walks at PEI is *Homestead*, kicking off just outside the campground. It is a stacked loop of either 3.4 miles or 5 miles that plunges into woodlands before emerging on open

paths along New London Bay. Driving across the island the urge to stop the car and romp across the impossibly green fields will grow steadily and this trail will satiate that yearning.

Most of this land was cleared by 1900 for farms, stripping the original Acadian forest mix of hardwood and softwood species. Trails through the regenerating forests can be enjoyed in the Brackley section of the park. Also here is a quiet trip along the *Reeds and Rushes Trail* into the heart of a vibrant salt water marsh community. Dogs are barred from the main *Greenwich Dunes Trail* but you can get a brief feel of the power of the shifting sands in a parabolic dune on the adjacent *Tlagatik Loop*. Out in the warm waters of St. Peters Bay you can see the oyster lines of aquafarmers.

Sidetrip: Black Marsh Nature Trail (at very end of Route 12 on North Cape)

The *Black Marsh Nature Trail* moseys along the top of North America's longest natural rock reef, making ten interpretive stops, including a fragile sub-arctic bog. The route incorporates the North Cape Wind Farm, where eight gigantic windmills generate 3% of Prince Edward Island's energy. Offshore is the "meeting of the waters" as the waves of the Gulf of St. Lawrence break against the waters of the Northumberland Strait.

Directions to Prince Edward Island National Park (Prince Edward Island):

Along the northern side of Prince Edward Island, the segmented park can be reached from six entrances off of highways 6, 13, 15 and 25.

Phone: (902) 672-6350
Website: parkscanada.pch.gc.ca/pn-np/pe/pei-ipe/index_E.asp

Gaspe Peninsula

Forillon National Park

The Park:

Jacques Cartier sailed along the snakehead-shaped Gaspé Peninsula in 1534 to claim the territory for France. Named for the Mi'kmaq Indian word meaning "land's end," the Appalachian Mountains tumble into the sea in Forillon National Park on the peninsula's northeast tip.

The Walks:

Dogs are welcome on all nine trails across Forillon's 95 square miles. The marquee trail is *Les Graves Trail,* a linear route that can be accessed by car at several points along its 8.9 kilometers. It bounds along Gaspe Bay through light forests and meadows; drops onto sandy beach coves for canine swimming; and passes through Grande-Grove National Historic Site where the homestead of generations of fisherman-farmers is preserved. The trail also tracks through two historic cemeteries. Les Graves Trail then climbs into the thick forest and finishes up on the last steps of the *International Appalachian Trail* that ends (or begins) its 4,555-kilometer journey at the very tip of Cap-Gaspé. The *Mont-Saint Alban Trail* visits both sides of the peninsula in its 8.5-kilometer loop ("boucle" in French) and passes an 80-foot high observation tower. The tower, whose wide steps can be climbed by a dog, overlooks the Gulf of St. Lawrence with a 360-degree view. Although named for the waterfall traversed top and bottom by the trail boardwalk, *La Chute Trail* is actually worth a visit more for its maple forest than the tumbling waters.

Directions to Forillon National Park (Quebec):

The park is at the extreme northeastern end of the Gaspe Peninsula on Route 132 East.

Phone:　(418) 368-5505

Website:　parkscanada.pch.gc.ca/pn-np/qc/forillon/index_E.asp

At the very end of Les Graves Trail another trail leads downhill for a kilometer to a small observation deck where you can see the very end of the Appalachian Mountains as the world's oldest mountain range cascades beneath the sea. In the waters off-shore you and your dog can watch some of the seven species of whales that haunt the region and maybe spy a harbor seal on the rocks.

Most travelling in the Gaspé Peninsula is done around the edges with the lure of the mountainous interior offered by Gaspésie National Park. No dogs, however, are allowed in the park.

Percé

The Town:

With a natural sheltered harbor, Percé began life as a thriving port but when the cod played out the town was reborn after tourists came to enjoy the area's natural splendors. Just offshore are two of Canada's most recognizable natural landmarks: the île-Bonaventure, home to a colony of 70,000 gannets and puffins, and the 288-foot high Percé Rock. You can walk to the rock at low tide but dogs aren't allowed on the beach so you'll have to make the short walk alone.

The Walks:

Percé is squeezed against the shore by the mountains and many trails climb to such attractions as the Grotto and the Crevasse. The most popular trail ascends 900-foot Mont St. Anne. The trek begins on a steep mountain road before branching off to a footpath with stunning overlooks of the town and six visible capes jutting into the sea. Interpretive signs describe the cultural and natural history of Percé along the way. Prominent throughout the walks are views of Île Bonaventure and Percé Rock.

Directions to Percé (Quebec):

The town is on Route 132 on the eastern tip of the peninsula.

Phone: (418) 782-5448
Website: None

Sugarloaf Provincial Park

The Park:

Sugarloaf is a year-round activity center on 2718 acres at the foot of the Gaspé Peninsula. The namesake gumdrop-shaped mountain is hard for canine hikers to resist as it comes into view and indeed the observation deck on the 925-foot summit provides seductive views of the rolling Gaspé hills in the distance.

The Walks:

Much of the 4-kilometer *Terry Fox Trail* to the top of Sugarloaf Mountain is easy hiking on a graded snowmobile trail around the mountain. The summit trail is short and steep and calls for the dog to negotiate boulders and an unusual metal ladder with a metal screen that may take some getting used to. The 360-degree view at the top includes the Restigouche River, Chaleor Bay and the backyards of Campellton below. A small reservoir at the trailhead is an ideal spot for a mountain-climbing dog to cool off.

At the campground is a detailed interpretive canine hike that identifies over 30 indigenous plants. There are also another 20 kilometers of multi-use trails at Sugarloaf that cut across ski slopes, through deep woods and around delightful Prichard Lake.

Directions to Sugarloaf Provincial Park (New Brunswick):

The park is in Campbellton on Highway 11. Take the exit marked Campbellton & Sugarloaf Park and continue off the exit going south on the Val D`Amour Road.

Phone: (435) 564-3633
Website: www.tourismnewbrunswick.ca/Cultures/en-CA/Products/ Attraction/04496792-F6F2-4602-BDDB-2FEEED484DBA.htm

"The best thing about a man is his dog."
- French proverb

Rocky Coast of Maine

Acadia National Park

The Park:

Samuel Champlain led a French expedition that landed here on September 5, 1604. In claiming the land for France, Champlain, noting the bare, rocky mountain humps, called his discovery "Isles des Monts Desert." Settlement came slowly to Mount Desert Island as the British and French bickered over ownership. Eventually, the British assumed control and the island became a farming and fishing and lumbering center. The wealthy barons of the Gilded Age began summering on Mount Desert Island and the Rockefellers, Astors, Fords, and Vanderbilts all built lavish estates. One of the wealthy elite, George B. Dorr, devoted 43 years and much of his family fortune to preserving the island. He offered more than 6,000 acres to the federal government and in 1916, Woodrow Wilson established the Sieur de Monts National Mounment. Three years later Lafayette National Park became the first national park east of the Mississippi River. Honoring its Acadian heritage, the park became Acadia National Park in 1929.

The Walks:

Acadia National Park is certainly one of the crown jewels in the National Park Service and dogs will not bark in dissent - this is the best national park to bring your dog for hiking. Except for the swimming beaches and ladder hiking trails like the *Precipice Trail*, dogs are allowed throughout the park.

Many of the more than 120 miles of hiking trails on and around more than a dozen small mountain peaks were blazed by early American Indians and subsequent European settlers. Still others were financed by wealthy benefactors from

Bubble Rock near the summit of South Bubble Mountain - to the north are views of Eagle Lake, around the corner are overlooks of Jordan Pond.

a master trail plan for the island that began in 1891.

Several park highlights come via easy canine hiking. The *Jordan Pond Nature Trail* is a mile-long loop leading to views of glacial mountains reflecting in the pond waters. The rounded mountains, known as the Bubbles, can be climbed on short trails. Other easy hikes include the *Ocean Trail* to Otter Cliffs that clings to the edge of lands' end over the Atlantic surf and exploratory walks atop Cadillac Mountain. The 1530-foot summit is the highest point on the Atlantic Ocean north of Rio de Janeiro, Brazil and sunrise hikes here will be the first to be illuminated in America.

The *Great Head Trail* loops across Sand Beach and most people go right at the head of the loop. But going left into the maritime forest saves the spectacular coastal views from one of America's highest headlands until the end. All these trails are easily accessed from the Park Loop Road and can get busy. Seek out trails across Somes Sound - America's only fjord - in the western reaches of the park to find fewer paw prints.

Sidetrip: Bar Harbor Shore Path (Town Pier in Bar Harbor)

Squeezed between the park and the Atlantic Ocean is the town of Bar Harbor, the hub of Mount Desert Island. In the 1800s wealthy vacationers began claiming homesites on the water but private landowners have provided a sliver of land for the public to enjoy the *Shore Path* for over 100 years. The curvilinear gravel path, starting at the Town Pier, is absolutely level and ideal for strolling. When the waves are gentle there are numerous spots for your dog to drop down and play in the tidal pools of the waters of Frenchman Bay.

Directions to Acadia National Park (Maine):

Take I-95 north to Bangor, Maine; from Bangor take Route 1A east to Ellsworth; from Ellsworth take Route 3 to Mount Desert Island.

Phone: (207) 288-3338
Website: www.nps.gov/acad/index.htm

> 🚫 *On Mount Desert Island save the dog paddling for the Atlantic Ocean - many of the freshwater lakes are used for the public water supply. One good place to let your dog swim is in the sheltered waters at Otter Cove.*

John D. Rockefeller, Jr. was no great fan of the horseless carriage. While on vacation he enjoyed outings on his horses and to travel around Mount Desert Island he directed the building of wide, motor-free carriage roads around the mountains. Forty-five miles of rustic broken stone roads were eventually built between 1913 and 1940 and the hand-built byways are the best examples of the construction technique still in use in America. In addition to the stone roads and stone guardrails, irregularly spaced granite slabs known locally as "Rockefeller's Teeth," there are 16 stone-faced bridges - each unique in design.

Camden Hills State Park

The Park:

The National Park Service purchased land on the shores of West Penobscott Bay in the 1930s and oversaw creation of a park destined for the state of Maine. Noted local landscape architect Hans Heistad did much of the design work for the park which now encompasses 5,700 acres, including ten named mountain peaks.

The Walks:

Twenty short trails - most less than 2 miles - run up and across the seaside slopes of central Maine. All allow dogs. The premier hike is a one-mile climb up Mount Megnticook, the highest mainland mountain on the Atlantic coast. Of the paths to 1300-foot Ocean Lookout, the *Megunticook Trail* is the one to take for its ex-

tended ocean views on the return route down the *Tablelands Trail*. Tablelands connects to Mt. Battie, that can also be reached by a popular auto road that makes for a crowded summit on busy days. The 360-degree view from the stone tower on Mt. Battie includes Megunticook Lake and the town of Camden, where the *Peyton Place* television series was filmed. All told the 30-mile trail system visits all ten named peaks in the park.

Directions to Camden Hills State Park (Maine):

The park straddles US 1 north of the town of Camden.

Phone: (207) 236-3109
Website: www.state.me.us/cgi-bin/doc/parks/
          find_one_name.pl?park_id=14

Quoddy Head State Park

The Park:

Perched on 80-foot black rock cliffs, Quoddy Head State Park is the easternmost point of land in the United States. The dark rock was forced up from below the ocean floor as hot liquid magma over millions of years. The softer surrounding rock has eroded away leaving the magma, known as gabbro. The State of Maine purchased the 532 acres of peninsula in 1962 to develop the park.

The Walks:

Some of the best canine hiking directly on the rocky Maine Coast is found at Quoddy Head. The *Coastal Trail* dips up and down along the clifftops for two miles before dropping to water level at Carrying Place Cove where your dog can play in the shallow waters. Your dog will love this rollercoaster walk at land's end; eagerly bounding to the top of the many hillocks to see

what awaits on the other side. The return trip can be made over the inland *Thompson Trail* through light forests of shallow-rooted white spruce and hardy balsam trees battling the wind and salt spray. Many of these arboreal warriors remain standing after losing the fight, leaving spectral sculptures along the coast. A side trip leads to the Carrying Place Cove Bog, a National Natural Landmark. This subarctic remnant is home to plants that survive in low temperatures and thin, non-nurturing soil. Here carniverous plants such as the sundew and pitcher plants gobble insects for nutrients unavailable in the soil.

Directions to Quoddy Head (Maine):

From US 1, take Route 189 towards Lubec and follow signs on South Lubec Road to the park.

Phone: (207) 733-0911
Website: www.state.me.us/cgi-bin/doc/parks/
          find_one_name.pl?park_id=10

West Quoddy Head Light, built in 1808 as America's easternmost lighthouse, still guides ships through the Grand Manan Channel with its original Fresnel lens. The moist climate around Quoddy Head is frequently foggy and the lighthouse was one of the first to employ a fog bell that was eventually replaced with a steam-powered foghorn. The lawn around the squat, red-and-white striped lighthouse is ideal for relaxing with your dog and look for whales in the channel.

New Hampshire's White Mountains

Crawford Notch State Park

The Park:

The Crawford family settled in this magnificent mountain pass in 1790 and two years later Abel Crawford and his son Ethan opened the Notch House, ushering in the hotel era in the White Mountains. In 1825 Samuel Willey brought his family to the notch to operate an inn on a farmstead along the Saco River. The next year, after watching a ferocious landslide in the mountains, Willey built a cave-like shelter for his family of seven to escape to in the event of another slide. He didn't have long to wait. On August 26, 1826 an epic storm shook the White Mountains, raising the river 20 feet and loosening thousands of tons of rock and debris. Rescuers found the house unscathed - apparently because it had been built beneath a ledge - but the family perished seeking safe ground. Today Crawford Notch State Park retains a family feel with many of the trail signs being hand-painted on boards.

The Walks:

Canine hikers come to Crawford Notch not to scale majestic peaks but to look at them. Some of the best views of the Presidential Range and Mount Washington can be had from Mt. Willard, an outcropping at 2,804 feet reached from a gradually rising 1.4-mile trail. Similar rewards await on the *Arethusa Falls/Frankenstein Cliffs Trail.* The exposed outcroppings offer sweeping views down the notch to the south and east. The trail completes a four-mile loop by visiting New Hampshire's highest waterfall - the 200-foot feathery plunge of the Arethusa River. The trail is rocky and rooty and can be slow going at times. Short, easy walks can be taken around the Saco River at the site of the former Willey Farmstead.

Directions to Crawford Notch State Park (New Hampshire):

US 302 runs through the gap in the Webster and Willey mountains.

Phone: (603) 374-2272
Website: www.nhparks.state.nh.us/ParksPages/CrawfordNotch/
CrawfordNotch.html

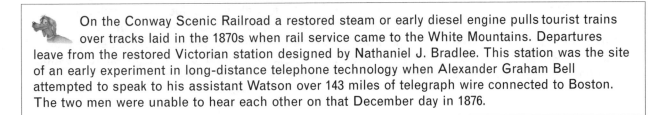

On the Conway Scenic Railroad a restored steam or early diesel engine pulls tourist trains over tracks laid in the 1870s when rail service came to the White Mountains. Departures leave from the restored Victorian station designed by Nathaniel J. Bradlee. This station was the site of an early experiment in long-distance telephone technology when Alexander Graham Bell attempted to speak to his assistant Watson over 143 miles of telegraph wire connected to Boston. The two men were unable to hear each other on that December day in 1876.

Franconia Notch State Park

The Park:

The Wisconsin Glacier scoured and gouged the granite mountains of the Franconia Notch, a deep slice between Franconia Ridge and the Cannon-Kinsman range. The retreating ice mass left behind an embarassment of natural wonders that began attracting tourists in 1808 with the discovery of the Flume, a natural 800-foot gorge with perpendicular granite walls less than 20 feet apart. Stagecoach roads to the area began opening in the middle of the 19th century when Nathaniel Hawthorne immortalized the Old Man of the Mountain, five layers of rock sticking out of Profile Mountain. The 40-foot ancient rock formation emerged from Hawthorne's writings to become the state symbol of New Hampshire. The greatest of the tourist camps was Profile Inn but after the hotel burned to the ground in 1923 its owners put their entire holdings of 6,000 acres up for sale to be cut as timber. A campaign began immediately to save the notch and the state of New Hampshire matched the $100,000 raised to create Franconia Notch State Park in 1928.

The Walks:

Canine hikers are not allowed down the *Flume Trail*, the most popular walk in Franconia, but with the abundance of other great hikes it won't even be missed. Entering the notch from the north, the first trail is *Artist's Bluff Trail*, where one short, rocky climb bags the 2,368-foot summit and superb views of beautiful Echo Lake. An easy walk along a lightly wooded ridge with plenty of filtering light tags Blue Mountain (2,320 feet) to close the loop.

In the heart of Franconia Notch is dog-friendly Lafayette Campground, a jumping off point for the best walks in the park. From the campground, the *Pemi Trail* traces the Pemigewasset River to the Basin, a smoothed-out pothole that has absorbed 25,000 years of pounding from the stream. For an engaging loop, abandon the level Pemi Trail and climb along the boulder-strewn *Cascade Brook Trail* to Lonesome Lake for views of the Kinsman Range. The mountains plunge to the alpine waters at 2,743 feet. Close the six-mile loop with a steep, rocky descent to the campground on *Lonesome Lake Trail*.

Across the parkway from the campground awaits a classic White Mountains hike for the hardiest of canine hikers - the loop to the *Franconia Ridge Trail*. Begin on *Falling Waters Trail*, boulder-hopping along and across several waterfalls. The ascent to the ridge is accomplished on the grueling "45," so named for the severity of the climb. Once on the ridge you join the *Appalachian Trail* and walk two shelterless miles above the treeline, crossing Haystack Mountain (4,840 feet), Lincoln Mountain (5,089 feet) and Lafayette Mountain (5,260 feet). Some of the rock formations can be challenging for a dog but there is nothing insurmountable on this spectacular hike. Return from the ridge down *Old Bridle Path* that features a long, rocky descent across open slopes before dipping into stunted pines. The full loop will cover 9 rewarding miles.

At the southern end of the notch, the summit trail to Mt. Pemigewasset offers views from ledges in three directions in little over one mile. The Indian Head profile is on the mountain.

Directions to Franconia Notch State Park (New Hampshire):

US 3 winds north and south through the gap.

Phone: (435) 564-3633
Website: www.nps.gov/acad/index.htm

The Old Man of the Mountain, or Great Stone Face, was a geological oddity some 200 million years in the making. It hovered regally 1,200 feet above the floor of the valley until crumbling in 2003. You can view the Old Man's ghost position from turnouts in the highway or leisurely from the 9-mile paved recreational trail that runs the length of the notch. Another natural formation nearby may not be so obvious. Just to the north, a rock formation can be seen suggesting a cannon profile poking from a fortress parapet, hence the name Cannon Mountain.

Mount Washington

The Park:

Mount Washington, at 6,288 feet, is the highest and most famous mountain in the Northeast. Darby Field, a British colonist from Exeter, made the first recorded ascent of Mount Washington in 1642. In 1819 Ethan Allen Crawford and father Abel built the first trail to the summit and it is the oldest continuously used mountain trail in the United States. Not long afterwards a bridle path was carved up the mountain and a hotel opened on the summit in 1852 (built by workers who had to hike 2 miles up Mount Washington each day to meet material hauled nine miles by horses over rough trails). In 1861 the 8-mile long Mt. Washington Auto Road opened for carriages. Mt. Washington Cog Railway, using the first rack-and-pinion mountain climbing system, later would haul passengers up one of the steepest railway tracks in the world.

The Walks:

At least 15 long, rugged hiking trails wind to the top of popular Mount Washington. The most travelled, and one of the most scenic, climbs the eastern slope on the *Tuckerman Ravine Trail* from Pinkham Notch. On the western face the *Ammonoosuc Ravine Trail* and *Jewell Trail* combine for an invigorating loop. Go up the Ravine and down the Jewell as the latter affords long exposed views as it works along cliffs; the Ravine Trail is thickly wooded and follows the plunging river all the way up. From the Appalachian Mountain Club Hut the original *Crawford Trail* climbs 1.4 open miles and nearly 2000 feet to the busy top. Much of the way is boulder hopping but your dog can make it without too much difficulty.

Directions to Mount Washington (New Hampshire):

The western assault trailheads can be found in the Mount Washington Cog Railway parking lot of SR 302; Pinkham Notch is on Route 16, 18 miles north of North Conway.
Website: www.mountwashington.com

The weather on Mount Washington is considered the worst in the world. The highest wind velocity ever measured - 231 miles per hour - was clocked on the summit on April 12, 1934. Winds average 35 mph every day with a hurricane force wind (75 mph) registered one day in three. Dense fog and clouds envelop the summit 315 days a year which makes your chances of enjoying the 130-mile views to New York, Quebec and even the Atlantic Ocean about 1 in 10.

Vermont's Green Mountains

Camel's Hump State Park

The Park:

There has long been a predilection for naming this distinctive double-humped mountain in the center of Vermont's Green Mountains. The Waubanaukee Indians called it "Tah-wak-be-deece-wadso" meaning "saddle mountain." French explorers in the 1600s named it "lion couchant" or "resting lion." When Ira Allen sketched out a regional map in 1798 he colorfully called the unique mountain "camel's rump." By 1830 the name "Camel's Hump" was in common usage.

The park began in 1911 from a gift of 1000 acres, including the summit, from Colonel Joseph Battell, who bought Camel's Hump to preserve the pristine views from his home. The State of Vermont has continued to adhere to Colonel Battell's ideals and Camel's Hump remains one of the few undeveloped peaks in the Green Mountain state.

The Walks:

Two routes ascend the 4,083-foot Camel's Hump summit to create a hiking loop. The climb starts with a rolling walk through light hardwoods and lifts gradually to the trail fork. Canine hikers will want to stay straight onto the *Monroe Trail*, which is a steady uphill path suitable for dogs.

The *Dean Trail* to the left climbs through thick birches and past a reflective beaver pond before joining the famous *Long Trail*. The Long Trail, a 265-mile scenic route from the Massachusetts state line to the Canadian border, was the first long-distance trail of its kind in the United States. Here, however, it approaches the open, rocky summit with steep rock faces that most dogs can climb only with a helping lift. Better to come down this eastern side of the mountain, not up. The full loop is 7.4 miles. Canine refreshment

The summit of Camel's Hump is characterized by bare rock and long views.

comes in the form of Camel's Hump Brook, that crosses both trails often.

After completing the summit loop, walk the *View Trail*, a wide grass trail, to admire what you and your dog have just accomplished.

Directions to Camel's Hump State Park (Vermont):

Camel's Hump is approached from the north. From I-89, take Exit 10 and go south on VT 100 to VT 2. Go east, or left, into Waterbury Village and take the first right on Winooski Street. Cross the Winooski River and then go right on River Road, a dirt road. Go 5.1 miles to Camel's Hump Road on the left, that follows Ridley Brook. Turn left here and climb 1.4 miles to a fork in the road, bear left and cross a bridge. Continue to climb another 2.4 miles to the eastern trailhead parking.

Smuggler's Notch

The Park:

In 1807 Thomas Jefferson signed an embargo act fordbidding trade with Great Britain and its North American colony, Canada. Not about to be cut off from their most lucrative market in Montreal, northern Vemonters began driving cattle north through a sliver of trail between the thousand-foot cliffs of Spruce Peak and Mount Mansfield, Vermont's highest peak at 4,395 feet. Thus was born Smuggler's Notch. Later, fugitive slaves used the notch as an escape route and in the 1920s illegal liquor flowed from Canada down through the notch. Today, Smuggler's Notch is part of Mt. Mansfield State Forest, Vermont's largest forest with 37,242 acres.

The Walks:

Underhill State Park is a gateway with several trails to ascend busy Mount Mansfield, inlcuding a paved road. *Laura Cowles Trail* (2.7 miles), *Sunset Ridge* (3.0 miles), and *Halfway House* (2.5 miles) are all moderate length climbs to the summit. From the "Chin" on Mount Mansfield are extensive 360-degree views. You'll know if it is a clear day if you can see Mount Royal and the skyscrapers of Montreal.

Across Smuggler's Notch is a rollicking hike on the *Elephant's Head Trail* to a small clearing at the top of a 1,000-foot cliff. The trail climbs stone steps from the roadway to Sterling Pond, the highest life-sustaining alpine pond in New England (trout are stocked by helicopter). The trail drops to the shoreline where canine hikers will meet a single impassable rock climb for most dogs. A bushwhacking detour through thick spruce will probably be in order. From this point the way is seldom level with plenty of hopping from root to rock. Keep an eye out for many species of plants found nowhere else in Vermont that reside happily among these moist, cold cliffs.

The views from Elephant's Head sweep up and down the rugged notch and directly across to hulking Mount Mansfield, scarred by a 1983 landslide. The return trip can be over the same route or continue down the hillside switchbacking across rocks and roots. This loop is completed only by walking the dog along the narrow, winding Route 108 through the notch. This trail is closed from February to mid-July to protect peregrine falcons.

Sidetrip: Stowe Recreation Path (starts in the village behind the Stowe Community Church on Main Street with various connecting places along the Mountain Road)

Stowe Recreation Path from Stowe Center, along a mountain stream towards Mount Mansfield, is a five-mile greenway notable as the first such path whose land was donated by individual owners rather than purchased by the government. This is an easy canine hike though farmfields, meadows and woodlands.

Directions to Smuggler's Notch (Vermont):

Form I-89, take Route 100 North into Stowe. Stay on Route 100 to Route 15. Turn left onto Route 15/Route 100. Turn left onto Route 108 South to the notch.

Phone: (802) 253-4014
Website: www.vtstateparks.com/htm/smugglers.cfm

"I can't think of anything that brings me closer to tears than when my old dog - completely exhausted after a hard day in the field - limps away from her nice spot in front of the fire and comes over to where I'm sitting and puts her head in my lap, a paw over my knee and closes her eyes, and goes back to sleep. I don't know what I've done to deserve that kind of friend."
- Gene Hill

The Adirondacks

Adirondack Park

Adirondack Park was established in 1885 to protect water resources but is now a favorite for lovers of all aspects of the land; trails are under the guidance of the Department of Environmental Conservation. Adirondack Park is the largest park in the lower forty-eight states. Blending public and private lands across its six million acres, the park dwarfs several American states. The Adirondacks support the country's largest and most elaborate hiking system featuring more than 2,000 miles of trails. Fortunately for the casual visitor, many of the best day hikes are conveniently close to developed communities, such as Lake Placid and Lake George.

Of course, this easy accessibility can make for crowded trail conditions. On busy holiday weekends rangers have been known to turn hikers away from popular trailheads. Right now dogs are allowed without restriction on any trails except in the Adirondack Mountain Reserve in the Ausable Lakes Region.

Lake George

The Town:

The strategic position of Lake George, so named by its European discoverer Father Jogues in 1609, between Lake Champlain and the Hudson River long made it of prime military importance. Fort William Henry, looming on a bluff above the southern shore, was constructed in 1755 and served as the backdrop for James Fenimore Cooper's *The Last of the Mohicans*. Battle plans eventually gave way to vacation plans with the arrival of many of America's wealthiest men who built summer retreats around Lake George.

The Walks:

The most spectacular - and grueling - hike in the Lake George region is the *Tongue Mountain Range Loop*. The range is a five-mile peninsula that thrusts down the middle of the lake. The loop tags the summit of five named mountains and several unnamed knobs on the eastern side of the peninsula before returning along lake level on the western edge. The mountains never reach 2000 feet in height but the ascents and decents make it

seem like climbing across the back of a stegosaurus. There are steep, rocky drops - nothing that a dog can't handle - but canine hikers are best served by taking the loop clockwise. Views from the lightly forested ridges are splendid up and down the lake, including memorable looks at some of Lake George's 365 islands, many clustered in the Narrows caused by the peninsula. Your destination is the very Tip of the Tongue, where the mountain range dips into Lake George. Here, wide rock perches make ideal diving boards for a well-deserved doggie dip. In the background will be the venerable Sagamore Hotel across Northwest Bay. The loop is closed with a 4.8-mile return trip along the sometimes-steep shoreline. The total distance for this invigorating exploration is about 13 miles. Bring plenty of water for the dog as there is none aside from the lake.

The tallest mountains surrounding Lake George are on the eastern shore. Trails to Buck Mountain (2,330 feet), Black Mountain (the highest at 2,646 feet) and others make good use of old bridle paths and logging roads and are technically easy for a dog to climb. Fires have visited most of the bare rock summits clearing views from the spruce and oak-beech forests. Mossy hemlocks proliferate on the damper lower slopes. The *Black Mountain Loop*, best tackled by canine hikers in a counter-clockwise direction so a tricky pick-your-way trail is encountered moving downhill, is enlivened by a series of valley ponds and beaver marshes.

Directions to Lake George (New York):

US 9 off of the New York State Thruway leads to Lake George Village. Scenic Lake Shore Drive (SR 9N) goes up the west shore to the Tongue Mountains; east shore hikes are off Route 22.

Phone: (800) 705-0059
Website: www.lgchamber.org

Islands pepper the Lake George Narrows as seen from the Tongue Mountain Range Loop.

"He is very impudent, a dog is. He never makes it his business to inquire whether you are in the right or in the wrong, never bothers as to whether you are going up or down upon life's ladder, never asks whether you are rich or poor, silly or wise, sinner or saint."
- Jerome K. Jerome

Lake Placid

The Town:

Lake Plaid is one of only three cities to host two Winter Olympic games, in 1932 and 1980. Melville Dewey, the genius behind the Dewey decimal system of library book classification, established Lake Placid as a resort community when he built the Lake Placid Club in the one-time ironmaking town. Today, although its winter heritage is much in abundance, Lake Placid is a year-round recreation destination.

The Walks:

Lake Placid is the destination of choice for canine hikers in search of spectacular views of the High Peaks in the Adirondacks. The premier area trail is the *Wilmington Trail*, a long, straight climb up and over Marble Mountain and across a rocky ridge to the summit of 4,867-foot White-face Mountain. The going can be wet and muddy on the well-worn path and views won't kick in until reaching the rocky glacial deposits but the 360-degree views at the top are unforgettable. After all the hard work from you and your dog on the 5.2-mile linear trail you will be sharing the summit with many others who have driven cars up the Whiteface Mountain Memorial Highway.

More outstanding views can be found on Haystack Mountain (of the High Peaks and the Saranac Lakes chain to the west); Mt. Van Hoevenberg (of the High Peaks and Mount Marcy to the south); and Mt. Jo (open vistas of the High Peaks Wilderness in three directions). All these hikes feature similar moderate woodlands walks before steep final climbs to exposed rocky ledges. Mt. Van Hoevenberg can be approached from the north or south - the northern approach tours the Olympic boblseld and luge runs. Mt. Jo is the only loop in the bunch (2.3 miles) and nearby is the trail to Rocky Falls, a series of tumbling cascades with a canine swimming hole.

When you want to take a break from scaling the Adirondack slopes you can relax on the *Brewster Peninsula Nature Trails*, a spiderweb of pleasant wooded trails on the shore of Lake Placid.

Directions to Lake Placid (New York):

From the New York State Thruway, Route 73 West runs into the village of Lake Placid, that is a central point for many of the best canine hikes in the area.

Phone: (800) 447-5224
Website: www.lakeplacid.com

Abolitionist John Brown farmed land south of Lake Placid before embarking on his inflamatory career in the years prior to the civil War. After meeting his fiery end in a bullet-ridden Harpers Ferry firehouse, Brown's body was returned for burial on his Lake Placid farm. A self-guiding trail winds through interpretive displays on the grounds and cross-country trails are available.

"Dog. A kind of additional or subsidiary Deity designed to catch the overflow surplus of the world's worship."
- Ambrose Bierce

Tagging New England Peaks

Dogs can make it to the top of New England on Mount Washington and are welcome at Vermont's high point on Mount Mansfield. Dogs cannot scale Maine's highest peak, Mount Katahdin at the terminus of the Appalachian Trail - no dogs allowed in Baxter State Park.

Another state ceiling your dog can experience is Mt. Greylock in Massachusetts. Long before Mt. Greylock became the first Massachusetts state park in 1898, it had attracted New Englanders with its panoramic five-state views. Great American writers and artists such as Edith Wharton, Nathaniel Hawthorne, Herman Melville and Henry David Thoreau regularly trekked up the trails to Mt. Greylock's 3,491-foot summit. (Sadly, the natural site most associated with Thoreau, Walden Pond, is not open to dogs).

Threatened by logging and industrial development in the late 1800s, a group of Berkshire County businessmen formed a private land conservation association and purchased 400 acres at the summit to preserve Mt. Greylock. The Massachusetts Legislature purchased Greylock as a State Reservation in 1898 and over the next century the park grew to encompass some 12,500 acres.

More than 45 miles of trails meander across Mt. Greylock State Reservation, including the *Appalachian Trail* that runs north-south over the summit. Many of the trails connect and it is easy to create looping circle hikes of any desired duration. An excellent trail map with elevation contours is available for planning a day's excursion.

One of the best ways to explore the park is with a circle hike around the Hopper, a U-shaped glacial ravine studded with old-growth spruce. The 7-mile loop combines several trails to the peaks of Mt. Prospect, Mt. Greylock and Mt. Williams with several outstanding vistas. Although most of the hiking is moderate, with elevation changes less than 1000 feet, the trail into and out of the Hopper, a designated Unique Natural Area, is the steepest in the park.

The *Thunderbolt Trail* leaves the Appalachian Trail opposite Robinson's point just north of the Mt. Greylock summit and follows the route of the Thunderbolt Ski Trail, an historic championship ski run down the eastern flank of the mountain. The Thunderbolt leads into Greylock Glen at the foot of the mountain where easy-walking trails explore wetlands, forests and farmlands. Side trails lead through Hemlock Gorge to Pecks Falls, one of several pleasing waterfalls at Mt.Greylock. Dogs are permitted in the 35-site campground in the Reservation.

A 100-foot tall stone War Memorial Tower commands the views at the summit of Mt. Greylock. Although your dog can't scale the tower the same sweeping views of the Hoosic River Valley are available from the stone wall and benches on the edge of the ridge. Also on the summit is a detailed three-dimensional sculpture of the Mt. Greylock Reservation.

Cape Cod

Cape Cod National Seashore

The Park:

Cape Cod, first sighted by the Pilgrims in 1620, became a national seashore in 1961, the first National Park to be purchased with federal monies. Senator John F. Kennedy co-sponsored the act that led to establishing the non-donated park. Cape Cod reigns as our most popular national seashore. Where once only fishermen and whalers came, the 40-mile stretch of sand dunes between Chatham and Provincetown at the tip of the cape attracts five million visitors a year. In addition to its sandy beaches, Cape Cod National Seashore features a number of interesting historic buildings, including the Old Harbor Lifesaving Station and five lighthouses.

The Walks:

Cape Cod National Seashore features 11 self-guiding nature trails - unfortunately dogs are banned from all park trails. But dogs are allowed on all non-nesting protected beaches year-round. Walking the beaches at Cape Cod is a special experience due to limited sight distance down the shore caused by the coastline's curvature. The effect is that of a series of private beaches as you move from beach alcove to beach alcove. In addition to Atlantic Ocean beaches backed by impressive highlands, the park extends across the cape to include bayside beaches with gentler waves for canine aquatics.

Canine hikers looking to shake the sand from shoe and paw can use one of three maintained bicycle trails, ranging from a modest 1.6 miles to a 5.45-mile loop on the *Province Lands Trail*. There is little wheeled competition for thse paths in the off-season. Harbor and grey seals can be sighted on Cape Cod beaches.

Directions to Cape Cod National Seashore (Massachusetts):

There are many access points to the national seashore off Route 6 heading to the land's end.

Phone: (508) 255-3421
Website: www.nps.gov/caco

Cape Cod is famous for its harvests of one of only three native American fruits - the cranberry. In addition to commercial harvesting, wild bogs can be found in places like the Province Lands dunes. Blueberries, blackberries, rose hips, raspberries and a choice variety of mushrooms can all be found in natural areas during summer and fall. Dogs enjoy fruit and bite-size chunks are a good trail snack. Dogs generally like apples - it is probably a dog's favorite fruit to eat. Any of the popular varieties will do. For dogs with a sweet tooth, an apple is a better option than candy or Oreos. Berries are another fruit dogs seem to enjoy. For easier digestion, use fruits as treats between meals rather than at mealtime.

Martha's Vineyard

The Park:

Human habitation is thought to have begun on Martha's Vineyard before it was an island in the time before melting glaciers raised the level of the Atlantic Ocean. Some are convinced that the Norsemen visited here around 1000 A.D. and in 1524 Verrazzano is known to have sailed by and named the island Indians called Noepe, "Louisa." Other explorers gave the island a name but its enduring moniker came in 1602 from Batholomew Gosnold, who immortalized one of his young daughters and the wild grapes that grew in abundance.

The Walks:

Just off the southern coast of Cape Cod, Martha's Vineyard is an extremely dog-friendly resort destination. For canine hikers, the Sheriff's Meadow Foundation has conserved over 2100 acres of land on Martha's Vineyard in more than 100 separate parcels. From these protected lands the Foundation has created eight sanctuaries open to the public, including dogwalkers. The largest trail system is at Cedar Tree Neck Sanctuary where two miles of paw-friendly trails visit hilly woodlands, secluded ponds and a small sandy beach.

Neighboring Nantucket Island is also a good choice for canine hikers. Dogs are allowed on island beaches the entire year, although there are restrictions during the summer. Dogs are even allowed on shuttle buses to the beach.

Directions to Martha's Vineyard (Massachusetts):

Martha's Vineyard is reached by ferry from Woods Hole on the southwest tip of Cape Cod at the end of Route 28.
Website: www.mvol.com

A good place for a seaside game of fetch, Ocean Park is one of many little parks set aside for open space in the town of Oak Bluffs on Martha's Vineyard.

Colonial Martha's Vineyard was a vibrant place with butter churning from its inland farms and its ports a constant whirl of activity. However, British raiders during the American Revolution torched the towns and stole 10,000 sheep and 300 head of cattle from Patriot farms. The island economy was crippled until a small congregation of Methodists staged a religious camp meeting in 1835. Within 20 years the yearly retreat was drawing more than 10,000 attendees and Martha's Vineyard was reborn as a resort destination. The tents from the camp meeting gave way to wooden cottages in Wesleyan Grove. Today more than 300 of these eclectic Victorian cottages remain clustered on the circular paths behind the main streets of Oak Bluffs. You and your dog can wander through the campground, placed on the National Register of Historic Places in 1979 on the Centennial of the historic Tabernacle, that served as the centerpiece of the camp meetings.

America's Most Spectacular Backyard Walk

In the late 1800s wealthy New Yorkers began coming to Newport, Rhode Island to escape the suffocating summer heat in the city. They build the most extravagant "cottages" ever seen in America on the rocky bluffs overlooking the Atlantic Ocean.

No matter how impressive the mansion or how rich the owner, however, no one's property could extend all the way to the shoreline. By virtue of "Fisherman's Rights" granted by the Colonial Charter of King Charles II and a provision in the Rhode Island Constitution, the public is always guaranteed the legal right to walk along a small sliver of cliff.

Not that the powerful residents on the other sides of the gate have always agreed with that right. In the past bushes were planted, walls erected and even bulls grazed to discourage use by the public.

Other owners embraced the Cliff Walk and helped devlop it from a mere footpath. Some tunnels were built and flagstones placed in muddy stretches.

Eventually the federal government stepped in to help rebuild the path after erosion during hurricanes. In 1975, the Cliff Walk was named the first National Recreation Trail in New England.

Today the Cliff Walk rambles for about 3.5 miles, about two of which are paved and easy to walk. Dogs are welcome all along the Cliff Walk and Poop Bags are even provided at the start on Memorial Boulevard.

Continuing past the paved path, the Cliff Walk turns rustic with some walking on unprotected, open cliff faces and boulder hopping. It requires concentration but any level of canine hiker can negotiate the trip.

If you continue to the end of the Cliff Walk you will drop to ocean's edge and small coves where the dog can get a swim (Newport's First Beach, at the start of the Cliff Walk, is open to dogs only in the off-season).

At the end of the Cliff Walk you have the option of returning by the same route along the black Atlantic rocks or exiting into the town and walking back on the sidewalks in front of the mansions whose backyards you have just walked through.

Catskill Mountains

Burroughs Range

The Park:

John Burroughs grew up on a farm in the Catskills in the 1840s and at an early age pledged to become an author. He honed his skills as a government worker but found himself being drawn away to his love of nature. Eventually he published a series of nature essays in 1871, extolling the simple pleasures of the outdoors. In short time he moved back to the Catskills to take up fruit farming. Burroughs would come to publish 23 influential volumes of collected essays. The "Father of the American nature essay" was one of the six charter members named to the Ecology Hall of Fame.

The Walks:

The red-blazed *Wittenberg-Cornell-Slide Trail* tags the three peaks in the Burroughs Range. The climb from the trailhead to the summit of 4180-foot Slide Mountain - the highest point in the Catskills - is a steady ascent on a rocky woods road, a technically easy hike for the dog. The final half-mile is an easy walk through a fragrant spruce alley that compensates for the general lack of overlooks. A loop can be formed for the return trip down Slide Mountain on the blue-blazed *Curtis-Ormsbee Trail*, one of the prettiest hikes in the Catskills. The descents through the birches and hemlocks plunge steeply at times so save this alternate route for athletic dogs.

Directions to Burroughs Range trails (New York):

The trailhead is 29 miles off I-87, the NY Thruway. Take the Kingston exit and pick up Route 28 to Phonecia. Use Woodland Valley Road to reach the Woodland Valley Campground area. The trail head is on the right just before the campground.

Just east of the Slide Mountain summit is the Burroughs Plaque. Beneath this small cliff overhang in a clearing, John Burroughs spent many a night. Walk the sandy path to the right to reach the site.

Devil's Path

The Park:

The *Devil's Path*, so-called for the rugged terrain it follows, slices through the heart of the Catskill Mountains, tagging seven mountain peaks in its 27-mile east-to-west journey. The eastern segment (over Overlook, Indian Head, Twin and Sugarloaf mountains) opened in 1930 and the western continuation over Plateau, Hunter and West Kill mountains was completed in 1935.

The Walks:

From start to finish, *Devil's Path* features an elevation gain of 18,000 feet - more than 3 1/2 miles of climbing. There are, however, ample opportunities to sample the central Catskills without experiencing the entire trail. On the eastern edge, a popular trail twists to multiple vistas and a nine-story, steel-framed lookout tower on Overlook Mountain. More adventurous canine hikers will want to tackle the crags and outcroppings of 3573-foot Indian Head Mountain. Do so, however, only with a liftable dog as the final ascent to the summit features several high steps and pull-ups.

There are plenty of opportunities along the Devil's Path to stop and take a look around.

On the western end of the Devil's Path range, four routes lead to a firetower atop Hunter Mountain, at 4040 feet the second highest peak in the Catskills. The route on Devil's Path rises to the summit from Stoney Clove notch, a climb of 2040 feet in just over two miles.

Although it is the steepest climb on the trail, the route up the mountainside is technically easy for a dog, using old service roads. There is scarcely a downhill step on the long, steady pull up Hunter Mountain. Don't expect many vistas on the way up but the tower on top offers long east-facing views.

Directions to Devil's Path Campground (New York):

From the New York State Thruway (I-87), take Exit 19 at Kingston. Follow Route 28 West to Phoenicia. At Phoenicia, follow signs for Route 214 and the campground is located about 9 miles on the left.

Kaaterskill Falls

The Park:

Kaaterskill Falls, a two-tiered water plunge with a slight lefthand turn, is New York state's highest waterfall. The upper ribbon of water drops a full 175 feet - the same as Niagara Falls - and the lower falls tumble another 75 feet into a rocky basin. Kaaterskill was an inspiration for landscape painter Thomas Cole, founder of the Hudson River School of painters, the first major art movement in the United States. The Catskill Mountains were introduced to the world by these artists in the mid-19th century. Thomas Cole can be seen at Kaaterskill Falls in Asher B. Durand's major work, *Kindred Spirits*. In the late 1800s, when the New York State Legislature designated lands "forever wild,"the Falls were in the first set of lands protected.

The Walks:

The trickiest part of this short hike for dog owners is the .2-mile downhill walk from the parking lot to the trailhead along a narrow roadway making a hairpin turn. At points this mountain road is scarcely wide enough for two vehicles. Once on the trail, it is a sometimes rugged .7-mile climb to the base of the falls. The beginning is a manufactured trail up the side of the fast-flowing Bastion Falls. From the top of these falls the walk becomes easier through the hemlock-filled gorge. Many of the dark giants are old-timers more than 200 years old. The trail ends splendidly at the Kaaterskill Falls.

Directions to Kaaterskill Falls (New York):

The trail to Kaaterskill Falls is located on Route 23A, near Palenville and Haines Falls.

North-South Lake

The Park:

North Lake Campground was first developed as a recreational destination with the construction of 10 tent sites and a small picnic area in 1929. Work during the Depression greatly expanded the camp and a beach was constructed on the lakeshore. In the 1980s a sliver of earthen dam between North and South lakes was removed to create today's large, island-speckled lake.

The Walks:

North-South Lake lies at the eastern edge of the Catskill escarpment where the elevation rises abruptly from 540 feet at its base of the cliffs to 2500 feet in elevation. The campground offers easy access to the trail along the escarpment where spectacular views of the Hudson River Valley can be purchased for very little effort. This *Escarpment Trail* scampers north along the cliffs for 24 miles with an almost continuous series of overlooks. In the immediate campground vicinity the trail covers 6 easy miles with vistas and geological oddities arriving at regular intervals, including Sunset Rock and one of the most scenic lookouts in the Catskills. Keep close control of your dog as you go since few of the ledges offer railings and the drop-offs are precipitous. Spur trails through leafy glens drop back to the campground from the escarpment often to create loop trails of varying length. Although centered around the North-South Lake, the trails don't visit the water; dogs are not allowed on the two small swimming beaches in the day use area.

Directions to North-South Lake (New York):

Take Exit 20 at Saugerties off the New York State Thruway (I-87). Follow Route 32 north for approximately 6 miles to Route 32A and then Route 23A west. Stay on Route 23A to the village of Haines Falls. Make first right turn in Haines Falls onto County Road 18 and go 2 miles to the end of the road.

Phone: (518) 357-2234
Website: www.dec.state.ny.us/website/do/camping/campgrounds/ northsouth.html

---

On a grassy flat, just up an old service road from the campground, once stood the grand Catskill Mountain Hotel. First built in 1823, it required a day-long stage coach ride to bring guests up to the hotel and its glimpses of five states on clear days. The view from the Greek Revival portico was the most famous in America and enjoyed by Presidents Chester Arthur, Ulysses Grant, Theodore Roosevelt and others. In its heyday during the 1850s to 1870s more than 400 guests stayed at the Catskill Mountain Hotel that inspired other great hostelries to be built nearby. The Hotel Kaaterskill was the largest mountain hotel in the world when it opened in 1881 with 1,014 rooms. The grand hotels are all gone now but their sites can be visited with your dog.

"We are alone, absolutely alone on this chance planet; and amid all the forms of life that surround us, not one, excepting the dog, has made an alliance with us."
- Maurice Maeterlinck

Minnewaska State Park Preserve

The Park:

Alfred and Albert Smiley opened the Shawangunk Mountains, the Catskills' close southern neighbor, to the vacationing public after the Civil War when they built the Mohonk Mountain House. Later, a disagreement caused Alfred to move on and build the Cliff House nearby. The last guest checked out in 1979 and the state of New York stepped in to prevent any further development in 1987 with the creation of Minnewaska State Park Preserve.

The Walks:

After decades of jostling for tourist dollars the Smiley brothers eventually reconciled and began building a network of carriageways between the two hotels. These wide, carefully graded roadbeds are where you will be doing most of your hiking with your dog. Expect to share the carriageways with plenty of bicyclists.

Several long parallel carriageways between Lake Awosting and Lake Minnewaska can be combined for loop hikes of several hours duration. For spectacular views of the Hudson Valley use the *Castle Point Carriageway* to Castle Point, the highest summit in the park. Looks at the Catskill Mountains come quickly on the short, steep *Sunset Path* near the entrance parking lots.

The narrow hiker-only paths are where the adventure begins for canine hikers at Minnewaska State Park Preserve. These trails are generally moving up and down, leading to treasures deep in the Shawangunks like Stony Kill Falls.

The trek to Gertrude's Nose bursts from a dark hemlock forest for extended walking on exposed clifftops. This is not the place for a rambunctious dog and inexperienced canine hikers may have trouble with the rock scrambles but otherwise is worth every step of the two-mile detour off the *Millbrook Mountain Carriageway*.

Directions to Minnewaska State Park Preserve (New York):

Take Exit 18 off the New York State Thruway at New Paltz. Head west across Route 32 to Route 299 to Route 44/55 and continue to the park entrance on the left hand side, a total of 11.5 miles from the Thruway.

Phone: (845) 255-0752
Website: www.nysparks.com

The canine hiking is easy on the beautifully crafted carriageways at Minnewaska Preserve.

The unique environment on the dramatic Shawangunk Mountain ridge is extremely sensitive and access to the park is limited to reduce the impact of human - and canine - intrusion. Capacity in the park on any given day is limited by the number of parking spaces in the lots. it is not unheard of for the park to be closed before it actually opens - so many cars are lined up for the 9:00 a.m. opening. When one car leaves, another is allowed in. Even with the restrictions the park averages more than 1,000 visitors per day. If you arrive early and get in, however, you will find the trails generally uncrowded, especially on the hiker-only footpaths.

Pocono Mountains

Delaware Water Gap National Recreation Area

The Park:

The Delaware Water Gap, a mile-wide break in the spine of the Appalachians, is renowned for its depth, width and dramatic beauty. Travellers and settlers have long taken advantage of the breach in the mountains, caused by a combination of continental drift, ages of mountain building and the relentless action of mountain rivers. A 40-mile stretch of the Delaware River, one of the last free-flowing rivers in the eastern United States, was declared a National Recreation Area in 1965. More than five million people come each year to explore the park's 70,000 acres.

The Walks:

More than 60 miles of trails are available to satisfy any taste in canine hiking - dogs are welcome on all trails and most anywhere in the park, save for the beach areas. On the Pennsylvania side of the Delaware River are a variety of shorter trails leading to hemlock-filled ravines and waterfalls. In New Jersey, the going is more strenuous. Day hikers can travel along 25 miles of the *Appalachian Trail* that skirts the Kittatinny Ridge and passes Sunfish Pond, one of New Jersey's "7 Natural Wonders."

Challenging canine hiking awaits at the southern end of the park where the Delaware River courses through the Gap. In Pennsylvania (southern side of the Gap), an old fire road climbs more than 1,000 feet to the top of 1,463-foot Mt. Minsi. The hike can be combined with the Appalachian Trail to form a four-mile loop hike. Its New Jersey twin, 1,527-foot Mt. Tammany, is ascended from the parking lot by the twisting *Red Dot Trail* that switches steeply up the rocky slopes for 1.5 miles. Both peaks serve up superlative views of the Delaware Water Gap below. A trail system leads off Mt. Tammany back down and around the Appalachian Trail.

Trails also take advantage of old railroad lines and historic military roads for easier canine hiking along the Delaware River in the Gap.

Directions to Delaware Water Gap National Recreation Area (New Jersey and Pennsylvania:

The jumping off point for explorations of the Delaware Water Gap is at the Visitor Center on I-80 at the Pennsylvania-New Jersey border.
Phone: (908) 496-4458
Website: www.nps.gov/dewa

"My dog can bark like a Congressman, fetch like an aide, beg like a press secretary and play dead like a receptionist."
- Gerald Solomon

Ricketts Glen State Park

The Park:

One of the most uniquely scenic areas in the Northeast, Ricketts Glen was slated to become a national park in the 1930s but World War II shelved plans for this development. Instead, Ricketts Glen opened as a state park in 1944. Gradually the Commonwealth of Pennsylvania continued purchasing blocks of land from the descendents of Robert Bruce Ricketts until the park spread across more than 13,000 acres.

Ricketts enlisted as a private in the United States Army in 1861 and after commanding a battery during the Civil War was discharged with the rank of Colonel. After the war Colonel Ricketts began acquiring inaccessible virgin timber until he controlled over 80,000 acres of land. His Central Penn Lumber Company began harvesting the old growth forest, with some trees 900 years old, when the railroads arrived in 1890. By 1913 the timber was exhausted and the lumber town of Ricketts deserted.

The Walks:

The spectacular attraction of Ricketts Glen is the magical *Falls Trail*, a Y-shaped exploration of 23-named waterfalls. Two branches of the Kitchen Creek slice through the Ganoga Glen to the left and Glen Leigh to the right before uniting at Waters Meet. The stem of the trail flows through Ricketts Glen, among towering hemlocks and oaks, before tumbling over three cascades at Adams Falls at the trailhead.

The remoteness of the land in the 19th century kept the waterfalls, ranging as high as the 94-foot Ganoga Falls, undiscovered until 1865. Colonel Ricketts hired a crew to build a trail along and across the plunging water and the project took 28 years. Today the Falls Trail remains a maintenance challenge and its steep grades can be muddy and slippery and your dog's four-wheel traction will be most welcome. The two prongs of the trail connect at the top of the twin falls via the 1.2-mile *Highland Trail*. The complete falls experience encompasses almost seven miles.

More than 20 miles of trails meander through the deep woods and mountain lakes at Ricketts Glen. The rocky *Cherry Run Trail* takes you away from the crowded Glens Natural Area into the eastern section of the park and the *Grand View Trail* is a 1.9-mile loop that reaches a fire tower with an almost complete 360-degree vista. Other less demanding trails mosey along near 245-acre Lake Jean.

Sidetrip: World's End State Park (south of Forksville on Route 154)

Twenty miles west of Ricketts Glen State Park is a much smaller, but no less dramatic landscape, Worlds End State Park. So named because the first road built here atop steep ridges left travelers feeling as if they were at the end of the world, these hiking trails wind to panoramic views of the Loyalsock Creek Gorge. The heart-stopping *High Rock Trail* is one of the most challenging short trails in Pennsylvania and features life-threatening drop-offs that mandate a tight leash on the dog. Across Loyalsock Creek are many more tough miles of hiking in the Wyoming State Forest. Another fifty miles further west is the Grand Canyon of Pennsylvania, with hiking along the west rim of the 800-foot Pine Creek Gorge and on the flat *Pine Creek Trail* through the chasm.

Directions to Ricketts Glen State Park (Pennsylvania):

The main park entrance is off Route 487 between Red Rock and Dushore. A good way to reach the Falls Trail is to travel on Route 118, east of its intersection with Route 487, and park in the lot on the right for the *Evergreen Trail*.

Phone: (570) 477-5675
Website: www.dcnr.state.pa.us/stateparks/parks/rickettsglen.asp

Jersey Shore

Gateway National Recreation Area: Sandy Hook

The Park:

Sandy Hook is a 7-mile sand spit dangling into the Atlantic Ocean off the northern tip of New Jersey. Ships sailing into New York harbor have always needed to navigate around the shifting sands of Sandy Hook. The first lighthouse, was built from lottery funds in 1764. The strategic peninsula has been fortified since the War of 1812 and the Hook was the site of the first United States Army Proving Ground. The last active military base, Fort Hancock, closed in 1974 but the United States Coast Guard still maintains an active presence at Sandy Hook.

The Walks:

The best canine hiking in the 1,655-acre Sandy Hook Unit is on the seven miles of ocean beach (No dogs from March 15 to Labor Day to protect nesting shorebirds). The open sands of North Beach curl around to reveal views of the Brooklyn skyline and the Verrazano Narrows Bridge, the longest suspension bridge in the world when it opened in 1964. Open all year to dogs are short nature trails through a 264-acre maritime forest that holds the greatest concentration of American Holly on the East Coast. When hiking around sand trails, steer your dog clear of low-lying prickly pear cacti that grow in abundance on the peninsula (No dogs on the *Old Dune Trail*).

In addition to the unspoiled natural areas at Sandy Hook, there are plenty of places to explore with your dog through historic Fort Hancock, much of which is used for educational purposes today. Interpretive trails describe missile testing sites, anti-aircraft defenses, and lead into overgrown gun batteries.

Other New Jersey Beaches to Enjoy with Your Dog:

Island Beach State Park (central New Jersey). The wide, white-sand beaches of the Jersey shore are some of America's most popular and there

You never know what treasure will wash ashore on a beach, like this coconut at Gateway National Recreation Area.

isn't much space for a dog to squeeze into in the summertime. For instance, dogs will never get to trot down the historic wooden planks of the Atlantic City boardwalk. Most of the beaches in New Jersey open to dogs in the off-season but in the summertime the dog lovers beach of choice is Island Beach State Park, one of New Jersey's last remaining natural barrier islands. The ten miles of pristine dunesland would look familiar to Henry Hudson, the first European to sail past this coast on the Half Moon in 1609. Dogs are allowed on the non-recreational beaches year-round at Island State Beach.

Sunset Beach (Sunset Boulevard, Cape May). While dogs in the popular Victorian seaside town of Cape May are not allowed on the beach, the boardwalk or outdoor shopping areas, they are welcome at Sunset Beach at the southernmost point on Cape May. Just off the beach are the remains of the *Atlantus*, a unique concrete ship built to transport soldiers in World War I. With steel at a shortage, reinforced concrete was tried as a shipbuilding material. The concrete ships worked but proved too slow and were scrapped after the war. The *Atlantus* was towed to Cape May in 1926 to be used as a Ferry slip but an accident dumped her on a sand bar where she remains today. From the center of Cape May take Lafayette Avenue to West Perry Street, which turns into Sunset Boulevard. The two-lane road deadends after three miles at Sunset Beach.

Directions to Gateway National Recreation Area: Sandy Hook (New Jersey):

Sandy Hook is located off Route 36 near the town of Highlands.

Phone: (732) 872-5970
Website: www.nps.gov/gate

The Sandy Hook Lighthouse has been guiding ships through the sandy shoals for 240 years. You can walk your dog around the grassy base of the National Historic Landmark and well-behaved dogs can even sit in on the short video history of the illumination of New York harbor. While looking at the old brick sentinel, you can grasp the dynamics of land-building at Sandy Hook - when first built, the lighthouse was a mere 500 feet from shore and today is more than one and one-half miles from the northern end of the peninsula. When leaving the National Recreation Area, in front of you on the highlands are the Twin Lights, a distinctive light that was built as dual beacons to distinguish it from the Sandy Hook Lighthouse and others. You can visit the historic Twin Lights, the first to use the navigational lens designed by French physicist Augustine Fresnel in 1841 that are still "state of the art" today, but your dog must remain in the car.

Wharton State Forest

The Park:

Wharton State Forest lies at the heart of New Jersey's mysterious Pine Barrens, a vast tapestry of impenetrable scrub pine, swamps and bogs. Today known for its cranberry and blueberry production, the area's bog ore once supported a nascent iron industry that supplied much of the weaponry and ammunition for the American Revolution. Many of the indecipherable sand roads through the Pine Barrens date to the Revolution. When the foundries followed the discovery of America's massive upper mid-western iron ranges in the mid-1800s, the area's economy became so depressed that Philadelphia financier Joseph Wharton was able to acquire over 100,000 acres of land here. Wharton died in 1909 and much of his land became the core of the Wharton State Forest in 1954, part of the Pinelands National Reserve. Wharton State Park is the largest slice of land in the New Jersey State Park system.

The Walks:

The main hiking trail among 500 miles of unimproved roads is the *Batona Trail*, a wilderness trail that begins at Ongs Hat to the north of the park and ends at Lake Absegami in Bass River State Forest. The original 30 miles of the Batona Trail were routed and cleared through white cedar and pitch pine forests by volunteers in 1961. Today the total length of the trail is 50.2 miles with many road crossings that make different lengths of hikes possible. The distinctive pink blazes on the Batona Trail were selected by Morris Burdock, then president of the Batona Hiking Club and chief advocate for the building of the trail.

The Batona Trail is easy walking on paw-friendly sand for most of its length. Despite the over-whelming flatness of the surrounding countryside, there are undulating elevation changes on the trail itself. An aquifer inside the Pine Barren's deep sand beds holds 17 trillion gallons of pure glacial water and often percolates to the surface in the form of bogs, marshes and swamps. The Batsto River is stained the color of tea by cedar sap, adding to the region's mystique. It makes a worthy canine swimming pool.

Traffic on the Batona Trail is restricted to hikers and dogs are welcome along the length of the trail. Most of the trails in Wharton State Forest are unimproved dirt roads that hikers share with on- and off-road vehicles. Near the center of the Batona Trail, and a popular parking place to access the trail, is Batsto Village. Thirty-three wooden structures have been restored to this bog iron and glassmaking industrial center which flourished from 1766 to 1867. There is a self-guided 1-mile nature walk around the lake at Batsto Village, that includes stops at the Batsto Mansion and an operating gristmill and sawmill.

Directions to Wharton State Forest (New Jersey):

Two offices serve the park, one at Batsto Village on Route 542 and the other in Atsion on Route 206, eight miles north of Hammonton.

Phone: (609) 561-0024
Website: www.state.nj.us/dep/parksandforests/parks/wharton.html

The chance to see New Jersey's version of Bigfoot, the legendary winged creature known as the "Jersey Devil." The Jersey Devil is a creature with the head of a horse supported by a four-foot serpentine body with large wings and claws. According to lore, the Devil appeared in the 1700s when an indigent woman named Mrs. Leeds was struggling to feed her 12 children in the darkest recesses of the Pine Barrens. Finding herself once again pregnant she is said to have exclaimed: "I want no more children! Let it be a devil." The devil-child was born horribly deformed, crawled from the womb, up the chimney and into the woods where it was rumored to survive by feeding on small children and livestock, haunting the countryside. When a person saw the Devil, it was an omen of disaster, particularly shipwrecks, to come. Sightings were common through the next two centuries and often breathlessly reported in the local newspapers. Once some local Pineys, as Pine Barrens residents are known, tried to claim a $10,000 reward for capturing the Devil by obtaining a kangaroo, painting stripes across its back and gluing large wings on the animal. But so far there have been no documented Jersey Devils captured. Perhaps your dog can sniff one out.

Delmarva Peninsula

Assateague Island National Seashore

The Park:

The first European settlers - a band of four men - came to Assateague Island in 1688. At times more than 200 people survived on the shifting sands of the barrier island, fishing or clamming or growing what crops they could. In 1833 the first lighthouse was built but ships still ran aground, including the *Dispatch*, the official yacht of five American presidents. The cruiser was ruined beyond repair when it reached the island shores unscheduled on October 10, 1891. A bridge to the mainland opened in 1962 and in 1965 Assateague Island became a national seashore.

The Walks:

Dogs are not allowed on the three short channel-side nature trails and can not go on lifeguarded beaches but that leaves miles of wide, sandy beaches to hike on with your dog any time of the year.

Drive to the furthest parking lot from the entrance gate and head up the boardwalk across the dunes. Make a right and ahead of you will stretch hours of unspoiled canine hiking in the surf and sand. Although the national seashore is within a few hours' drive of tens of million of Americans don't be surprised if you have most of this beach to yourself and your dog.

⊘ Assateague State Park in Maryland is one of the best state parks in America - but your dog will never know. When coming on to the island turn right and avoid going straight into the state park. No dogs allowed there.

Directions to Assateague Island National Seashore (Maryland):

Assateague's north entrance is at the end of Route 611, eight miles south of Ocean City, Maryland.

Phone: (410) 641-1441
Website: www.nps.gov/asis

⊘ There is a second entrance to the national seashore, a southern access through Virginia. Avoid this entry - dogs are not allowed on the Virginia side of Assateague Island, even in the car.

Assateague Island is the famous home of the free-roaming "Chincoteague Ponies," a present-day reminder of Assateague Island's past. Although no one is certain when or how the ponies first arrived on the island, a popular legend tells of ponies that escaped a shipwrecked Spanish galleon and swam ashore. However, most historians believe that settlers used the island for grazing livestock (including ponies and other farm animals) in the 17th Century to avoid fencing regulations and taxation. The ponies rule the island and you can see them on the roads or even meet them in the surf.

Cape Henlopen State Park

The Park:

Cape Henlopen has the distinction of being one of the first parks in America: in 1682 William Penn decreed that Cape Henlopen would be for "the usage of the citizens of Lewes and Sussex County." The area had been Delaware's first permanent settlement 50 years earlier by ill-fated Dutch colonists who were massacred by local Indians.

Cape Henlopen's strategic location at the mouth of the Delaware Bay led the United States Army to establish Fort Miles among the dunes in 1941. Lookouts scanned the Atlantic Ocean for German U-boats during World War II and although the fort's huge guns were never fired in battle, a German submarine did surrender here after the war. In 1964, the Department of Defense declared 543 acres on the cape as surplus property and the State of Delaware established Cape Henlopen State Park. Today the park boasts more than 5,000 acres, including four miles of pristine beaches where the Delaware Bay meets the Atlantic Ocean. The park's 80-foot high Great Dune is the highest dune on the Atlantic shore between Cape Cod and Cape Hatteras.

The Walks:

Cape Henlopen State Park features three self-guided interpretive trails of varying length. All three natural surface trails can be completed in a day with plenty of time left for the dog to play in the ocean. The shortest of the trails is the .6-mile *Seaside Interpretive Trail*, that loops through dunes and a mixed forest of pitch pines and hardwoods. The 2.1-mile *Pinelands Nature Trail*, Delaware's first National Recreation Trail, travels through a maritime forest of old cranberry bogs, drained wetlands and pine woods.

The 3.1-mile *Dune Overlook Trail* includes a short spur to the famous "walking dunes" of Cape Henlopen. The walking is generally easy, save for extra exertion through the soft sand surfaces.

Dogs are allowed on the beach at Cape Henlopen from October through April and in the early morning and evening through the summer. Dogs - and people - are not permitted in designated bird nesting areas or on seaside dunes. One good way to explore the beach areas at Cape Henlopen is on the 1.8-mile *Beach Loop Trail* that begins opposite the parking lot in the southernmost section of the park and leads to overlooks of Gordon's Pond Wildlife Area, a unique saltwater impoundment.

Sidetrip: Trap Pond State Park (Road 449 in Laurel)

Trap Pond State Park is an arboreal buffer zone where many northern tree species begin to reach their southern limits and southern species find the end of their northern range. Trap Pond harbors one such species, the northernmost natural stand of baldcypress trees in the United States. A flat, easy-walking 5-mile trail circles Trap Pond, created in the 1700s to power a sawmill that harvested the area's cypress trees. In addition to stunning views of the bald cypress trees, the trail meanders through dense stands of another southern stalwart - the stately loblolly pine.

Directions to Cape Henlopen State Park (Delaware):

Cape Henlopen is one mile east of Lewes, via Route 9.

Phone: (302) 645-8983
Website: www.destateparks.com/chsp/chsp.htm

Remnants of Cape Henlopen's military past remain nestled among the massive sand dunes. Bunkers and gun emplacements were camouflaged deep in the sand and concrete observation towers were built along the shoreline to bolster America's coastal defenses during World War II. These silent sentinels remain scattered along Delaware's beaches and one has been restored to provide visitors with a panoramic view of the park and the ocean.

Virginia Beach

First Landing State Park

The Park:

The Commonwealth of Virginia obtained more than 2,000 acres near Cape Henry in 1933 at the cost of $157,000. Depression-era public work programs set out to shape the land into the park that was dedicated in 1936. In 1965 the park was included in the National Register of Natural Landmarks as the northernmost location on the East Coast where subtropical and temperate plants grow and thrive together.

The Walks:

The trail system at First Landing State Park, designated as part of the National Recreation Trail System, features 19 miles of dog-friendly hiking. The marquee walk is the *Bald Cypress Trail* that circles a cypress swamp for 1.5 miles, much of the way on elevated boardwalks. Airborne Spanish moss drapes many of the ancient giants. Looping off the red-blazed Bald Cypress Trail is the 3.1-mile blue *Osmanthus Trail*, named for the American olive tree that grows abundantly on the fringes of the dark lagoon along the trail. Another worthwhile detour from the Bald Cypress Trail is the quarter-mile *High Dune Trail* that uses wooden sleeper-steps to ascend a steep, wooded dune. It is easy walking on these packed sand and soft dirt trails that are further cushioned to the paw by pine straw from towering loblolly pines. There are gentle undulations that spice up the flat canine hiking along the 8 hiker-only trails and the 6-mile Cape Henry multi-use trail.

First Landing State Park stretches to the edge of the Chesapeake Bay where swimming is allowed on unguarded sandy beaches. Dogs are allowed on this beach year-round, the only such Virginia state park allowing dogs in the beach/swimming areas.

Directions to First Landing State Park (Virginia):

The park is north of Virginia Beach on US 60, about six miles from the Chesapeake Bay Bridge-Tunnel.

Phone: (757) 412-2300
Website: www.dcr.state.va.us/parks/1stland.htm

Boardwalks are used at First Landing State Park to navigate through jungle-like cypress swamps.

Just off-shore are views of the Chesapeake Bay Bridge-Tunnel, one of the seven modern engineering marvels of the world. Each span of the 17.6-mile crossing utilizes more than 2,500 concrete piles to support the trestles. Construction of the bridge-tunnel complex required undertaking a project of more than 12 miles of low-level trestles, two 1-mile tunnels, two bridges, almost 2 miles of causeway, four man-made islands and 5-1/2 miles of approach roads, totaling 23 miles.

The Strip

The Town:

The first English settlers made their first contact with America on Cape Henry at the tip of Virginia Beach in 1607. That party, led by John Smith, pressed further on but enough people have settled here in the next four centuries that Virginia Beach is now the most populous city in Virginia. When a railroad spur linked the beach to Norfolk after the Civil War and the first hotel was built in 1883, Virginia Beach took off as a major resort.

The Walks:

The heart of Virginia Beach is a 3-mile paved boardwalk stretching from 1st to 40th streets known as "The Strip." Fronted mostly by high-rise hotels and resorts, this clean and wide beach permits dogs between Memorial Day and Labor Day. During the summer months dogs are not allowed on the beach, boardwalk, grassy buffer zones or access roads at any time. On the residential beaches in the North End above 41st Street to 80th Street, dogs are allowed on the sand before 10:00 a.m. and after 6:00 p.m. Continuing north, the beach runs through Fort Story to its end on Cape Henry where the Atlantic Ocean meets the Chesapeake Bay. Fort Story is an active military base, the only installation devoted to coastal operations, but its uncrowded, pristine beaches are open to the public and dogs.

Chesapeake Bay. Fort Story is an active military base, the only installation devoted to coastal operations, but its uncrowded, pristine beaches are open to the public and dogs.

Sidetrip: Back Bay National Wildlife Refuge (south of Sandbridge, Virginia at the southern end of Sandpiper Road)

South of the developed area of Virginia Beach lies 8,000 protected acres on a sliver of barrier island. The refuge features two short scenic trails leading to the coastline and a beach trail that continues south nine miles to the North Carolina border. Along the way the hike leads through False Cape State Park with 7.5 miles of hiking through maritime forests, swamps and dunes. There is no vehicular access to False Cape, so named because its land mass resembled Cape Henry, luring northbound ships into treacherous shallow water. Land access to the park is only via this beach trail. No dogs are allowed in the refuge from April 1 until October 1; dogs can visit False Cape State Park during this time only by boat. In addition, public trails can be closed during nesting seasons. Canine hiking is easiest at low tide and you must be off the refuge property before nightfall.

Directions to Virginia Beach (Virginia):

US 60 runs directly to The Strip in downtown Virginia Beach.
Website: www.vbfun.com

On a hillock just off the beach at Fort Story is the Old Cape Henry Lighthouse, the first lighthouse authorized to be built by the United States Congress. Completed in 1792, the 90-foot sandstone tower is the third oldest lighthouse still standing in the United States. Across the street is Memorial Park - a dual memorial marking the first landing of the settlers who continued up the Chesapeake Bay to found Jamestown and the commemoration of the Battle of the Capes, the most important open seas naval battle of the American Revolution. The French fleet under Admiral de Grasse turned back a British sailing force headed to Yorktown and insured the triumph of General Washington's troops to end the war.

Outer Banks

Cape Hatteras National Seashore

The Park:

For centuries storms, shifting sands and war have visited the turbulent waters off the coast of the Outer Banks. More than 600 ships have wrecked in the seas that have earned Cape Hatteras the ghostly moniker of "Graveyard of the Atlantic." Eventually people, more than mangled ships, began arriving on the shore and in 1953 Cape Hatteras was protected as America's first National Seashore. The narrow bands of sand between the Atlantic Ocean and the Pamlico Sound stretch for 70 miles across three islands connected by a free bridge and a free ferry.

Cape Hatteras looks much different today than in the days when pirates like Blackbeard, who favored Ocracoke Island as a hide-out, cruised these beaches. Hundreds of dunes have been built along the shore to protect the Cape.

The Walks:

Dogs are welcome on the Cape Hatteras beaches year-round. There are only four swimming beaches (in season) on the entire national seashore and that leaves plenty of open sand for the dog to roam. There are short 3/4-mile nature trails on each of the three islands: the *Dyke Trail* on Bodie Island, the *Hammock Hills Nature Trail* on Ocracoke Island, and the *Buxton Woods Nature Trail* on Hatteras Island. The interpretive trails emphasize the harshness of the saltwater environment and the struggle for suvival of the plants and animals that colonize the dunes. These bounding wooded walks on soft sand are a shady treat for a dog after a day in the sun on the sand. Dogs are not allowed on the trails in the Pea Island National Wildlife Refuge on the northern end of Hatteras Island.

Sidetrip: Fort Raleigh National Historic Site (National Park Road in Manteo)

The expeditionary force that set out from England in the 1580s to establish the first English settlement in America was comprised of scientists, merchants and other gentlemen of standing. Conspicuously missing were farmers and craftsmen whose skills might have proved valuable in a strange new land. Perhaps it is not surprising then that when a supply ship returned to the settlement on Roanoke Island there was no trace of the "Lost Colony." Your dog is welcome to explore the Roanoke Colony site, including the recreated earthworks of Fort Raleigh and the birthsite of Virginia Dare, the first English-speaking baby born in the New World. The *Thomas Hariot Nature Trail*, named for a scientist from that first ill-fated voyage, rolls through a maritime forest and emphasizes the natural riches found on the island that the English hoped to exploit for riches rather than adapt for survival.

Directions to Cape Hatteras National Seashore (North Carolina):

Access to the seashore is from the north on Highway 12, about 25 miles south of Nags Head.

Phone: (252) 473-2111
Website: www.nps.gov/caha

Each of the three islands sports its own historic lighthouse, the queen of which is the 208-foot Hatteras Light, the tallest brick lighthouse in America. The Ocracoke Lighthouse, a squat 75-foot tower tucked into a residential neighborhood, has been in service since 1823 and is the oldest operating lightouse in North Carolina. The least known of the Hatteras lightouses is the Bodie Island Lighthouse, the northernmost. Located away from shore behind a freshwater marsh and partially ringed by tall pine trees, the Bodie Light's beam reaches 19 miles out to sea from its 156-foot crown. Dogs are allowed to hike the grounds of all three lighthouses.

Jockey's Ridge State Park

The Park:

Jockey's Ridge is an example of a medano—a massive hill of shifting sand that lacks vegetation. It is the tallest natural sand dune system in the Eastern United States, varying from 80 to 100 feet, depending on weather conditions. The bottom layers of sand retain enough moisture to keep the sand pile from blowing completely away. In addition, winds shift directions seasonally so the grains of sand on the hilltops are simply blown back and forth. Local citizen groups fought encroaching development on the dunes in the early 1970s by getting Jockey's Ridge declared a National Natural Landmark and in 1975, the dunes became a state park.

The Walks:

Your dog is welcome to play anywhere throughout this vast sand box. The soft sands, steep dunes and stiff winds can make for invigorating canine hiking at Jockey's Ridge. For those who like their walking more structured there are two interpretive nature trails marked by posts across the dunes. The 1.5-mile *Tracks in the Sand Trail* departs from the Visitor's Center and highlights the plants and animals that have adapted to these nutrient-deprived dunes. The 1-mile *Soundside Overlook Trail* explores the four different environments of the park including shrub forest and brackish marsh. Both trails lead to the sandy edge of the Roanoke Sound estuary where the gentle waters make an ideal canine swimming pool.

Jockey's Ridge is the ideal place to hone your skills in tracking. Signs in the sand are left by small mammals, reptiles, birds, insects and even plants. Carefully observe the size and shape of each print and study the distance between the prints to determine if the animal was walking, running or hopping. By process of elimination you can make an educated guess of what has walked the dunes before you and your dog.

Directions to Jockey's Ridge State Park (North Carolina):

The entrance to the park, Carolista Drive, is in the town of Nags Head at milepost 12 on the Highway 158 Bypass (South Croatan Highway). From I-95, exit onto US 64 east, which merges with US 264 east before Roanoke Island. Continue on US 64/US 264 to Bodie Island and turn north on US 158. The entrance to the park will be on the left after the town of Nags Head.

Phone: (252) 473-2111
Website: www.ils.unc.edu/parkproject/visit/jori/home.html

There is no need to stick to the trails at Jockey's Ridge; the massive dunes are one giant sandbox for your dog.

Flamboyant kites, model planes and hang gliders frequently fill the skies above Jockey's Ridge State Park. It is an enduring legacy. A century ago, two Dayton, Ohio bicycle mechanics tamed the skies just north of here on Big Kill Devil Hill. Orville and Wilbur Wright were lured to the Outer Banks - then a near wilderness - to test their experimental fliers by the high dunes, blustery winds and the promise of soft, sandy landings. At the Wright Brothers National Memorial your dog can walk along the rubber mats that mark the path of the first four powered manned flights in history on December 17, 1903.

Gulf Coast

Wakulla Springs State Park

The Park:

Legend has it that when Spanish explorer Ponce de Leon claimed to have discovered the "fountain of youth" in 1513 it was Wakulla Springs he was sampling. One of the world's largest and deepest freshwater springs, the bowl of the main spring covers approximately three acres. The water temperature remains a relatively constant 70 degrees year-round. A record peak flow from the spring on April 11, 1973 was measured at 14,325 gallons per second - equal to 1.2 billion gallons per day!

So crystal clear are the waters that objects 185 feet down on the bottom can still be clearly seen. In 1850, a woman reported seeing bones of an ancient mastodon at the bottom of the Springs and scientists have since discovered the remains of at least nine Ice Age mammals. The source of Wakulla Springs remains a mystery. An extensive underwater cave system has been explored to a depth of over 300 feet and mapped for more than a mile without revealing the tap of the great flow.

Today the spring is the centerpiece of 2,860-acre Wakulla Springs State Park.

The Walks:

Your dog won't be able to experience the mystical Wakulla waters - dogs are not allowed beyond a chain link fence that lines the shore. The fence was actually erected by landowner Edward Ball more than fifty years ago to keep boaters away from the springs. He was sued for fencing a navigable waterway but he won and the fence survives, as does the opulent Ball Mansion. Still, there is plenty of interest for the canine hiker in Wakulla Springs State Park. Two trails - the *Short Trail* and *Long Trail* - combine for a total of about three miles through pine and hardwood forests, cypress wetlands and other indigineous Florida plants. The trails are wide and soft and, like most of Florida, universally flat. Around you are a wide variety of Florida wildlife including bobcat, alligator, deer and wild turkey. More hiking is available along the natural surface service roads.

Sidetrip: St. Andrews State Park (east of Panama City off Highway 392)

The Wakulla River empties towards the Gulf of Mexico and you will no doubt be heading that way as well. Save for Apalachicola, there are few Gulf beaches that welcome your dog and St. Andrews State Park, once named the best beach in America, is no exception. But ignore the sugary white sands of the Gulf and head for the mostly ignored Grand Lagoon side of the park where you and the dog can enjoy a narrow strip of sand and leisurely swimming in the shallow, gentle waters. The Grand Lagoon is reached by the *Heron Pond Trail*, a rolling exploration of the scrubby dunes. Closer to the crowds, just on the other side of the famous dunes in fact, is the *Gator Lake Trail*, a surprisingly quiet half-mile trail through a sandy waste area on the edge of the park.

Directions to Wakulla State Park (Florida):

Wakulla Springs is 14 miles south of Tallahassee at the junction of SRs 61 and 267.

Phone: (850) 224-5950
Website: www.abfla.com/parks/Wakulla/wakulla.html

Hollywood came to Wakulla Springs early with several of the early *Tarzan* movies starring Johnny Weismuller being filmed here. Most famously the South American jungle was recreated at Wakulla Springs State Park for the B-movie classic *Creature From The Black Lagoon*. All three "Creature" movies would be filmed here and horror buffs will no doubt recognize the terrain.

Apalachicola National Forest

The Park:

In 1936 the federal government put an end to destructive logging and turpentine practices in the Florida panhandle with the establishment of the Apalachicola National Forest. More than half a million acres were eventually protected and healthy pine and cedar trees now mingle with large cypress trees in a healthy forest stretching from Tallahassee nearly to the Gulf of Mexico. On the edges of the national forest's two rivers, the Ochlockonee and the Sopchoppy, you can find rare hardwood swamps. The Apalachicola National Forest is one of the three most popular national forests east of the Rocky Mountains.

The Walks:

About 69 of the 85 miles of trails through the Apalachicola National Forest come on the long-distance *Florida Trail*. This orange-blazed, shady footpath is unpaved and paw-friendly its entire length; numerous trailheads slice the route into day-hike chunks but backpackers don't need a permit to set up a campsite for longer canine hikes. Most of the Florida Trail is easy-going with an occasional rolling hill. One of the most challenging stretches is an 18-mile trek through the swamps of the Bradwell Bay Wilderness Area. In times of heavy rain, portions of the trail may disappear under waist-deep water.

Canine day hikers will want to focus on three main trails: the 4.5-mile *Wright Lake Trail*, the 6-mile *Trail of the Lakes*, and the 5.4-mile *Leon Sinks Geological Trail*. Wright Lake and the Trail of the Lakes are large loops with plenty of places for your dog to slip through the pine trees and into the water. Take care with your dog at the Leon Sinks, unique sinkholes with steep sides and treacherous footing. The area contains several wet and dry sinkholes, numerous depressions, a natural bridge, and a disappearing stream accessed by three trails. Both humans and dogs have drowned in the sinks.

Directions to Apalachicola National Forest (Florida):

The forest is located southwest of Tallahassee; the Apalachicola Ranger district is on Florida Highway 20 in Bristol.

Phone: (850) 942-9300
Website: www.southernregion.fs.fed.us/florida/recreation/
          index_apa.shtml

Conscientious forest management has brought back many a tree but wildlife can't always be restored to the forest. Such is the case with the red-cockaded woodpecker, a cardinal-sized, black-and-white bird with a red-streaked black hood, that depends on mature pine trees for its survival. A fully grown pine tree often suffers from a fungus that makes the heart wood soft and easy to excavate for the woodpecker. Old growth pine forests have been mostly decimated and regenerated forests aren't allowed to keep their most mature trees so today the red-cockaded woodpecker has lost more than 99% of its liveable habitat. It is estimated only 15,000 birds survive today and the largest red-cockaded woodpecker population in the world lives in the Apalachicola National Forest.

De Soto National Forest

The Park:

Deep in the Mississippi delta is an unexpected place to stumble across remnants of America's military heritage. General Andrew Jackson marched through what would become the De Soto National Forest along the Old Federal Road from Mobile to New Orleans during the War of 1812, steps that would take him to military glory and all the way to the back of the $20 bill. A short loop trail near Janice interprets Jackson and the Battle of New Orleans. During World War II, one of five German Prisoner of War camps in Mississippi was located here. More than 20,000 prisoners, including all but a few German generals, were interned in the state. The remnants of the camp have been converted into a recreation area in the De Soto National Forest where your dog can hike around old ammunition bunkers.

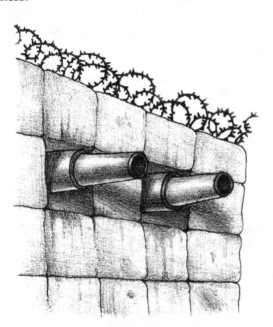

The Walks:

At just over 500,000 acres De Soto National Forest is the largest of six national forests located in Mississippi. The moist climate and warm days have created a lush, semi-tropical woodscape that is penetrated by two main long-distance hiking trails. The *Black Creek Trail* traces the lanquid Black Creek for 40 miles. The slow-moving river, stained the color of tea by tannic acids leaking from trees, has been declared Wild and Scenic and is an extremely popular float trip. Overland, more than 90 bridges and walkways have been constructed to cross feeder streams and ponds. The trail is limited to foot traffic only and is a quiet and easy hike in the shady dells.

An abandoned rail line that once served a busy sawmill kicks off the 22-mile *Tuxachanie Trail*. This trail also shadows a meandering river that produces hardwoods in its bottomlands unique to the region. Also growing amidst the dense broadleaf pines is the occasional wild orchid. This is more easy canine hiking with soft trails, slight rises and plenty of timeouts for a doggie dip.

Directions to De Soto National Forest (Mississippi):

The trail can be accessed from three different trailheads: Highway 49 north of Saucier, Airey Lake Recreation Area, and P.O.W. Lake Recreation Area. Parking is available at these trailheads. Rows of live oaks mark the trail's entrance on Highway 49.

Phone: (850) 523-8500
Website: www.southernregion.fs.fed.us/mississippi

"To err is human, to forgive, canine."
- anonymous

Blue Ridge Parkway

Blue Ridge Parkway

The Park:

Begun as a Depression-era public works project, the Blue Ridge Parkway was America's first rural parkway. When ultimately completed it was also the nation's longest - 469 miles of uninterrupted mountain roads linking Shenandoah National Park in the north to the Great Smokey Mountains National Park in the south. Designed for leisurely motoring, the speed limit never exceeds 45 mph on the parkway and roadside parking is permitted on the shoulders the entire way. Much of the beautiful road is lined by low stone walls. Parks and recreation areas - several spanning thousands of acres - appear roughly every 30 miles, although most are located on the Blue Ridge Mountains, the 355 miles that comprise the northern part of the route. The lower 114 miles wind through the powerful Black Mountains, named for the dark green spruce that cover the massive slopes. The Blue Ridge Parkway is far and away the most popular destination in the National Park System - more than 19 million recreation visits per year.

The Walks:

Dogs are allowed on the more than 100 varied trails throughout the Blue Ridge Parkway, ranging from easy valley strolls to demanding mountain summit hikes. From the north, an early highlight comes within the first ten miles at the Humpback Rocks where the *Greenstone Nature Trail* leads to the unusually shaped boulders. A strenuous climb accesses the *Appalachian Trail* in 2 miles. Canine hikers will look forward to the Peaks of Otter, in the vicinity of the highest mountains on the Virginia section of the Parkway, beginning around the 75-mile mark.

Three mountains - Sharp Top (3,875 feet), Flat Top (4,004 feet), and Harkening Hill (3,364 feet) comprise the Peaks of Otter, a popular hiking destination since Colonial days. The 4.4-mile trail to the Flat Top summit is graded most of the way until jumbled rocks provide athletic dogs a tail-wagging workout. Also in the Peaks of Otter are a quick loop hike threading through rhododendron and mountain laurel on Onion Mountain and the 1.6-mile loop of the *Fallingwater Cascades National Scenic Trail*. Both offer splendid views in exchange for moderate effort.

At the 167-mile mark comes Rocky Knob, with 15 miles of trails across 4,800 acres. The marquee walk here is the rugged 10.8-mile *Rock Castle Gorge National Recreation Trail*. Just down the road is picturesque Mabry Mill with an easy, self-guiding trail spiced with interpretive exhibits and in-season demonstrations on rural Appalachian life. The first canine hiking in North Carolina comes on Cumberland Knob at the 217.5-mile mark. A quick 15-minute loop leads to the knob and a more challenging 2-mile loop that traces Gully Creek. Next up is 7,000-acre Doughton Park, the largest recreation area on the Blue Ridge Parkway. More than 30 miles of trail and a dog-friendly campground are the prime attractions here. All the 9 first come, first served campgrounds on the Parkway welcome dogs.

The Moses H. Cone Memorial Park is a popular stopping point for relaxing or exploring. Many miles of horse and carriage trails jump off from the Historic Cone Manor House and many

While it is not a prime destination for dog owners, you may want to make arrangements to visit the Biltmore Estate in Asheville, America's largest private home.

more trails criss-cross neighboring Julian Price Memorial Park, which includes Price Lake, one of the few lakes along the Parkway. In another 10 miles you cross the Linn Cove Viaduct, an engineering marvel skirting the side of Grandfather Mountain. You and your dog can pick your way along an interpretive trail to close-up views of the viaduct.

A most-anticipated highlight of the Blue Ridge Parkway will be the upcoming Linville Gorge, one of the most remote locations in the Appalachians. Unblazed trails lead deep into the wilderness but most canine hikers will stick to the two main hiking trails surrounding Linville Falls. *Erwins View Trail* is a sporty walk that takes in four distinct overlooks of the plunging waters in its .8-mile journey. More challenging is the hike on the opposite side of the water into the gorge that descends through a virgin hemlock forest to the water's edge.

South of Linville Falls the elevations climb and the canine hiking opportunities fade away. *Craggy Pinnacle Trail* at 364.4 miles is a narrow ridge trail that tunnels through purple rhododendron to a hilltop opening in a veritable sea of trees. A second moderate trail here is the *Craggy Gardens Nature Trail*. Nearby, a spur road leads up Mount Mitchell. Your dog can make the final paved ascent to the 6684-foot summit on foot and stand on the highest point of ground east of the Mississippi River.

The last major recreation area on the Parkway comes south of Asheville at Mount Pisgah, once part of the 125,000-acre Biltmore estate owned by George W. Vanderbilt. Vanderbilt directed trail building efforts across his vast property to provide access for hunting and horseback riding in the first example of managed forest land in America. The trail to summit views of Mt. Pisgah is a hardy 1.26-mile climb.

The final gasps for canine hiking on the Blue Ridge Parkway before entering Great Smoky Mountain National Park - where dogs are not allowed on the trails - occur at Milepost 431 where *Richard Balsam's Self-guiding Trail* wanders through the remnants of a spruce-fir forest on the highest point on the Parkway (6,047 feet) and at Waterrock Knob at Mile 451.2. Here a mountain trail leads to the knob and its panoramic, 4-state views of the Great Smokies.

Phone: (828) 271-4779
Website: www.nps.gov/blri

🚫 *One of the most popular hikes on the East Coast is up Old Rag Mountain in the Shenandoahs. Do not drive out of your way to do this hike with your dog however. Dogs are not allowed on the trail and probably could not negotiate some of the rock passages anyway.*

Ground was broken on the Blue Ridge Parkway on September 11, 1935 at Cumberland Knob on the North Carolina-Virginia border, near the mid-point of the proposed route. By 1967 all but seven and one-half of its 469 miles were complete. The final section, around the rocky slopes of Grandfather Mountain, one of the world's oldest mountains, would not be finished until 1987. To finish the Parkway without massive cuts and fills on the fragile mountainside would call for the most complicated concrete bridge ever built - the serpentine Linn Viaduct.

The 12 bridges of the viaduct were constructed from the top down at an elevation of 4100 feet to eliminate the need for a pioneer road. In fact, the only trees cut down during the entire project were those directly beneath the roadbed. The only construction on the ground was the drilling of seven permanent piers upon which the Viaduct rests. Exposed rock was covered to prevent staining from the concrete epoxy binding the pre-cast sections. To further minimize the intrusion on the mountain, concrete mixes were tinted with iron oxide to blend with existing outcroppings. Trails lead to views underneath this engineering marvel and access the 13.5-mile *Tanawha Trail* from Beacon Heights to Julian Price Park.

Appalachian Highlands

Spruce Knob-Seneca Rocks National Recreation Area

The Park:

Legend has it that the spectacular crags of white/gray quartzite that soar 900 feet above the flat valley of the North Fork of the Potomac River were the childhood playground of Snowbird, beautiful daughter of Seneca Indian chief Bald Eagle. To determine the warrior who would win her hand in marriage she staged a contest to see who could scale the magnificent cliff. The first documented roped ascent of the Seneca Rocks, however, took place in 1935. Today there are nearly 400 mapped climbing routes on the rocks. In 1969 the federal government purchased the West Virginia landmark and pieced together the national recreation area with Spruce Knob within the Monongahela National Forest.

The Walks:

A switchbacking 1.3-mile hard-packed trail ascends the north edge of the Seneca Rocks to a wooden viewing platform. Sure-footed dogs can climb a bit further up bare rock to notches at the very top of the rocks for views of the Allegheny Mountains to the west. The trail is a steady climb but within the means of even the novice canine hiker.

More extended trail time can be found in the Dolly Sods area of the park. The going is not nearly so smooth on the *Boar's Nest/South Prong Loop Trail* that picks up 1,500 feet in elevation over the six-mile trip. Come prepared for wet trails conditions and slippery rocks. Pay close attention to the blazes on the trail.

Isolated canine hiking can be found in a dead-end gorge known as Smoke Hole Canyon where the South Branch of the Potomac River is forced into a 180-degree turn by North Mountain and Cave Mountain. The *Big Bend Loop Trail* is a one-mile circle over a hill and around the Big Bend Campground where the river bends back on itself. The *South Branch Trail* is a 3.5-mile loop that climbs out of the half-mile deep canyon and into meadows and cedar barrens. Stay on the blue-blazed route when encountering old mountain roads.

Spruce Knob is the highest point in West Virginia at 4,861 feet. The *Whispering Spruce Trail* winds through wind-sculpted rocks and boulders on a wide, gravelly 1/2-mile loop around the summit. Down below the *Gatewood Nature Trail* shares time in a typical Northern hardwood forest and a Southern red pine plantation during two tranquil miles.

Directions to Seneca Rocks (West Virginia):

The Visitor Center is located in the town of Seneca Rocks off US 33 and West Virginia Route 28.
Phone (Seneca Rocks): (304) 567-2827
Website: www.fs.fed.us/r9/mnf/map_information.shtml

There are enough switchbacks and steps to enable any dog to conquer the 900-foot high Seneca Rocks.

Spruce Knob may be the best place in the East to bring your dog to howl at the moon. The remote summit is perenially ranked #1 on amateur astronomers' Dark Sky Sites lists east of the Mississippi River. With nothing more than binoculars or even the naked eye you can spot streaking meteors and even the Northern Lights.

Catoctin Mountain Park

The Park:

It took an offer of 200 acres of land rent free for three years and a penny an acre thereafter by Lord Baltimore to lure settlers into this remote region. When they finally came so much wood was cut for charcoal, tanning and lumber that eventually people left the mountains. This time there was no effort to populate the region and in 1935 over 10,000 acres were acquired by the Federal Government and developed as the Catoctin Recreational Demonstration Area. The land regenerated into an eastern hardwood climax forest looking again as it did before the original European settlement.

The Walks:

You could fill up a day of canine hiking at Catoctin Mountain Park just by checking off the many easy self-guiding interpretive trails as you learn about mountain culture and forest ecology.

There is plenty of more challenging fare in the park as well. Three of the best vistas - Wolf Rock, Chimney Rock and Cat Rock - are connected by a rollercoaster trail on the eastern edge of the mountain. There is little understory in the woods and views are long. Many of the mountain slope trails are rocky and footing can be uncertain under paw on climbs to 1500 feet.

In the western region of Catoctin Mountain, near the Owens Creek campground, are wide horse trails ideal for contemplative canine hiking. The grades are gentler for long hikes through mixed hardwoods of chestnut oak, hickory, black birch and yellow poplar. Dogs are allowed in the campground and on all national park trails but not across the road in the popular Cunningham Falls area.

Directions to Catoctin Mountain Park (Maryland):

The Visitor Center, where you can pick up many of the park trails, is on Maryland Route 77, west of US Route 15 in Thurmont.

Phone: (301) 663-9388
Website: www.nps.gov/cato

A short hike on the Blue Blazes Whiskey Trail leads to a reproduction of a working still.

The forests deep in the rugged Catoctin Mountains provided ideal cover for a whiskey still, made illegal by the onset of Prohibition in 1919. On a steaming July day in 1929 Federal agents raided the Blue Blazes Whiskey Still and confiscated more than 25,000 gallons of mash. Today the airy, wooded *Blue Blazes Whiskey Trail* along Distillery Run leads to a recreated working still and interprets the history of whiskey making in the backwoods of Appalachia.

Canine Hiking In Presidential Footsteps

How would you like to hike with your dog where Presidents hike with their dogs? When an American President leaves the White House for the presidential retreat of Camp David, there is almost always an eager dog in tow. Franklin Roosevelt's Scottish Terrier Fala was the first in a steady procession of Presidential dogs to romp in the woods of Camp David. President Reagan once complained that when he took a break at Camp David, his dog Rex would beat him to the window seat in the helicopter.

Everyone has heard of Camp David but where exactly it is? Surprisingly it is located right here in Catoctin Mountain Park. When you take your dog there, you will never see Camp David or any evidence that the presidential compound is hidden among the trees but the trails you can hike on are of Presidential quality nonetheless. Just don't expect to see President George W. Bush and Spotty.

George Herbert Bush with dogs Ranger and Millie.
(photo courtesy of The George Bush Presidential Library and Museum)

Bluegrass Country

Mammoth Cave National Park

The Park:

Not named for extinct wooly elephants but rather the length of its passageways, Mammoth Cave is by far the longest known cave system in the world. There may be no traces of mammoths in the vast underground world but archeologicalists have unearthed evidence of human occupation in Mammoth Cave from as far back as 4,000 years ago. In the early days of the country, Mammoth Cave was used commercially to produce saltpeter needed to manufacture gunpowder and in 1941 the cave was protected as a national park. In 1981, Mammoth Cave was named a World Heritage Site.

The Walks:

Your dog won't be able to sniff around the 336 miles of underground passages in Mammoth Cave but there are more than 70 miles of trails above ground to explore in the park. A variety of leg-stretching hikes less than two miles are available around the Visitor Center, including the *Green River Bluffs Trail* that snakes through thick woods to a promontory above the Green River. For prolonged canine hiking head for the *North Side Trails*. A half-dozen mid-length day hikes launch into the dark hollows and hardwood forests from the *Maple Spring Trailhead* (North Entrance Road). This labyrinth of trails cuts through rugged terrain that has been left in its natural state. In the Big Woods (Little Jordan Road), you can hike the *White Oak Trail* through one of the last remaining old growth forests in Kentucky.

Directions to Mammoth Cave National Park (Kentucky):

From I-65, take Highway 31 West, and Highway 31 East from the north.
Phone: (270) 758-2180
Website: www.nps.gov/maca

Along Highway 255 (the East Entrance road) is a small parking lot for a short trail to Sand Cave. For several weeks in the 1930s, this remote section of woods was the most famous spot in America. A local cave explorer named Floyd Collins became trapped in the cave and the nation became fixated on the rescue efforts that were ultimately unsuccessful in freeing him from a leg-pinning rock.
The incident spawned books and a movie starring Kirk Douglas, *Ace In The Hole*.
The small entrance of Sand Cave is wired off today and there is little to remind visitors of the drama that once gripped America here.

Big South Fork National River and Recreation Area

The Park:

Flowing north from Tennessee into Kentucky, the Big South Fork of the Cumberland River and its tributaries have been carving up the Cumberland Plateau into cliffs, natural arches and rock shelters for tens of thousands of years. In 1974 Congress placed 123,000 acres of wilderness under the management of the National Park Service in the Big South Fork National River and Recreation Area. The centerpiece of the park is the Big South Fork River with 90 miles of free-flowing, navigable water through gorges and valleys.

Straddling the Tennessee-Kentucky border, the 150 miles of hiking trails through mixed hardwood and pine forests are uncrowded - a stark contrast to Great Smoky Mountains National Park, America's most-visited national park, to the southeast. Plus, dogs are allowed on trails here.

The Walks:

Save for the 6.5-mile *Blue Heron Loop*, the top hikes at Big South Fork are in the Tennessee portion of the park near the Bandy Creek Visitor Center. At the Visitor Center is the *Oscar Blevin Trail*, an easy 3.2 mile loop through mature forest to an historic farmstead that was worked until the National Park Service took over into 1974.

To the east of Bandy Creek is the Leatherwood Ford, the trailhead for the popular *Angel Falls Trail*, an easy two-mile lope along the west bank of the Big South Fork Cumberland River. Continuing another .8 mile, the trail winds to the top of a jagged limestone bluff with a commanding view of Angel Falls, actually a series of rapids. The cliffs are unprotected but the climb can be negotiated by an agile dog. The Angel Falls Trail is a small segment of the *John Muir Trail* that stretches 50 miles across the park.

The seven miles upstream from Leatherwood Ford on the Big South Fork to its confluence with the New River contain the greatest concentration of rapids in the gorge and trails lead to outstanding river views in the hardwood forests.

Sidetrip: Pickett State Park (Highway 154, northeast of Jamestown)

The 16,500 acres of Pickett State Park, once owned by the massive Stearns Coal & Lumber Company, became one of Tennessee's earliest state parks in the 1930s. Here are botanical and geological wonders found nowhere else in Tennessee; more than 58 miles of hiking trails skirt deep gorges and lead through thick stands of laurel and rhododendron. Many of the more accessible trails are short, ranging from 1/4 mile to three miles, and lead to unique natural formations.

Directions to Big South Fork National River and Recreation Area (Tennessee):

From I-75 southbound: take KY 461 south to KY 80 west to US 27 south. The Kentucky visitor center is south of Whitley City off KY 92. Continuing south to Oneida, follow TN 297 west into the Tennessee visitor center.
Phone: (423) 569-9778
Website: www.nps.gov/biso

In the remote western region of Big South Fork National River and Recreation Area are a sandstone double archway known as the Twin Arches. Trailheads are reached by unpaved roads off Highway 154. A short, but hardy, trek of less than a mile leads to the largest natural sandstone bridges in Tennessee. Rock shelters like these deep in the woods were once popular harbors for moonshine stills and old still equipment is on display in the park. The walk can be extended into a 6.0-mile loop to the historic farm at the Charit Creek Lodge. A hunter in the area, Jonathan Blevins built a log cabin here in 1817 that is now incorporated into the rustic lodge. Charit Creek Lodge, which sports no electricity, can be reached only on foot or by horseback.

Daniel Boone National Forest

The Park:

The Treaty of Fort Stanwix in 1768 during the French and Indian War triggered a rush to settlement of the wilderness, then part of the great Virginia Colony, that stretched to the Mississippi River. The most prominent pioneer was Daniel Boone from Berks County in Pennsylvania, thanks in part to an autobiographical narrative he published in 1784. After the American Revolution veterans received land grants for their service and by 1796 nearly a quarter of a million people came into the area on the Wilderness Trail, little more than a horse path. Some mined coal, some mined saltpeter necessary to manufacture gunpowder, and some logged but most farmed small plots of cleared land. When the Daniel Boone National Forest was established in 1937, 98% of the dwellings were of log and pole construction and the average number of acres on a farm in cultivation was only 17.

The Walks:

There are more than 500 miles of trails in the 700,000-acre national forest that occupies a 140-mile slice of eastern Kentucky. The great variety of trails from flat and easy to steep and twisting help spread out the five million annual visitors. Save for the designated swimming areas, your dog is welcome everywhere in the Daniel Boone National Forest.

The *Sheltowee Trace National Recreation Trail* courses through the entire forest for 269 miles. The footpath, blazed in white turtle markers (Sheltowee is the Indian name given Boone when he visited the area meaning "big turtle"), connects the major day-use areas as it visits deep canyons, long ridgetops and craggy rimrock cliffs.

The first destination for many canine hikers in the Daniel Boone National Forest is the Red River Gorge where 300-foot sandstone cliffs and overhangs are decorated with grotesque rock formations. The more than 100 natural stone arches in the area give the feel of a southwestern canyon country trek with trees.

Easy explorations include the *Natural Arch Trail* that reaches a bridge of sandstone more than 100 feet across and seven stories high and the *Nathan McClure Trail* along the shores of Cumberland Lake. The lake is graced by towering sandstone cliffs.

Directions to Daniel Boone National Forest (Kentucky):

Park headquarters are located in Winchester, Kentucky at 1700 Bypass Road.

Phone: (859) 745-3100
Website: www.southernregion.fs.fed.us/boone/

Great Lakes

Niagara Falls

The Park:

Of all the crown jewels in America's natural tiara - Yellowstone, the Grand Canyon, Yosemite - none is as dog-friendly as Niagara Falls. Save for special guided tours, your dog can walk anywhere you walk to view the world-famous Falls in both New York's Niagara Falls State Park and Ontario's Queen Victoria Park.

One of the first Europeans to see the Falls was 51-year old French priest Father Louis Hennepin in 1678. Hennepin is reported to have dropped to his knees in prayer and muttered, "the universe does not afford its parallel." The French military, while perhaps appreciating the romantic sentiment, was more interested in defending the natural trade route between Lake Erie and Lake

The walking paths on Goat Island lead right to the edge of the wild Niagara River above the Falls.

Ontario and built a key fort here.

Travelers did not begin to arrive in western New York in great numbers until the opening of the Erie Canal in 1825 and the coming of the railroads in the 1830s. Many enjoyed the same reaction as Father Hennepin. The tradition of honeymooners coming to Niagara where "the love of those who honeymoon here will last as long as the Falls themselves" dates to this time when members of the French ruling Bonapart family came on wedding trips. Soon the area around the Falls was a confused hodgepodge of water-powered mills and private resorts.

Following the Civil War, a small group of visionaries sought to heal the scars inflicted on Niagara's natural beauty. A "Free Niagara" crusade led to the creation of Niagara Reservation, America's first state park in 1885. Frederick Law Olmsted, designer of New York City's Central Park and one of the leaders of the movement, laid out the park's network of wooded footpaths. Olmsted's belief in retaining natural beauty while providing public access - for human and dog - endures at Niagara Falls to this day.

The Walks:

Niagara Falls reigns as one of the world's premier sightseeing destinations and your dog is welcome along. Due to the crush of visitors near the edge of the Falls it is best to begin your explorations of Niagara Falls State Park with the dog in the early morning hours when it is easier to maneuver to the various vantage points. Even in the busiest times there are grass fields and shady promenades for the dog to romp.

Begin your tour on the paved paths of Goat Island in the middle of the Niagara River, flanked by ferocious rapids on all sides. Pedestrian bridges lead to the Three Sisters Islands and Green Island for close-up looks of the wild river as it approaches the Falls. Descend a flight of stairs to Luna Island, nestled in between the American Falls and the Bridal Veil Falls, before crossing back across Goat Island to the precipice of the Horseshoe Falls on the Canadian side. You and your dog can stand at the edge of all three falls and drink in the spray of water before the droplets fall 18 stories over the crest into the gorge. Forty million gallons of water spill over Niagara Falls every minute.

For panoramic views of the three falls you will need to walk your dog across the gorge into Canada. Ontario's Queen Victoria Park actually predates Niagara Falls State Park. Landscaping of the area began in 1837 and it became a park in 1882. Both parks are free to visit, as are the nightly light shows illuminating the Falls.

While dogs are banned from many popular natural tourist destinations, they can go right to the edge of Niagara Falls.

Niagara Falls has plenty in store for the serious canine hiker as well. The thrills of the Niagara River are not completely spent when the water crashes 170 feet down the Falls into the gorge. The river, one of the shortest in the world, rumbles another turbulent 7 miles before disgorging its contents into Lake Ontario. The rapids in the river are among the fiercest in the world, rated a 6 on the navigable scale of 1-6. The dangerous waters have historically gripped daredevils as securely as the Falls themselves. Matthew Webb, the first man to swim the English Channel, perished in attempt to swim across the Niagara River in 1883. Today, whirlpool jet boats ply the tamer of the rapids for thrill-seeking tourists.

The flat, paved *Niagara Gorge Rim Trail* runs six miles from the American Falls at Prospect Point along the canyon, linking a necklace of New York state parks along the way. Several sets of 300+ steps descend into the gorge to reach connecting trails along the river's edge. Much of the trail below the rim follows the roadbed of the historic Great Gorge Railway that operated until September 17, 1935 when 5000 tons of rock slid down the gorge and buried the tracks. Part of the trail crosses this rubble and involves considerable rock-hopping for an athletic dog. These periodic rock falls - seldom of this magnitude - are more common in the winter and early spring and canine hiking in the gorge is recommended only between mid-May and November 1.

The trail leads to the edge of the waves where the 35-foot deep river can reach speeds of 22 miles per hour. While the views of the water

It is no problem for you to stand with your dog right at the precipice of Niagara Falls. From these vantage points you can stand and contemplate the first recorded person to jump into the Falls. That was Sam Patch in October 1829, who leaped twice from a platform 110 feet high. He survived both jumps. The first person to successfully ride over the falls in a barrel was a woman, Annie Taylor, who survived the stunt on October 24, 1901. Of the 16 known attempts to ride the Falls in a barrel or similar capsule - a stunt that is now illegal - 10 survived. And dogs going over Niagara Falls? Sadly, there is one recorded account of just such an event. In December of 1874 some local hotel owners purchased an old Great Lakes schooner and planned to send it over the Falls to lure visitors to Niagara. To add drama to the spectacle the organizers loaded the ship with a buffalo, three bears, two foxes, a raccoon, a dog, a cat and four geese and cut their "Reverse Noah's Ark" loose in the rapids. The animals were observed scampering around the deck as the schooner slipped over the edge of the falls and smashed into hundreds of pieces on the rocks below. Only two geese were believed to survive the stunt.

churning through Devil's Hole Rapids and Whirlpool Rapids can be mesmerizing, don't forget to look up now and then and perhaps spot the occasional bald eagle circling about, no doubt looking for an easy meal of dazed and battered fish.

The northern-most park along the Niagara Gorge is the Earl W. Brydges Artpark in Lewiston, where the cocktail was invented by a local tavern owner who stirred one of her concoctions with the tail feather of a handy stuffed cock pheasant. The river has calmed down enough by this point to permit a cautious swim for the dog.

The cliffs of the gorge at Lewiston are where Niagara Falls began some 12,000 years ago at the end of the Ice Age. Torrents of water from melting glacial ice poured over the edge of the Niagara Escarpment, as the cliff is known. The sheer force of the water has slowly worn away the rock and moved the falls to their present position seven miles upstream. Today, the falls are eroding at the rate of an inch per year and you can trace the travels of the falls in the rocks that line the gorge.

The Niagara Gorge Trail System ends at the imposing concrete dam of the Robert Moses Power Plant, completing a journey from the beauty of Niagara Falls to the hard reality of its practicality. Power plants on the American and Canadian sides of the Falls use water diverted from the Falls to generate enough electricity to light 2,500,000 100-watt light bulbs. As impressive as the Falls are today, they are only a fraction as mighty as our ancestors saw - as much as half of the Niagara River's flow is diverted for hydroelectric production. River's flow is diverted for hydroelectric production.

Some day in the next 3,000 years Niagara Falls will wear away entirely and the power will dry up as water flows placidly between Lake Erie and Lake Ontario. Until that day, however, there is ample opportunity to take the dog and marvel at the power of Niagara.

Directions to Niagara Falls (New York/Ontario):

The Robert Moses Parkway leads directly into the town of Niagara Falls.

Phone: (716) 278-1796
Website: www.niagarafallsstatepark.com/

Presque Isle State Park

The Park:

Pennsylvania's most popular state park is believed to have formed 11,000 years ago from the deposits of sand carried by wind and water across Lake Erie. This "flying spit" of sand is the largest in the Great Lakes region and the only one in Pennsylvania. Presque Isle State Park is estimated to be moving eastward at the rate of one-half mile per century. Although Presque Isle is French for "almost an island," the area has often been completely surrounded by water. One such breech in the sand peninsula lasted 32 years.

During the War of 1812 Commodore Oliver Hazard Perry used a harbor on the east side of Presque Isle as a base of operations for the critical Battle of Lake Erie on September 10, 1813. After the clash with the British fleet, Perry returned to Presque Isle for the winter, using a shallow pond to bury American dead. The harbor was named Misery Bay in light of the hardships suffered that winter. Today the Perry monument on Crystal Point remembers the heroic American exploits here.

The 3,200-acre peninsula was designated a National Natural Landmark in 1969.

The Walks:

Presque Isle is unique in that plant succession from sandy shoreline to climax forest can be seen in less than one mile. This transformation can be viewed from the 5.8-mile *Multi-Purpose Trail*, a National Recreation Trail. The path begins at the park entrance and shadows the Presque Isle Bay shoreline until it ends at the Perry Monument. As this main pathway is popular with cyclists, skaters and joggers, dogwalkers may want to migrate to one of the park's many other trails. Dogs are welcome on all trails but ticks are heavy so avoid the trail fringes. Dogs are also allowed on any beach not designated a swimming beach.

There are more than a dozen short trails radiating across the peninsula that offer a pleasing variety of easy hiking. The *Sidewalk Trail* was constructed of wooden boards by a lighthouse keeper to reach the Presque Isle Lighthouse from his boat over a mile away in Misery Bay; it is now a concrete strip down the center of the trail that was resurfaced in 1925. The *North Pier Trail* traces the shoreline along a sand ridge and the *Long Pond Trail* hugs the shoreline of one of the park's several lagoons. Longer trails such as the *Fox Trail* (2.25 miles) and the *Dead Pond Trail* (2 miles) traverse distinct ecological zones as they move from sandplains to oak-maple forests.

Presque Isle is a key resting point for both migratory land and shore birds. As many as 320 species of birds have been identified here, arriving from the Arctic to South America. One of the best spots in the park to study this great ornithological stew is on the observation platform at the end of the *Gull Point Trail*. The 1.9-mile circle hike is at the farthest tip of Presque Isle where changes to the sand spit are most dramatic.

Directions to Presque Isle State Park (Pennsylvania):

The park is in southwest Erie; PA 832 leads into the park at land's end.

Phone: (814) 833-7424
Website: www.presqueisle.org/

Pictured Rocks National Lakeshore

The Park:

The "pictured rocks" on the south shore of Lake Superior were painted by mineral stains on exposed cliffs scoured by glaciers. The colorful streaks on the cliffs - as high as 200 feet above the water - result from groundwater that seeps out of cracks in the rock. The oozing water contains iron, limonite, copper, and other minerals that brush the cliff face with colors as they trickle down. The pictured rocks were the inspiration for William Wadsworth Longfellow's "The Song of Hiawatha." In 1966, the Pictured Rocks were preserved as America's first national lakeshore. The park stretches along Lake Superior, the world's largest freshwater lake, for 40 miles.

The Walks:

Dogs are not allowed to trot everywhere in Pictured Rocks National Lakeshore's 72,000 acres (a detailed pet area map is available) but there is plenty of superb canine hiking on tap here. Day hikes lead to clifftops and cobble beaches through hardwood forests and windswept dunes. Some of the best walks are around kettle lakes where massive blocks of ice melted down - such as the *Chapel Falls Loop*. One short trail that should be on any canine hiker's menu is the *Grand Sable Dunes Trail* at the Sable Falls Parking Area. These dunes once fronted an ancient predecessor of Lake Superior. Dogs are also permitted on most of the park's 21 miles of ski trails during the snow-free season.

When hiking in Pictured Rocks during the summer, if the winds blow warm from the southwest, they can blow in hordes of stable flies. These biting pests are impervious to insect repellent and prefer to hover close to the ground - and your dog. In times of invasion, the inland, forested trails are your best bet.

Sidetrip: Grand Island (western end of national lakeshore)

Less than one mile off shore, is Grand Island, the largest island in the southern waters of Lake Superior. The 22-square mile island has been a National Recreation Area since 1968 and is reached by regular ferry passenger service in season. Leashed dogs ride free. On the island you'll find deep woods, lakes, sandy beaches and dramatic rocky shorelines. A spiderweb of old, unmaintained logging roads penetrate the island and a 23-mile perimeter route circles it.

Directions to Pictured Rocks National Lakeshore (Michigan):

Route 28 across the Upper Peninsula will take you to the Munising entrance to the park on the western end. To reach the eastern access point at Grand Marais, take Route 77 North from Route 28 in Seney.

Phone: (906) 387-3700
Website: www.nps.gov/piro

Sleeping Bear Dunes National Lakeshore

The Park:

Long ago, according to the Ojibway Indian legend, a racing forest fire ravaged the Wisconsin shoreline driving a mother bear and her two cubs into the waters of Lake Michigan. The three bears swam for safety across the entire lake. The worried mother reached the shore and climbed a high bluff to wait for her cubs who tired and drowned before her eyes just off shore. The Great Spirit Manitou created two islands to mark the spot where the exhausted cubs disappeared and then created a solitary dune to represent the faithful mother bear. The national lakeshore, established in 1970, protects 35 miles of dunes - the highest 480 feet above the lake - that are the product of several glacial advances and retreats that ended 11,000 years ago.

The Walks:

Your dog isn't allowed to make the *Dune Climb* up a mountain of sand but she may thank you for that. Otherwise dogs are welcome on Sleeping Bear Dunes National Lakeshore trails. The best canine hike is the *Cottonwood Trail* off the popular Pierce Stocking Scenic Drive. The loop leads out into dunes speckled with the bleached remains of overwhelmed trees and the hardy survivors adapting to their sandy world. The rollicking trail, open May to October, is completely on thick sand that, while soft to the paw, can tire an unfit dog.

In the north section of the park the *Good Harbor Bay Trail* is a flat, wooded walk. Most of the starch has been taken out of the Lake Michigan waves here for gentle canine swimming. More adventurous dog paddlers will want to test the frisky waves in the southernmost Platte Plains section. You have your choice of trails here to choose how much you want to hike before reaching the surf. The 13 mid-length trails are all hiker-only. Dogs are not allowed on North or South Manitou Island.

Directions to Sleeping Bear Dunes National Lakeshore (Michigan):

Located on the western coast of Michigan's Lower Peninusla, Route 22 runs through the national lakeshore from south to north, connected by US 31 from the east.

Phone: (231) 326-5134
Website: www.nps.gov/slbe

The *Dunes Trail* at Sleeping Bear Point leads past the Sleeping Bear Point Coast Guard Station, one of some 60 life-saving stations that once served Great Lakes mariners. Shipwrecks in the United States were once considered a concern mostly for Atlantic sea captains but after 214 people perished in shipwrecks on the Great Lakes in 1870-1871, Congress authorized money to train professional life-saving crews on the land-locked lakes. Now restored to its early 1900s appearance, the life-saving station now operates a museum.

Indiana Dunes National Lakeshore

The Park:

The Indiana Dunes National Lakeshore is a park of striking contrasts. More than 1,400 plant species have been identified within park boundaries, ranking it 7th among national parks in native plant diversity. Growing zones clash here at the southern base of Lake Michigan so southern dogwood mixes with arctic bearberrry and northern conifer forests thrive alongside cacti. The park itself stands in stark relief from the industrial surroundings of Gary, Indiana and Chicago. The national lakeshore was designated in 1966 and preserves 25 miles of Lake Michigan shoreline.

The Walks:

Canine hikers will also find the dog-friendly trails, with dips and climbs, to be of a different style than the generally flat northern Indiana area. The high point on the dunes is 123-foot Mt. Baldy at the extreme eastern point of the park - you can make this short, sandy climb your first or last stop. If you take your time, even older dogs can make it to the top or you can hike a trail around Mt. Baldy directly to the beach.

Other trails highlight the natural and cultural significance of the Indiana Dunes National Lakeshore. You won't even realize you are mere yards from Lake Michigan on the *Cowles Bog Trail*, three stacked loops totalling 5 miles. The trail goes past the sub-arctic bog, declared a National Natural Landmark.

The similarly inland *Little Calumet River Trail* leads to the Bailly Homestead, a National Historic Landmark from the pre-Colonial fur trading era and the Chellberg Farm settled by Swedish immigrants.

No dogs are allowed on the *Ly-Co-Ki-We Trail* but can spend the night in the Dunewood Campground.

More superb canine hiking can be found in Indiana Dunes State Park, entombed by the national lakeshore. There are many numbered trails - some quite challenging - that ascend high vista points such as Mt. Tom. The best trails on the lake's edge can be found in the state park.

Directions to Indiana Dunes National Lakeshore (Indiana):

Visitors can access the national lakeshore via Interstate Highway I-94, the Indiana Toll Road, I-80/90 U.S. 20, or Indiana State Hwy 12 and various state roads.

Phone: (219) 926-7561
Website: www.nps.gov/indu

The industrial setting of the Indiana Dunes make the natural delights found in the park even more special.

The Indiana Dunes are considered the birthplace of the science of ecology. University of Chicago professor Dr. Henry Cowles used the dunes to develop his theories of plant succession, the process of botanical colonization and development. The one-mile *West Beach Succession Trail* illuminates the natural processes that over thousands of years have created oak forests on once barren sand.

Ozarks

Hot Springs National Park

The Park:

Andrew Jackson was still in the White House and Arkansas was not yet even a state when Congress set aside the springs and surrounding mountainsides as a park-like federal reservation in 1832. Designated a national park in 1921 and protecting 47 thermal springs, "the American Spa" is the oldest park in the national park system. The namesake springs begin as rainwater absorbed into nearby mountains and carried more than a mile underground where it is heated to about 143 degrees. Now purified, the water percolates slowly towards the surface and is released through cracks in the earth's crust. By this time the original rainwater is about 4,000 years old.

The Walks:

Unlike other national parks, Hot Springs is part town and part nature preserve and unlike most other national parks, dogs are allowed to enjoy the groomed trails. Your first stop will likely be a dog walk down the *Grand Promenade*. Designated a National Recreation Trail, the red-and-yellow brick half-mile walkway provides a smooth flow from the bathhouse area to the mountains.

You will leave most of the tourists behind by leaving the Grand Promenade for the *Peak Trail*. This trail pulls to the top of Hot Springs Mountain and views of the verdant Ouachita Mountains in less than a mile. Another choice from the Grand Promenade is the *Dead Chief Trail* behind the Fordyce Bathhouse Visitor Center. This hardy canine hike intersects with the *Short Cut Trail* and also leads to the summit of Hot Springs Mountain.

The longest hike in Hot Springs is *Sunset Trail* that tackles a ridge to the top of Music Mountain. At the summit you are standing with your dog at 1,420 feet, the highest point in the park. The ridge is an open-ended arc with Sugarloaf and West mountains on the points.

There are many more short explorations on foot and paw, including a ramble through a wildflower meadow to a massive rock outcropping on the *Goat Rock Trail* and several paths leading from the scenic driving roads.

Directions to Hot Springs National Park (Arkansas):

The national park is in downtown Hot Springs. Visitors traveling north-south on I-30 take the Hot Springs US 70 West exit south of Benton, the Hot Springs US 270 West exit at Malvern, or the Hot Springs Ark. 7 North exit near Arkadelphia. The Visitor Center is located downtown on Highway 7 North or Central Avenue.

Phone: (501) 624-2701
Website: www.nps.gov/hosp/

You can fill your dog bowl with the tasteless, odorless pure water of the hot springs free of charge from Jug Fountains located near the corner of Central and Reserve streets. Just let it cool before serving.

Mark Twain National Forest

The Park:

For hundreds of years the Osage Indians hunted and farmed these lands but European settlers had other things in mind when they arrived here in the 1800s. Soon the land was exhausted by lead and silver mining and the harvesting of hard, sturdy oak. It was so depleted that during flooding on the Mississippi River in 1927 the Ozarks contributed 38% of the water flow despite being only 4% of the Mississippi basin acreage. Depression-era restoration began and the Mark Twain National Forest was established in 1939. The nearly 1.5 million acres of land stretch across 29 Missouri counties.

The Walks:

The Ozark Mountains are not soaring peaks but tucked inside the folds are many sharp, sporty canine hikes among nearly 750 miles of trail. For easy walking head to one of the lakes in the national forest. The *Pinewoods Lake Trail* winds gently around a 31-acre lake and is paved part of the way. More spirited trotting can be found on the stacked-loop, 5-mile ramble around Crane Lake in the Fredericktown Ranger District. The *Crane Lake Trail* is one of three National Recreation Trails in the Mark Twain National Forest.

Another national trail is the 24-mile *Berryman Trail* in the Potosi Ranger District. Created as a horse trail, there are no steep climbs as the undulating path switchbacks to ridges from dark, leafy hollows. The loop can be broken down to a day hike from the three trailheads.

Experienced canine hikers will gravitate to the Bell Mountain Wilderness in the St. Francois Mountains, one of the oldest rockpiles on the continent. Streams cutting deep into hard-rock gorges here form what are known as "shut-ins" amidst the oak-hickory and soft-pine forests.

One of the most dramatic water-sculpted features of the forest is the Devil's Backbone in the North Fork Recreation Area where the Crooked Branch of the White River twists through six miles of limestone to gain scarcely half that distance. The *Devil's Backbone Trail* travels on two loops for 11 miles of challenging canine hiking.

Directions to Mark Twain National Forest (Missouri):

Forest headquarters are located in the college town of Rolla at 401 Fairgrounds Road, off I-44 at Route 63. Rolla is at the center of the seven Mark Twain ranger districts.

Phone: (573) 364-4621
Website: www.fs.fed.us/r9/marktwain/

Although named for Mark Twain, the Missourian most associated with the Ozark hills is not the humorist but outlaw Jesse James. James was reputed to have used the limestone caves as hiding places, including a prominent rock room along the Berryman Trail of today. The James-Younger gang's first Missouri train robbery took place in the Fredericktown District near a small town called Gads Hill when five men robbed the Little Rock Express on its way from St. Louis, MO to Little Rock, AR on January 31, 1874. The gang brought with them a pre-written press-release that was left with the crew on the train to relay to the local newspapers.

Black Hills

Mount Rushmore National Monument

Few visitors to the Black Hills leave without at least taking a look at Mount Rushmore. And if you are traveling with a dog, that is about all you will be able to do. Dogs are restricted to the parking lot area in the shadow of the world-famous mountain carving that took sculptor Gutzon Borglum 14 years to complete.

The closest recreation area to Mount Rushmore that allows dogs on its trails is Horsethief Lake in the Black Hills National Forest, two miles past the entrance to the monument on Highway 244. *Horsethief Lake Trail*, National Forest Trail #14, is an easy 3-mile ramble that leads to Mount Rushmore until dogs are banned. Your dog will be able to drown his disappointment at not seeing the granite likenesses of Presidents Washington, Jefferson, Lincoln and Roosevelt with the swimming available in Horsethief Lake.

The most stunning sculpture by nature in the Black Hills is Devils Tower National Monument, established as the nation's first National Monument by Theodore Roosevelt in 1906. Dogs are also not allowed on the *Tower Trail* that encircles the 867-foot fluted monolith but there is no restriction for dogs elsewhere in the southeastern Wyoming park, including the camping area.

Custer State Park

The Park:

General George Armstrong Custer led an expedition into the Black Hills in 1874, then considered one of the last unexplored regions of the United States. Custer and his men discovered gold and the region was a secret no more. Precious metals are just part of the cornucopia of riches found in the Black Hills. Custer State Park, the largest state park in the Continental United States, is able to support its 73,000 acres without government money.

Entrance fees are supplemented by harvesting timber, selling special hunting licenses for unique game like big horn sheep and buffalo, and renting park attractions to private concessionaires. The park's annual buffalo sale can yield $250,000 alone.

The Walks:

The bounty at Custer State Park extends to canine hikers as well. One of the best places to begin are the trails in the small arm of the park around Sylvan Lake, a calendar-worthy pool of water flanked by giant granite boulders that formed when Theodore Reder dammed Sunday Gulch in 1921. A pleasant one-mile loop circumnavigates the lake and offers plenty of dog-paddling along the way. Hardy canine hikers will want to make a detour to the demanding *Sunday Gulch Trail* that passes over massive boulders and along splendid light walls of granite.

Water-loving dogs will spend more time dog-paddling than trotting on the Sylvan Lake Trail.

Sylvan Lake is also a popular jumping off point to climb Harney Peak, at 7,242 feet the highest point in America east of the Rocky Mountains. The most traveled route to the summit is on *Trail 9*, a 6-mile round trip. There is some rock scrambling near the top but your dog can make it all the way and even go up the steps into the observation tower.

The craggy rocks atop Harney Peak are a good place to rest after climbing the highest point in America east of the Rockies.

Back in the main body of Custer State Park, you will find the French Creek Natural Area in its center. There are no marked trails along this 2200-acre swath of protected land but paths meander along the creek. There are many stream crossings and the sheer canyon walls narrow practically to the width of a greyhound at one point.

One of the biggest attractions in Custer State park is one of the world's largest free-ranging buffalo herds that grazes on over 18,000 acres of mixed prairie grasslands. The 3-mile hillside *Prairie Trail* off the Wildlife Loop Road is a rolling loop that explodes into a spectacular wildflower display in the summer.

For a short woodlands walk, take your dog to Badger Hole, home to Badger Clark, South Dakota's first poet-laureate. Clark planned part of this footpath behind his four-room cabin that picks its way along rocky hillsides through a mixed pine and hardwood forest.

Sidetrip: Wind Cave National Park (adjacent to Custer State Park southern border on Route 385 North)

America's seventh national park. Wind Cave was discovered in 1881 when Jesse Bingham heard a whistling sound in the ground and had his blown off by a small hole when he went to investigate. Subsequent explorations have uncovered more than 100 miles of underground passages making Wind Cave the sixth longest known cave system in the world. Above ground are more than 30 miles of trails but canine hiking can be had on only two short trails, each about one mile in length. *Elk Mountain Trail* is a sporty loop around the campground that traverses a beautiful prairie with expansive views. A second option for your dog is the *Prairie Valley Trail* surrounding the Visitor Center.

Directions to Custer State Park (South Dakota):

Highway 87 runs through Custer State Park from north to south. From the town of Keystone or Custer, take Highway 16A.

Phone: (605) 255-4515

Website: www.custerstatepark.info/

In the summer of 1927 President Calvin Coolidge was looking to get out of Washington. The government was shut down for the heat and the bugs and the White House was scheduled for a major renovation. He decided to travel to the Black Hills and make the State Game Lodge in Custer State Park his "summer White House," the first President to ride out the heat west of the Mississippi. South Dakota was thrilled to have him and went overboard in welcoming the Coolidges. They showered the First Couple with gifts and overstocked the creek with so much trout that the President, a novice fisherman, could scarcely get his line in the water before getting a strike. The Grace Coolidge Creek that spills out of Center Lake is named for the former First Lady and features an easy three-mile walk on a dirt path along the creek and past seven lowhead dams. The Coolidge family loved their pets and historic photographs often feature their white collies, Rob Roy and Prudence Prim. Other dogs in their family included Blackberry and Tiny Tim - both Chows; Bessie, a Yellow Collie; Boston Beans, a Bulldog; Calamity Jane, a Shetland Sheepdog; Paul Pry, an Airedale; Peter Pan, a Terrier; Ruby Rough, a Brown Collie.

Spearfish Canyon

The Park:

Scientists estimate that Spearfish Canyon is six times as old as the Grand Canyon. The limestone cliffs of the 400-foot canyon lord over some of the greatest botanical diversity in the region. Of the 1,586 identified plant species in South Dakota, 1,260 grow along the Spearfish Creek. Bits and pieces of Spearfish Canyon began being incorporated into the Black Hills National Forest in 1897.

The Walks:

From a common trailhead along little Spearfish Creek, two sporty trail systems explore the upper reaches of Spearfish Canyon. The *Rim Rock Trail*, the more difficult of the two, traces the canyon rim, climbing sharply through Ponderosa pines in some areas. To the south is the *Little Spearfish Trail*, about six miles of more gradual hiking that visits the creek and rim. For a canine hiking challenge, head for the '76 Trail that rises almost vertically to the north rim at Buzzard's Roost in less than one mile.

Nearby are the *Eagle Cliff Trails*, carved by ski enthusiasts in the 1980s as a way to reach deep into the isolated mountains of the western Black Hills. More than 20 short trails totalling 27 miles loop and intertwine under Ponderosa pines and majestic white spruce trees. Any challenge of canine hike is on the menu here, especially in the winter.

Snow pack readings are taken in this area of the Black Hills to help with spring runoff predictions. It is not unusual for 180 inches of snow to fall on the Eagle Cliff Trails during a winter.

Directions to Spearfish Canyon (South Dakota):

The Spearfish Canyon Scenic Byway, Highway 14A, leads from I-90 south to the canyon. The trailhead is on FDR 222 out of Savoy. To reach the Eagle Cliff Trails from Spearfish Canyon, follow Highway 14A to the intersection with Highway 85 at Cheyenne Crossing. Go south on Highway 85 for 7.4 miles to the first of several trailheads.

Website: www.spearfish.com/canyon

For the 1990 Oscar-winning *Dances With Wolves*, star/director Kevin Costner filmed the Indian winter camp in Spearfish Canyon; the exact spot of the final scene where Costner and Mary MacDonnell leave the tribe was once marked by signs that have long since succumbed to souvenir-hunters. The opening sequence, where Costner receives his orders at Fort Hays to travel to Fort Sedgewick, was filmed on a private ranch east of Rapid City. Two of the set pieces, the major's house and the blacksmith shop have been moved to a tourist spot known as the Fort Hays Film Set (four miles south of Rapid City). The Sage Creek Wilderness Area in the Badlands National Park was the backdrop for the wagon trip through Sioux Indian country to Fort Sedgewick.

Centennial Trail & Mickelson Trail

Two long distance trails travel the Black Hills for over 100 miles from north to south. The 111-mile *Centennial Trail* was developed in 1989 as a monument to South Dakota statehood. From the north, the trail launches from the top of Bear Butte, a sacred mountain of the Lakota Sioux on its way through several major recreation areas. Elevations range from 3,200 feet to 5,600 feet and the going can be rugged at times. The route passes many streams and seven lakes to give your dog a refreshing swim. Twenty-two trailheads break the Centennial Trail into walkable chunks.

In 1889 it took railroad workers just 255 days to lay more than 100 miles of track, build 100 wooden trestle bridges and blast four hardrock tunnels to run a line from Deadwood to Edgemont. Under the guidance of then-Governor George S. Mickelson the rail line abandoned by the Burlington Northern in 1983 was converted to a multi-use trail in 1998. The total length of the Mickelson Trail is 114 miles, spread across 14 trailheads, as it rolls from town to town. Much of the way the wide, crushed limestone path advances at a gentle grade of less than 4%.

The northern terminus of the Mickelson Trail is in the town of Deadwood, so named because miners who arrived here in 1876 to chase gold had to clear so many dead trees from the narrow canyon before panning the river. The man synonomous with Deadwood is Wild Bill Hickok - showman, scout, buffalo hunter, frontier lawman, gambler. And it was in Deadwood that Wild Bill breathed his last. Hickok was uncharacteristally caught with his back to the door during a poker game in Saloon No. 10 and was ambushed by Jack "Broken Nose" McCall. Shot dead with a .45 Colt revolver, Hickok died holding a pair of black aces, black eights and a 9 of Diamonds - forever afterwards known as the "Dead Man's Hand." There are several sculptures of Wild Bill in town and the moment of his death is re-enacted on Main Street several nights a week for visitors. James Butler Hickok is buried at Mt. Moriah Cemetery in Deadwood, where dogs are not allowed.

Your Dog And The Badlands

America's badlands received their ominous name when early settlers found it impossible to safely roll a wagon through the cracked lunar landscape in the Upper Midwest. Our most famous badlands are preserved in national parks in the Dakotas - and off limits to canine hikers.

To give your dog a chance to explore these unique lands of sculpted rock, head south from the Dakotas to the lesser-known badlands of the Nebraska panhandle. Here in the Gala National Grasslands you will find Toadstool Geologic Park where the relentless tag-team of water and wind have carved fanciful rock formations into the stark hills.

The "toadstools" form when underlying soft clay stone erodes faster than the hard sandstone that caps it. A marked, mile-long interpretive loop leads you on an educational adventure through these badlands. Your dog is welcome on the hard rock trail but you can also explore off the path for close-up looks in the gullies at fossil bone fragments that lace the rocks and 30-million year-old footprints preserved in the stone.

There are some rocks to be scaled along the route but this ramble under banded cliffs of clay and ash is suitable for any level of canine hiker. There is only sporadic shade and seasonal streams in this ancient riverbed so bring plenty of water for your dog, especially in the summer months. Take a break at the end of the hike in the small fenced yard of the reproduced sod house beside the parking lot.

For extended hikes, Toadstool Park connects to the world-renowned Hudson-Meng Bison Boneyard via a three-mile trail. This archeological site seeks to unravel the mystery of how over 600 bison died nearly 10,000 years ago in an area about the size of a football stadium. Human predation is the leading suspect.

Toadstool Geologic Park is located 19 miles NW of Crawford, Nebraska on US Forest Route 904 off State highway 2/71. The trail begins at the back of the six-unit campground.

Colorado Rockies

The Front Range - Boulder

The Town:

Dogs are not allowed on the trails in Rocky Mountain National Park but after a trip down the road to Boulder that disappointment will be most likely forgotten.

On the outwash plain of Boulder Creek a small settlement sprung up in 1858 for no other reason then, according to founder Captain Thomas A. Aikens, "the mountains look right for gold." The tiny mining camp limped along for the better part of twenty years and was rescued from oblivion only by the founding of the University of Colorado in 1876.

Today Boulder is a receational mecca where the town has preserved and protected over 37,000 acres of Open Space and Mountain Parks (OSMP). One hundred and twenty miles of trails are used by walkers, hikers, bicyclists, horseback riders and dog walkers. It has been said that Boulder sports more bicycles per capita of any city in the world. And probably as many dogs.

Dogs are welcome in most parts of the OSMP, and in many places are allowed off leash if sight and voice control can be demonstrated. A detailed Dog Regulations Map delineates exactly what dog restrictions are in force throughout the different areas of the OSMP. Dogs are not permitted on rock climbs. One place dogs are not allowed in Boulder is on the downtown outdoor mall on Pearl Street.

The Walks:

There are 28 trailheads in the OSMP; 27 of them are open to dogs. One of the most popular dog walking spots is Chautauqua Park on Baseline Road, at the base of the Flatiron Mountains, Boulder's trademark rocks on the western edge of town. The Ranger Cottage here is a starting point for several area circle hikes, including easy walks through the foothills along the *Chautauqua, Bluebell-Baird,* and *Mesa* trails. Beyond the Flatirons, the *Gregory Canyon Trail* climbs steadily through Ponderosa pine and Douglas fir on a former route used by gold miners. A short detour leads to Realization Point and the summit of Flagstaff Mountain, 1,600 feet above Boulder. Past the Green Mountain Lodge, the *Ranger Trail* leads to the 8144-foot summit of Green Mountain and sweeping views of the Front Range.

Another OSMP trailhead with a wide variety of hiking opportunities with your dog is *Mesa Trail South Trailhead,* 1.7 miles west of Highway 93 on Eldorado Springs Drive. The southern region of the *Mesa Trail* here lies in an overlapping band of diverse plant communities as the Great Plains blend into the forested mountains.

Directions to Boulder (Colorado):

Boulder is located northwest of Denver, reached via US 36 off I-25.

Phone: (303) 441-3440

Website: www.ci.boulder.co.us/openspace/

The city of Boulder Parks and Recreation Department operates three dog parks inside the city. The largest is a 3.5-acre, fenced dog park in an undeveloped park called Valmont near the airport, .25 miles east of the intersection of Airport and Valmont Roads. Outfitted with drinking spigots for dogs, the park at Valmont is lighted for night play. In East Boulder Community Park at 5660 Sioux Drive is a 1.5-acre fenced dog park with access to a portion of a pond. Both dog parks feature four-foot high chain link fencing, double entrance gates, benches, tables and trashcans. A third dog park is an off-leash area near the creek in Howard Heuston Park, off 4th Street. This dog exercise area is unfenced.

Pikes Peak

The Mountain:

Pikes Peak, with its height and position in the Front Range, was the first landmark seen by settlers heading west. Explorer Lieutenant Zebulon Pike, on assignment by Thomas Jefferson, first saw the mountain in 1806. He was thwarted by a blizzard in his attempt to scale the "Great Peak." The first recorded successful ascent was made by a scientist named Edwin James in 1820. In 1858 Julia Archibald - sporting bloomers - became the first woman to tag the summit and spent two days on top. The footpath up the eastern face was re-worked and built by Fred Barr between 1914 and 1918. It was pick-and-shovel duty, with an occasional dash of black powder for moving rocks and trees.

The Walks:

Dogs are welcome to tackle the *Barr National Recreation Trail* all the way to the summit. Near the top there are rock steps that most dogs can negotiate. The 13-mile pull to the 14,110-foot summit of Pikes Peak begins in Manitou Springs at an elevation of 6,300 feet. It is the biggest elevation gain of any trail in Colorado, with an average grade of 11%. Serious canine hiking indeed.

Barr Camp, where Fred ran a burro concession, is at the halfway point and makes a handy turn-around point for those not prepared to make the assault on the summit. There are three miles of hiking above the treeline and the peak gets afternoon storms nearly daily so come prepared.

The *Barr Trail* is well-trod and well-marked. It gets extremely hot in the mid-summer and there is no natural water for your dog on Pikes Peak.

Directions to Pikes Peak (Colorado):

In Colorado Springs, take Colorado Boulevard into Manitou Springs and turn left onto Ruxton at the west end of town. Follow Ruxton past the cog railway and turn right up a short hill to the Barr Trail parking lot.
Phone: (719) 545-8737

Pikes Peak is the most-visited mountain in the United States - a half-million people make their way to the summit every year, most in their cars. When it opened in the Fall of 1888, the 14-foot wide Pikes Peak Carriage Road was billed as the highest road in the world. The first automobile chugged to the summit in 1901 - today the climb is 6,710 feet over 19 miles on the toll road. Not many people go through the toll to hike.
But at the base of Pikes Peak is a one hour out-and-back ramble through the aspen groves, pine forests and impressive boulders of Crowe Gulch. This land was opened to homesteading in 1862 and the Crowe family was one that tried but farming was difficult in a place where snow could come in July. The Crowes abandoned their 160-acre parcel before the five years of residency required for ownership. There is no charge for this peaceful canine hike; just tell the folks at the toll booth that you don't want to drive to the top, just hike in Crowe Gulch.

Switzerland of America

The Park:

The mountains of southwestern Colorado are so rugged they earned the nickname, "Switzerland of America." Still, the promise of gold and silver brought prospectors to blaze trails and build roads deep into the mountains. In 1892 President Benjamin Harrison created the Grand Mesa National Forest as the third such reserve in America. The Uncompahgre and Gunnison forests soon followed and together the three parcels of public land, managed as one unit, contain more than three million acres - the largest national forest in the Rocky Mountains.

The Walks:

This is the place to come for challenging canine hiking. And there is a surprising amount of hiking and not climbing on some of the highest mountains on the continent.

Uncompahgre Peak is a stand-alone "fourteener" at 14,309 feet that can be reached with a seven-mile round-trip ascent. About half the mountain is above the treeline and this is an open hike that begins with a long, steady gain before a steep scamble to the flattish top above the Big Blue Wilderness.

Near the Victorian mining town of Ouray you can test the 4.2-mile *Bear Creek National Recreation Trail*. Steep inclines early in the hike serve up views of town before the trail picks its way through Bear Creek Canyon. Pay attention because the footpath, built by miners, shrinks to two feet wide in places. Your destination is the Yellow Jacket Mine but backpackers can penetrate deeper into the mountains.

On the Grand Mesa, one of the world's largest flattop mountains, a top destination is the *Crag Crest National Recreation Trail*. This 10-mile circle trail climbs to over 11,000 feet on a boulder-strewn crest affording great perches for views of alpine lakes and drops for good meadow walks and canine swimming holes on the lower loop.

On the eastern edge of the national forests is Black Canyon of the Gunnison National Park where uplifted hard rock is being gouged by a river dropping an average of 96 feet per mile in the park. Dogs are not permitted in the gorge but can walk on all the short nature trails and overlooks on the South Rim save for the *Warner Point Nature Trail*.

Your dog will enjoy short, flat hikes at the South Rim of the Black Canyon.

Directions to America's Switzerland (Colorado):

The three national forests are managed from a central office in Delta, on Route 50.

Phone: (970) 874-6600
Website: www.fs.fed.us/r2/gmug/

Bones of seventeen different dinosaurs - including some of the largest skeletons ever found - have been unearthed in the Uncompahgre National Forest since their discovery in 1971. You can visit the Dry Mesa Dinosaur Quarry (on gravel roads with vehicles of high clearance) anytime although all the fossils are buried when researchers are not present. Free guided hikes of the fossil beds are offered on Fridays and Saturdays when digs are in process.

Yellowstone

Yellowstone National Park

It is possible to visit Yellowstone National Park with your dog and still see many of the sights for which America's first national park is celebrated: Old Faithful, the Grand Canyon of Yellowstone, the Paintpots, Yellowstone Lake, etc. The park is designed so these attractions can be reached within a short walk from a parking lot. So, weather permitting, you can leave your dog briefly in the car and check out these wonders. But there won't be any canine hiking in Yellowstone - dogs are not permitted on any trails, the backcountry, the boardwalks around the hot springs and are not permitted more than 25 feet from any roadway. After driving around Yellowstone, you and your dog are going to want some places to stretch your legs.

Flaming Gorge National Recreation Area

The Park:

Continuing south out of Yellowstone and through Grand Teton National Park (also not a place for trail dogs) on US 191, you reach Flaming Gorge National Recreation Area in 250 miles. John Wesly Powell named the Flaming Gorge after he saw the sun shining off the red canyon walls on his epic 1869 exploration of the Green and Colorado rivers. Butch Cassidy and other outlaws often used the isolated valleys along the Green River as hideouts. Nearly a century later there were still only primitive roads in the aea when construction began on the Flaming Gorge Dam to store water and generate electricity. The 502-foot high dam, backing the Green River up 91 miles, was completed in 1964 and the Flaming Gorge National Recreation Area established four years later.

The Walks:

The best way to see the 1400-foot deep Red Canyon is on the *Canyon Rim Trail*, a multi-use trail accessed at the Red Canyon Visitor Center. In addition to the quiet overlooks at the canyon, this trail, that loops for nearly three miles past the campground, is also a good place to observe moose, elk and deer that graze here. Along the Green River is the *Little Hole National Recreation Trail*, a delightful seven-mile one-way walk below the Flaming Gorge Dam. Your dog may spend more time in the clear green waters than on the level, easy-hiking path. High altitude canine hiking is also available on Dowd Mountain and Ute Mountain while at Spirit Lake Campground a 3-mile loop visits a trio of alpine lakes above 10,000 feet.

Directions to Flaming Gorge National Recreation Area (Wyoming):

The Red Canyon Visitor Center is off Route 44, west of the Route 44, US 191 intersection.

Phone: (435) 789-1181
Website: www.fs.fed.us/r4/ashley/recreation/flaming_gorge/index.shtml

Outside the recreation area, just downstream from the Green River Trail at Indian Crossing Campground is the John Jarvie Historic Site. In 1880, Scottish immigrant John Jarvie set up shop in the Browns Park area of the Green River. He also later operated a ferry on the river. In 1909, Jarvie was robbed and murdered and his body dumped in a boat and shoved out on the Green River. It floated for eight days before being discovered. The frontier buildings Jarvie used for his enterprises have been preserved by the Bureau of Land Management.

Gallatin National Forest

The Park:

John Bozeman opened the first wagon trail into a valley American Indians called "Valley of the Flowers." Revered as a sacred hunting ground, the Sioux killed Bozeman and no one dared try his trail again for nine years. Eventually in 1899 President William McKinley established the Gallatin Nationa Forest with 45,000 acres. Today, the national forest encompasses almost 1.8 million acres, including most of the northern and western boundaries of Yellowstone National Park, and contains six mountain ranges. Gallatin shares much of the restless geology of its famous neighbor - on August 17, 1959, at 23 minutes before midnight, two massive blocks of the earth's crust dropped 10 feet tilting lakes, dropping houses into giant sinkholes and triggering a landslide that buried 19 campers. The city bearing John Bozeman's name is a gateway for approaching Yellowstone Park from the north and a base point for exploring the the Gallatin National Forest.

The Walks:

Any type of canine hike can be sculpted on the more than 2000 miles of trails in the Gallatin National Forest. Popular short trails penetrate the Hyalite Canyon (out of Bozeman on South 19th Avenue) to reach refreshing waterfalls. The hikes can be extended to take as much of a mountain ascent as you want; the *Hyalite Peak Trail* leaves a deep glaciated valley at 7,000 feet and tops out on the summit seven miles later at 10,299 feet. Grotto Falls is 2 miles into this trek and Hyalite Lake comes another three miles up the trail.

One of the marquee canine hikes near Bozeman is the 3.5-mile journey to Lava Lake (south of town off US 191). It is a steady climb along Cascade Creek on a rocky path - sturdy wooden bridges over rushing waters make appealing rest stops. Your destination is a secluded alpine lake tucked into the Spanish Peaks. Also south of Bozeman on US 191, through media mogul Ted Turner's ranch, is the trailhead for the South Fork of the Spanish Creek. This Forest Service trail rolls along easily until more challenging fare at the *Falls Creek Trail*. For mountain-climbing canines the tallest peak in the Bridger Range,

9,670-foot Sacajawea, can be tagged by a steep, 2-mile climb at the Fairy Lake Campground.

It is not all climbing for dogs in the Rocky Mountain as the trails along the Madison River attest.

Around Bozeman, check out Peet's Hill, a ridgeline trail designed for dogs to be walked under voice control. North of town, on the flank of Mount Baldy is a great letter "M," constructed of rocks by the Montana State University Class of 1918. Two trails, each about one mile, lead to the highly visible landmark, that requires 80 gallons of white paint each year. The "M" rests only part of the way up the summit and miles of more rigorous canine hiking await beyond.

In the Absorka/Beartooth Mountain Range the premier canine hike is the *Beaten Path*. The well-maintained trail crosses the range from east to west for 26 miles, although there are many off-shoots for day-hikers. Any level of canine hiker can handle the climbs along the way and scores of lakes await for a refreshing break. Many lakes cascade into each other via tumbling waterfalls. The route stretches from the East Rosebud Trailhead at 6,208 feet to the Clark's Fork Trailhead at 8,035 feet with climbs to 10,000 feet in between.

Directions to Gallatin National Forest (Bozeman, Montana headquarters):

Bozeman is located off I-90 west of US 89 and east of US 191.

Phone: (406) 587-6701

Website: www.fs.fed.us/r1/gallatin/

Idaho Panhandle

Lake Coeur d'Alene

The Lake:

By 1878 enough miners and homesteaders had filtered into the Coeur d'Alene Mountains that the United States government constructed Fort Sherman at the mouth of the Spokane River on Lake Coeur d'Alene. By the time the military outpost shuttered in 1901, tourism was entrenched along the lake. So many vacationers arrived by steamship that Lake Coeur d'Alene was America's busiest inland port west of the Mississippi River. Several times the lake, whose literal translation from French is the meaningless "heart of the awl," has placed highly on lists of the world's most beautiful lakes.

The Walks:

The best place to enjoy the shoreline of Lake Coeur d'Alene are the downtown parks. Manicured City Park features paved trails, including the 24-mile *North Idaho Centennial Trail*. The eastern terminus of this multi-use trail is on the north shore of the lake and traces the Spokane River heading west into Washington. At the south end of 3rd Street Tubbs Hill Park offers several miles of canine hiking in 120 acres. A 2.2-mile interpretive trail follows the perimeter of Tubbs Hill. No vehicles are allowed on these trails.

On the eastern shore of Lake Coeur d'Alene are several trails overlooking Beauty Bay. The easiest is Beauty Bay *USFS trail #257* at a picnic area off Highway 97. The half-mile loop trail climbs gently through the trees to the most photographed spot on the lake. Hearty canine hikers can access a 15-mile Forest Service Trail here as well, with a 3-mile day hike option.

From the campground at Beauty Bay Creek *Caribou Ridge Trail #79* grinds up four switchbacks to the top of Mount Coeur d'Alene. There is an elevation gain of more than 2,300 feet on this 4.6-mile-climb through the timber with glimpses of the lake along the way before reaching extensive views of Beauty Bay from the lookout at the 4,439-foot summit.

The must-do hike for dog owners on the shores of Lake Coeur d'Alene is the *Mineral Ridge National Recreation Trail*. Prospecting began on this slope in the 1890s with lead-zinc being the big draw. Construction on the 3.3-mile interpretive trail began in 1963 and two decades later it was designated a National Recreation Trail. The dirt trail switches up 660 feet to the 2,800-foot summit through lush stands of Ponderosa pine and Douglas fir and past old mining pit excavations. Views can be had of Wolf Lodge Bay and Beauty Bay and spur trails can add a few miles to your exploration of Mineral Ridge.

Directions to Lake Coeur d'Alene (Idaho):

The town of Coeur D'Alene is located directly on I-90. Beauty Bay trails can be reached by taking Exit 22 off I-90 to Highway 97 South seven miles east of town. The trailheads are all within five miles of the Interstate on Highway 97.

Phone: (208) 664-3194
Website: www.coeurdalene.org/

Along Caribou Ridge is a good place to hunt for huckleberries, the state fruit of Idaho. Huckleberries are wild blueberries common in coniferous forests, solitary plump, dark fruit dangling from bushes that can grow head-high. Idaho's bluish fruit is the black huckleberry that is most productive at elevations between 4,000 and 6,000 feet. Sweet and ripe in early summer, huckleberries are a favorite of bears.

Hells Canyon National Recreation Area

The Park:

Along the Idaho-Oregon border the Snake River has carved the continent's deepest gorge. The East Rim of Hells Canyon is 8,043 feet above the river and in places can be 10 miles across from rim to rim. Established in 1975, the Hells Canyon National Recreation Area showcases 652,488 acres of remote, rugged landscape. The Hells Canyon trail system is extensive - more than 900 miles - but doesn't lend itself easily to day hikes. Trailheads are often at the end of steep, single-lane unimproved roads and many trails are multi-day affairs on both sides of the canyon.

The Walks:

The easiest way to hike into Hells Canyon with your dog is to drive up the paved Snake River Road to Hells Canyon Dam. Here, a narrow band of dirt pushes into the canyon downstream from the visitor center. Beware of rattlesnakes that live in the rocky terrain.

The best access to rim trails is on the Idaho side of the gorge at Pittsburgh Landing on Deer Creek Road, Forest Road #493. At the Upper Pittsburg Landing Campground you'll find the trailhead for the *Snake River National Recreation Trail #102*. The path traces the Wild and Scenic Snake River upstream for 26.6 miles to Granite Creek, keeping the water in view during most of the hike. The trail starts at 1,200 feet in elevation and dips down to the shoreline in several places. Heaven's Gate Overlook at the end of Forest Road #517, where a 660-yard trail climbs sharply to views of Hells Canyon and parts of four states, is a popular jumping off point for hikes into the canyon. Deep in the Seven Devils Mountains, this is the area of highest elevation above the water. *Little Granite Trail* is the shortest route from this alpine country to the Snake River, a steep canine hike of six miles that drops 5,710 feet. Another wilderness trail to try is the 2.1-mile trek to Dry Giggins Lookout, one of the few places above Hells Canyon where you can actually see the Snake River.

Directions to Hells Canyon National Recreation Area (Oregon/Idaho):

Access to the Hells Canyon NRA in Idaho is from Highway 95 that parallels the Snake River. In Oregon the Hells Canyon Scenic Byway, a 218-mile loop through the Wallowa Mountains, leads to wilderness roads and remote trailheads.
Website: www.fs.fed.us/hellscanyon/

Canine hiking along the Snake River is at the bottom of the deepest gorge in North America.

Canadian Rockies

Banff National Park

The Park:

In the fall of 1883, three Canadian Pacific Railway construction workers stumbled across a cave containing hot springs on at the foot of Sulphur Mountain, known today as the Cave and Basin. Almost immediately the area was protected as a federal reserve and in 1887 "Rocky Mountains Park" was increased to 673 square kilometers to become Canada's first national park and the world's third. A town was built to entice tourists to the area and named Banff after "Banffshire," a village in Scotland that was the birthplace of two Canadian Pacific Railway officals. In the 1930s the park was renamed Banff and has since expanded to 6,641 square kilometers (2,564 square miles) of valleys, mountains, glaciers, forests, meadows and rivers. With more than eight million visitors annually, it is one of the world's premier vacation destinations.

The Walks:

Banff National Park is a hiking wonderland, containing over 1,600 kilometers (1,000 miles) of trails, more than any other mountain park. Your dog is allowed almost everywhere. Some favorite canine hikes include:

Fairview Mountain Lookout Trail. This healthy climb up a forested trail with a steep descent to the South shore of fabled Lake Louise is a good trail to get away from the crush of people you will find in the parking lot. This wide and soft dirt trail narrows as it jaunts along the lake with excellent water access for your dog.

Johnston Canyon. This popular tourist walk is paved over early sections with board-walks clinging to canyon walls; it leads to Lower Falls and Upper Falls and can go further up Johnston Creek into woodlands and meadows.

Moraine Lakeshore. An easy, flat walk along the north shore of Moraine Lake stares into of the Valley of Ten Peaks. The trail stays right on water most of the way. You can also take the dog on the Rockpile with large boulders to scramble on at east end of lake.

Mistaya Canyon. This short paved descent into a limestone gorge sculpted by rushing meltwaters of Mistaya River is worth having to navigate your dog through the tourists.

Parker Ridge. This is a steep, open climb through rocky tundra that switches 800 feet up the mountain to a treeless ridge with spectacular views of Saskatchewan Glacier. The rocks scattered along the trail contain fossil corals indicative of an ancient seabed.

Sunshine Meadows. This is a ski area accessed by shuttle bus. You can walk your dog up the road to the ski lodge and pick up the trails from there. Save this effort for athletic dogs ready for a long, rewarding day on the trail. These trails skip over ridges of the Great Divide, completely above the treeline with flower-filled meadows, eventually leading to Rock Isle Lake and loops around for a trip of several miles.

Directions to Banff National Park (Alberta):

Trans-Canada Highway (#1) runs west from Calgary into the park and through Banff and Lake Louise.

Phone: (403) 762-1550
Website: www.parkscanada.pch.gc.ca/pn-np/ab/banff/index_E.asp

"If your dog is fat, you aren't getting enough exercise."
- anonymous

Jasper National Park

The Park:

Fur trader David Thompson explored the Athabasca Pass in 1811 and helped establish Canada's first transcontinental route. The park began in 1907 as Jasper Forest Park, named for longtime trading post clerk Jasper Hawes. In 1930, with the passage of the National Parks Act, Jasper became an official national park. It is the largest of Canada's four Rocky Mountain national parks - there are 660 miles of trails in more than 400 square miles. Located on the eastern slope of the Continental Divide, the landscape is characterized by plunging valleys, deep forests and broad alpine meadows.

The Walks:

Dogs are allowed throughout this magnificent park - even crowded trails, such as the dirt Maligne Canyon footpath up the limestone gorge carved by the Maligne River. Canine hikers can bypass the multitudes by crossing the gorge on roads at either end and using an unblazed trail on the opposite side. Mountain climbing dogs will pant over *Whistlers Trail*, a steep and narrow route that gains 4,000 feet in elevation to unobstructed views of the Miette Valley and Athabasca Valley high above the treeline. Near the town of Jasper is an extensive trail system leading the Pyramid Lake and Patricia Lake; a wide climb from the back of the town leads to overlooks from Pyramid Bench, and another convenient canine hike is the Valley of Five Lakes. After walking through a lodgepole pine forest and across a boardwalk through Wabasso Creek wetlands, this trail loops around a series of secluded bluegreen lakes, each a different depth and hue.

Directions to Jasper National Park (Alberta):

The Trans-Canada Highway #16 (also called the Yellowhead Highway) runs through the park and is the main route to and from Jasper. The Icefields Parkway connects Jasper with the Trans-Canada Highway #1 near Lake Louise and Banff.

Phone: (780) 852-6176
Website: www.parkscanada.pch.gc.ca/pn-np/ab/jasper/index_E.asp

---

Athabasca Glacier is the most accessible glacier in North America. A short, barren walk on the *Forefield Trail* will take you and the dog to the toe of the glacier in the Columbia Icefield. The Columbia Icefield is the hydographic apex of the continent where water flows to three different oceans from a single point.

Desert Lands

Petrified Forest National Park

The Park:

The mineralized remains of an ancient Mesozoic Forest were tens of millions of years in the making but the nation's largest field of petrified wood wasn't formally described until 1851. The Atlantic and Pacific Railroad built though this area in the 1880s bringing profiteers to the forest. They carried off petrified wood specimens and dynamited the largest logs in search of quartz and purple amethyst crystals. In 1895 the state of Arizona began petitioning for federal protection and on December 8, 1906 Theodore Roosevelt designated the petrified forest as America's second national monument. In 1962, with the addition of the scenic landscape of the Painted Desert, the Petrified Forest became America's thirty-first national park.

The Walks:

Pets are banned from the 93,533 acres of backcountry and the popular *Painted Desert Rim Trail* near the Visitor Center but there is ample opportunity to experience the petrified forest with your dog.

Three paved loops - all less than a mile long - lead into the barren desert amidst remains of the petrified forest. Although short and easy to hike, these interpretive trails are completely without shade so have a supply of water ready on hot days.

The *Crystal Forest Trail* meanders through the remains of obliterated petrified logs, leaving you to only imagine what these crystalized trees once looked like before the pillaging that led to the creation of the Petrified Forest National Monument. Some of those prehistoric trees can be seen on the *Long Logs* path. Extinct conifers form the largest concentration of petrified wood left in the park.

The *Agate House Trail* leads up a slight rise to a reconstructed Anasazi Indian Pueblo built entirely of colorful petrified wood sealed with mud.

Also available to canine hikers is the one-mile *Blue Mesa Trail*. A sharp drop in the path leads to an ampitheater surrounded by banded badlands of bluish clay called bentontite. Rainwater is the brush that creates streaky patterns in the porous hills.

Directions to Petrified Forest National Park (Arizona):

Just southwest of the Four Corners, the park curves between I-40 to the north and Route 180 to the south.

Phone: (928) 524-6228
Website: www.nps.gov/pefo

White Sands National Monument

The Park:

Covering almost 200,000 acres, White Sands National Monument is the world's largest area of gypsum sand dunes. The gypsum dissolves in nearby mountains during rainstorms and, instead of being carried off by a river (this is an arid environment) wind sends the gypsum crystals downwind, where they accumulate in brilliantly white sand dunes. After much lobbying for the development of the dunes as a national park, White Sands instead was designated a national monument in 1933.

The Walks:

White Sands offers 6.2 miles of marked trails but there is no need to limit your explorations. Any dune is open to a canine hike. There are no maps - the sand dunes are constantly shifting. Stay alert for reptiles and rodents scampering on the dunes that have adapted to the white sands and are now a funny bleached white color.

During the summer, on the nights when the moon is full, the park stays open until midnight. The desert cools off then and the sands are haunting by moonlight.

Directions to White Sands National Monument (New Mexico):

The park is on I-70, about 20 miles west of Almogordo.

Phone: 678-538-1200
Website: www.nps.gov/chat/index.htm

White Sands Missile Range is where America's space age began with the firing of a Tiny Tim test booster at Launch Complex 33 on September 26, 1945. When testing missiles, it was important to retrieve small missile parts to analyze success or failure. These searches routinely wasted countless man-hours as ground recovery crews scoured vast expanses of desert for often-buried missile fragments. That all ended in 1961 with the introduction of the Missile Dogs: Dingo, a Weimaraner, and Count, a German Shorthair. For up to a year before firing, important components of a missile were sprayed with squalene, a shark-liver oil that the dogs could smell from hundreds of feet away. After a missile firing, the dog team was sent out for recovery as Dingo and Count sniffed out the scent object. With a 96% recovery rate, the program was so successful that other military and scientific agencies requested the services of the original Missile Dogs of White Sands.

White Sands Monument is one giant sand box for a playful dog.

Catalina State Park

The Park:

A small Hohokan Indian village was established on a wide ridge above Sutherland Wash, now known as Romero Ruin, about 1,500 years ago. The small community flourished for more than 1,000 years before being abandoned. The early Spaniards called the Santa Catalina Mountains "La Inglesia" for their cathedral-like appearance. The first European settlement in these foothills came around 1850 when cattle ranchers Francisco and Victoriana Romero established a homestead along the wash. The ranch grew to 5,000 acres but did not survive two generations. Gradually the forgotten property came to the attention of scientists and historians. In 1983 Catalina State Park, sprawling across 5,483 acres, was established, including 34 distinct archeological sites.

The Walks:

Eight trails of varying length and difficulty traverse the park's more than 8 square miles. Most - including the longer and most strenuous hikes - are off-limits to dogs. The best canine hike at Catalina State Park is the 2.3-mile *Canyon Loop Trail* that visits the differing habitat types found in this beautiful desert terrain. The trail rolls gently up and down through riparian arroyos and past stands of stately saguaros. Keep an eye to the sky for a chance to see any of the more han 170 species of birds that call the park home. The loop winds up with an unexpected hidden stream complete with a delightful doggie swimming hole.

Directions to Catalina State Park (Arizona):

The park is located on State Highway 77 (Oracle Road) at mile marker 81, just 9 miles north of Tucson.

Phone: (520) 628-5798
Website: www.pr.state.az.us/Parks/parkhtml/catalina.html

Tucson Mountain Park

The Park:

Your dog won't be able to trot among the giant cacti of Saguaro National Park but she can still see the best of the Sonoran Desert in neighboring Tucson Mountain Park. The national park, in fact, was once part of the local park. Originally, 60,000 acres were withdrawn from the Homesteading Act of 1873 to be used as Tucson Mountain Park. About half was returned for use by World War I veterans and part of that land became Saguaro National Park.

The Walks:

Miles of old desert roads and trails crisscross through boulders, palo verde and ocotillo plants in the park. Some of the best stands of giant saguaro cactus outside the national park can be found on the 5.4-mile out-and-back *David Yetman Trail*, named for a local television host and desert authority. Other long linear trails include the 4.4-mile *Gates Pass Trail* and the *Star Pass East Trail* along a route to early copper mines.

The namesake mountains in the park are more like large hills and most of the canine hiking is easy going on gentle grades. Moonlight hikes are popular in the desert but the park closes at 10:00 p.m due to vandalism and cactus theft. Come sundown find yourself a hillside to sit with your dog and admire the memorable sunset for which the park is known.

Directions to Tucson Mountain Park (Arizona):

The park is west of Tucson, reached via Gates Pass Road or Ajo Road to Kinney Way.
Phone: (520) 883-4200

The Sonoran Desert trails in Tucson Mountain Park run through rugged hillsides of volcanic rock.

In 1939 Columbia Pictures sought a real-life backdrop for its big budget ($2.5 million) epic *Arizona*, to star William Holden and Jean Arthur. They chose a site inside Tucson Mountain Park and after referring to historical records began to build a clay facsimile of 1860's Tucson. Without benefit of running water in the area, local builders erected more than 50 buildings using 350,000 adobe bricks. When the movie wrapped the sets were deserted and the buildings abandoned in the desert.

The arrival of the television era developed the Western into the most popular genre on the small screen. Hollywood remembered the *Arizona* set and Old Tucson Studios became a favorite filming location. More than 70 feature films were shot here including *Gunfight at the OK Corral* (Kirk Douglas/Burt Lancaster), *Rio Bravo* (John Wayne/Dean Martin), *Outlaw Josie Wales* (Clint Eastwood, Sandra Locke) and *Three Amigos* (Chevy Chase/Steve Martin). Eventually more feature films, television movies, and television series would be filmed at Old Tucson Studios than any other man-made location outside Hollywood.

The studio began its next life in 1960 under the auspices of entrepreneur Robert Shelton, who transformed the ghost town into a family fun park as well as movie studio. Today at Old Tucson Studios, after a fire destroyed half the buildings in 1995, you will find western town sets along Front Street and Kansas Street; the Mexican Plaza courtyard, the High Chaparral Ranch, a ghost town and a railroad.

Canyon Country

Grand Canyon National Park

Dogs are not allowed on trails below the rim at the Grand Canyon but there is a surprising amount of canine hiking you can do otherwise considering the immense popularity of the park. Dogs are allowed on trails throughout the developed areas of the South Rim, including the *Rim Trail* that stretches from the Village Area to Hermit's Rest. There are plenty of canyon views from the partially paved 2.7-mile trail. For dog owners wanting to hike into the canyon a kennel is available on the South rim; call (928) 638-0534 for details.

The less visited North Rim is also less inviting for canine hikers. You can get the dog only on a bridle path between the lodge and the *North Kaibab Trail* for a bit of exercise.

Kaibab National Forest

The Park:

Spanish conquistadores discovered the Grand Canyon in 1540 but the land was still unsettled by non-Indians until the late 1800s. Protection began in 1893 with the establishment of Grand Canyon Forest Reserve and eventually land on both sides of the canyon, part of the largest contiguous Ponderosa pine forest in the United States, became the Kaibab National Forest. Dogs are welcome on all trails until they run into national park land.

The Walks:

There are about 370 miles of trails in the 1.6 million acres of Kaibab National Forest, pronounced "KY-bab" from the Paiute Indian word meaning "mountain lying down." Some trails run to remote lookouts, others to historic cabins and still others along fabled stagecoach routes. You can even get views of the Grand Canyon itself. On long distance trails you can begin in desert sand and wind up frolicking in mountain snow.

The more rugged and less inviting trails are found in the North Kaibab section where the high elevations can bring snow from September to May. Some of the easiest canine hiking on the north rim is at the *Lookout Canyon Trail System* where a half-day's hiking runs through bottomlands and ridges of three forested canyons.

South of the Grand Canyon the plateau flattens out at about 7000 feet and the terrain in the forest is mostly rolling. The star canine hike in the Tusayan District is the *Red Butte Trail*. The butte is an odd geologic relic where a dark layer of hard volcanic basalt protects the butte from eroding like the surrounding landscape. The 1.2-mile trail gets going quickly before steep switchbacks in the final half-mile slow your progress. The vistas go in every direction at the top.

Directions to Kaibab National Forest (Arizona):

The Kaibab Plateau Visitor Center is in Jacob Lake, Arizona on HC 64.

Phone: (928) 635-4707
Website: www.fs.fed.us/r3/kai/

Dixie National Forest

The Park:

Father Silvestre Veles de Escalante, an adventurous Spanish priest searching for an overland route to California, was the first to describe the topography of southern Utah in 1776. Within a generation the Old Spanish Trail was busy moving settlers through these canyons and mountains. In 1850, shortly after their arrival in Utah, Brigham Young sent Mormon settlers south into the region.

The Dixie National Forest and its two million acres of land watch each year as millions of visitors flock to its neighbors: three national parks and two national monuments - none of which allow dogs on trails. Yet canine hikers can find much of the same beauty in the more than 600 miles of trails in the Forest, named because early Mormon settlers thought the pines and spruce that grow here looked like the Deep South.

The Walks:

One of the most popular canine hiking destinations in the Dixie National Forest is Pine Valley, with over 100 miles of trails between St. George and Cedar City. The marquee canine hike is the *Whipple Trail*, designated a National Recreation trail. The full trail is 8 miles long with plenty of ups and downs for flavor as it climbs to big views of Zion National Park. Except in early summer after snow melts don't expect much water time for your dog in the meadows and spruce forests along the way.

At Navajo Lake dog owners will find recreation and nearby the *Pinks Trail* and the *Virgin Rim Trail*, with views of the river that cuts the great Zion canyon. The *Pinks Trail* is a healthy 1/2-mile climb to looks at pink cliffs and a stand of bristlecone pine. These gnarled trees are among the oldest things on earth and can be more than 4,000 years old.

In Red Canyon canine hikers can get a taste of the fanciful red sandstone formations for which Bryce Canyon is famous. A variety of short and long trails here can easily fill a full canine hiking day. Heading out from the Visitor Center the *Pink Ledges Trail* is an easy, albeit noisy (road traffic) way to see brilliant red rock formations known as hoodoos. More red rocks await in Casto Canyon where a multi-use trail (including off-road vehicles) runs 5.5 miles along the bottom of the canyon. It connects to other roads, including one allegedly used by Butch Cassidy, for long loop hikes. Red Canyon is ten miles west of Bryce Canyon on SR 12.

Directions to Dixie National Forest (Utah):

The main headquarters for the five districts in the Dixie National Forest is in Cedar City, Utah at 1789 NorthWedgewood Lane.
Phone: (435) 865-3200
Website: www.fs.fed.us/dxnf/

Coral Pink Sand Dunes State Park

The Park:

The great national parks of Zion and Bryce and Capitol Reef that are the backbone of Utah's "Color Country" can be seen by your dog only from a parking lot. The same iron oxides and minerals that produce that color are responsible for the coral-colored Navajo sandstone that has eroded and blown into this notch in the mountains over thousands of years. The winds are pinched in the mountains so much they can't sustain enough speed to carry the grains of sand.

The Walks:

A quick introduction to dune formation comes on a 1/2-mile nature trail at the day-use lot. The *Two Dunes Trail* visits a wind-blown barchan (crescent-shaped dune) and a star-shaped dune caused by winds coming from several directions before returning in less than two miles.

Longer canine hikes are possible on the open, windy dunes. Check with the ranger station for latest maps as the shifting sands constanty cover old trails. As with all dune hikes, keep an eye on your dog's paw pads for irritation.

Coral Pink Sand Dunes is a magnet for noisy off-road vehicles so consider early morning hikes here since the onslaught cannot begin until 9:00 a.m. The cooler sands of the morning will be welcome to your dog's paws as well.

Directions to Coral Pink Sand Dunes State Park (Utah):

The park is 12 miles west of U.S. 89 near Kanab.

Phone: (435) 648-2800
Website: utah.com/stateparks/coral_pink.htm

Goblin Valley State Park

The Park:

Cowboys searching for lost cattle were the first to report on the bizarre gnome-like rock formations that cover this remote valley. The goblins form by uneven weathering of sandstone rocks of varying hardness. Water erosion and the smoothing action of windblown desert dust conspire to shape the hoodoos and spires in the valley. The state of Utah acquired 3,000 acres to create the park in 1964.

The Walks:

The park does not maintain many formal trails but you are free to drop into the Valley of the Goblins and explore the intricately balanced rock formations with your dog close-up. The valley is flat and any level of canine hiker can enjoy weaving in and out of the goblins.

More spirited canine hiking lies just outside the park on the vast lands of the Bureau of Land Management. The *Bell Canyon/Behind the Reef Road/Little Wild Horse Canyon* trails can be welded to form an eight-mile loop into dry wahses and slot canyons. The walls of these canyons constrict to barely the body width of a Golden Retriever at times.

Your dog can hike right next to the Goblins in central Utah.

Directions to Goblin Valley State Park (Utah):

The park is 36 miles southwest of Green Valley, the nearest town. From I-70 take 24 south to Temple Mountain Road and follow signs into the park.

Phone: (435) 564-3633
Website: www.stateparks.utah.gov/park_pages/
          scenicparkpage.php?id=gvsp

After visiting Goblin Valley it is hard to believe that Hollywood did not arrive until 1999 to use the park as a backdrop for alien planets. You can see the rounded rock formations on screen as the hostile planet Thermia in *Galaxy Quest* as Tim Allen and Sigourney Weaver star as actors in a popular space travel television series who are kidnapped by aliens to fight a real war.

High Sierra

Yosemite National Park

Dogs are not allowed on trails or in the backcountry of Yosemite. This prohibiton includes ski trails in winter. Dogs are, however, allowed to walk anywhere on the Yosemite Valley floor between the Happy Isles Nature Center or Mirror Lake parking lot and the Pohono bridge. You can also take your dog on any paved path not designated as a foot or horse trail. The park does operate a first-come, first-served kennel where you can leave your dog to hike some of Yosemite's legendary trails solo.

Yosemite is generous to dogs in its campgrounds - four whole campgrounds allow dogs in each of the major sections of the park and another four have sections of the campground set aside for dog owners.

Your dog can take a short walk on the paved parking lot paths that lead to some of Yosemite's famous landmarks.

Dogs are free to hike on much of the Yosemite Valley floor near the Merced River.

The Yosemite High Country is tackled by the Tioga Road, Highway 120, culminating in Tioga Pass at the park's entrance. Tioga Pass is California's highest automobile pass at 9.945 feet. Just outside Yosemite is a 3/4-mile nature trail around a glacial lake called the Nunatak Trail, or "Island of Life." If your dog is itching to get on a trail after a visit to Yosemite this is a refreshing leg-stretcher.

Nelder Grove

The Park:

One of the star attractions of Yosemite National Park is the Mariposa Grove of Giant Sequoias. It was these massive cinnamon-colored trees, the largest living things on earth, that inspired our national park system. In 1864 Abraham Lincoln set aside the Mariposa Grove as a protected state reserve "for the pleasuring of the people." Eight years later the world's first national park was created at Yellowstone and Yosemite was transferred to national guidance in 1890.

Your dog can't get on the trail through the Mariposa Grove but the closest place to get him to walk among giant sequoias is five miles south of Yosemite in the Nelder Grove. Naturalist John Muir discovered this redwood grove in 1875 and as he investigated he happened upon a retired miner named John Nelder who was homesteading there. The area was heavily logged thereafter, mostly sugar pines, firs and cedar and the largest sequoias still stand.

The Walks:

The *Shadow of the Giants Trail*, now a National Recreational Trail, was built in 1965. The self-guiding interpretive path meanders for about a mile through the Nelder Grove, one of eight (the most famous is the Mariposa Grove) growing above the Kings River. Unlike sequoias in national parks, the 100 giants here remain in dense forest and you can walk right up to the largest trees.

Those would be Old Granddad and the Kids, a grouping of giant sequoias on a ridgeline and Bull Buck, one of the world's five largest arboreal monarchs. After a half-mile hike from the lower campground you reach Bull Buck, nearly 250 feet tall, 99 feet around at the base and probably 2700 years old.

Directions to Nelder Grove (California):

From Oakhurst, go north of Route 41. Take Sky Ranch Road for seven miles and follow signs for the Nelder Grove after the pavement ends.

The Nelder Grove outside of Yosemite National Park is one place your dog can get up close to explore a Giant Sequoia.

Converse Basin

The Park:

Like Yosemite, its neighbors to the south, Kings Canyon and Sequoia national parks, boasting the largest concentration of giant sequoias in the world, do not allow dogs on the trail. About five miles north of Kings Canyon National Park and the famous General Grant Grove, however, is the Converse Basin Grove where your dog can get up close to a famous giant sequoia, the Boole Tree.

Converse Basin is a giant sequoia graveyard. This area was once quite possibly the finest sequoia grove that ever was. Massive trees over 300 feet high were enthusiastically felled by loggers - often for little more than shingles. One 285-foot sequoia known as the General Noble Tree was cut in 1893 to display at the Columbian Exposition in Chicago and the Chicago Stump can be seen today. Among the trees destroyed in the Converse Basin was the oldest known giant sequoia to have been cut down - 3200 annual growth rings were counted. So many trees were taken that the area is known as Stump Meadow.

This fallen sequoia in a Sequoia National Park parking lot was once used as a road; for real canine hiking you will need to go north of the park to the Converse Basin.

The Walks:

The hiking trail in the Converse Basin is a 2 1/2 mile loop to reach the Boole Tree. Leading straight out from the parking lot you are quickly on the edge of Kings Canyon and you'll enjoy open, sweeping views as you switchback up the ridge. Shortly after finishing your climb you reach a short side trail that leads into a depression containing the Boole Tree, once thought to be the largest giant sequoia in the world but more exacting measurements have placed it eighth. No one knows why this great tree was spared when equally large trees were brought down.

If you have spent the day looking at giant sequoias in the landscaped national parks, your encounter with the Boole Tree might come as a bit of a shock. It is related to its brothers in Kings Canyon National Park like the wolf is to your dog. Surrounded by dense forest growth, it is actually possible to not immediately recognize the Boole Tree from the main trail. But once you see your dog up against its massive trunk - its ground perimeter of 113 feet is the greatest of all giant sequoias - there is no mistaking this special tree.

Directions to Converse Basin (California):

Converse Basin is a few miles north of the Grant Grove Visitor Center in Kings Canyon National Park on the main road to Cedar Grove Visitor Center, Highway 180. The Chicago Stump and Boole Tree are reached by separate dirt roads off Highway 180.

Phone: (559) 565-3341
Website: www.nps.gov/seki

Mt. Whitney

The Park:

Mt. Whitney is the highest point of the High Sierra - at the very top of the continental United States. The 14,496-foot peak was discovered in 1864 by a California biological survey team and named for its leader, Josiah Whitney. The first people to stand on the summit were three fishermen who climbed to the top in 1873 and the highest mountain in the Lower 48 almost carried the head-scratching name "Fishermen's Peak" when a bill was introduced into the California Legislature to commemorate the ascent. The governor, however, vetoed it.

The *Whitney Portal Trail* up Mt. Whitney was completed in 1904 and the stone shelter at the summit built in 1909. Wood was dragged to the summit by mules and the stone shaped and cemented on site with hand tools. The trail is typically snow-free from July to October and hikers cram the slope for a chance to tag the summit making this one of the most popular hikes in the United States. Permits are doled out up to six months in advance; contact the Inyo National Forest Wilderness Reservation Service at 888-373-3773 or 760-938-1136.

The Walks:

The first thing canine hikers will want to know about the Whitney Portal Trail is whether dogs are allowed. Yes. The most important thing to know is that dogs will not be allowed to make the final ascent to the summit. Most of the trail is in the dog-friendly Inyo National Forest but the summit itself is in Sequoia National Park, that doesn't allow dogs on the trail. Dogs can go as far as Trail Crest at about 14,000 feet so to tag the summit you will need a partner staying in Outpost Campground with your dog.

The route to the top of Mt. Whitney is well-marked and graded, 11 miles one way.

An overnight permit is required to stay in one of the overnight campgrounds. Expect some rock scrambling and some strenuous stretches but well-conditioned dogs will have no problems with this trail. A permit is not required to hike the first 2.8 miles from Whitney Portal to Lone Pine Lake.

Sidetrip: Death Valley National Park (to the southeast on Route 190)

Just down the road to the east from Mt. Whitney is Death Valley National Park, America's largest national park outside of Alaska. There are more than three million acres of spectacular desert terrain but dogs are not allowed on trails or the vast backcountry.

Your dog can't hike in Death Valley but he can walk out to the lowest point in the Western Hemisphere.

Directions to Mt. Whitney (California):

The nearest town to Mt. Whitney and Whitney Portal is Lone Pine on Highway 395. From here it is a 13 mile, paved trip to the trailhead.

Phone: (760) 876-2000
Website: www.nps.gov/seki/whitney

A Canine Hike Through Movie History

Lone Pine rests in the shadow of Mt. Whitney, founded in the early 1800s to supply pioneer ranchers and, later, miners. The town got its name from a single pine tree that grew in the boulder-strewn foothills of the Cascades, beside the creek meandering through an area known as the Alabama Hills. The Alabama Hills consist of rounded, weathered granite boulders placed across a desert flatlands that form a sharp contrast with the sharply sculptured ridges of the Sierra. These majestic backdrops and rugged rock formations began attracting the attention of Hollywood, 212 miles to the west, in the 1920s.

You can hike with your dog along Movie Flat Road, a wide, dusty dirt road that runs through the Alabama Hills and is one of the most recognizable movie sets in Hollywood history. Beginning with Tom Mix in the silent era, every major Western star rode down the road on horseback at one time or another.

Roy Rogers appeared here in his first starring role in *Under Western Stars* and Bill Boyd, known on the screen as Hopalong Cassidy, filmed so many roles in Lone Pine that he moved here. The Alabama Hills hosted one of the largest location shoots in history when 1200 extras staged the climactic battle scene in *Gunga Din*. Other notable westerns among the more than 100 films shot here include *The Lone Ranger*, *How The West Was Won*, and *The Gunfighter*.

Although the golden age for Lone Pine has gone the way of the Hollywood western, film crews occasionally still appear. *Bad Day at Black Rock* (Spencer Tracy/Ernest Borgnine) used the area to build an entire town along the railroad tracks in 1955 and, more recently, Fred Ward and Kevin Bacon battled giant earthworms in the Alabama Hills in *Tremors*.

Lake Tahoe

Tahoe Rim Trail

The Lake:

The Washoe Indians named the lake, with 72 miles of shoreline, "big water." Native legend maintained that the Great Spirit gave a young man a branch of leaves to help him elude the pursuing Evil Spirit. Each time the man dropped a leaf from the branch it would create a pool of water the Evil Spirit would be forced to race around. In the heat of the chase, however, the young man became frightened and dropped the entire branch in one spot - creating Lake Tahoe.

At its deepest point the floor of Lake Tahoe is 1,645 feet beneath the surface, making it America's third deepest lake. At 6,229 feet above sea level, Tahoe is one of the world's largest alpine lakes. The glacial water is so clear - 97% pure - that if you dropped a meatbone over the edge of a boat your dog could watch it drop for 70 feet.

The water is so clear in Lake Tahoe your dog may wonder why she can't touch the ground when she's swimming.

The Walks:

The *Tahoe Rim Trail*, a footpath completely around Lake Tahoe, was the inspiration of USFS oficer Glenn Hampton. He built a coalition of support that would attract more than 10,000 volunteers working 200,000 hours before the 165-mile trail was completed in 2001. The Tahoe Rim Trail visits two states, six counties, three national forests, state parkland and three wilderness areas. It stands as one of the largest volunteer projects ever completed in the United States.

The lowest point of the ridge-running route is 6,300 feet at Tahoe City and the trail reaches its apex at Relay Peak where the summit is tagged at 10,333 feet.

Dogs are welcome to enjoy hiking on the Tahoe Rim Trail; the going is often on soft, sandy terrain as you pass through lush forests and playful meadows.

Directions to Tahoe Rim Trail (Nevada/California):

There is access to the Tahoe Rim Trail at numerous points around the lake; eight trail-heads with parking can be found around Lake Tahoe.

Website: www.tahoerimtrail.org

If you hike the entire trail you become eligible for the "165-Mile Club." These long-distance hikers receive a patch from the Tahoe Rim Trail Association but no word yet on laurels for your dog's completing the trail.

East Shore Trails

Winnemucca Lake:

This trail goes through Carson Pass, pioneered by hunter and trapper Christopher "Kit" Carson. When his team made the first successful winter crossing of the Sierras in 1844, the gap at 8,754 feet was called simply "The Pass." Gold-seekers who came several years later started calling this passageway "Carson Pass" even though the pioneers probably went through the mountains a mile or so to the south.

The hike through Carson Pass tags a string of jeweled alpine lakes, the most popular being emerald green Winnemucca Lake. The trail is a delight for humans and dogs alike - wide and sandy with no severe climbs for more than a mile. This is the Lake Tahoe hike to take for wildflower lovers in summer - Lupine, Mules Ear and Indian Paintbrush color the ground.

Canine hikers in search of a more spirited walk can continue past Winnemucca Lake. Another mile down the trail - and 400 feet higher - is Round Top Lake and behind it Round Top Mountain is waiting to be climbed. The scenery is some of the best in the Northern High Sierra.

Directions to Winnemucca Lake (Nevada):

Carson Pass is Highway 88. Turn right and follow to the parking area on the right, at the crest of Carson Pass.

Prey Meadows/Skunk Harbor:

Part of this easy-going canine hike reveals an old railroad grade built in the 1870s to supply lumber to the Virginia City building boom. The path forks but is short enough that canine hikers will want to take both routes. The left fork takes you into Prey Meadows with waves of springtime wildflowers; to the right is Skunk Harbor, a twinkling cove on the Tahoe shore. Along the way come glimpses of Lake Tahoe through thick pine and fir trees. If the meadows and mountains look familiar it is because this is where Ben, Adam, Hoss and Little Joe Cartwright rode for years on *Bonanza*.

Directions to PreyMeadows/Skunk Harbor (Nevada):

The trailhead is not heavily marked. Follow Highway 431 to where it ends at Highway 28, then turn left, toward Incline Village. Follow Highway 28 through Incline Village and past Sand Harbor to the iron pipe gate on the right side of the highway, about 6 miles past the Ponderosa Ranch. There are turnouts along the highway where you can park, make sure not to block the gate.

Very little of the canine hiking at Lake Tahoe leads to the water's edge on the East Shore.

South Shore Trails

Tallac Historic Site:

The southwest shore of Lake Tahoe was a favorite playground to the wealthy and the Tallac Historic Site features three separate rustic estates built from the 1890s through the 1920s. One belonged to Lucky Baldwin, a California real estate investor who operated "the greatest casino in America" here at his Tallac Resort. The Forest Service acquired the area between 1969 and 1971, and has been restoring and renovating ever since.

Pine-scented paths meander around the three estates and poke out to Kiva Beach on the lake, a free beach. Your dog is welcome to trot easily through charming buildings and gardens, man-made ponds and an arboretum. The Tallac Historic Site is linked by a short trail to the Lake Tahoe Visitor Center where dogs are welcome to enjoy a variety of short nature trails.

The *Rainbow Trail* is the feature trail, an interpretive 1/2-mile loop that illuminates the importance of marshes and meadows to the unrivaled clarity of Lake Tahoe. The *Forest Tree Trail* focuses on the life cycle of the Jeffrey Pine, the dominant tree in the Lake Tahoe basin. Across the road is the *Trail of the Washoe*, dedicated to life of Tahoe's original settlers.

Directions to Tallac Historic Site (California):

The twin parking lots for the Tallac Historic Site and Lake Tahoe Visitor Center are located three miles north of South Lake Tahoe on Highway 89.

Mt. Tallac Trail:

Mt. Tallac is the monarch of the Lake Tahoe shoreline, rising over 3,000 feet above the water. Many trails lead to its summit and the *Mt. Tallac Trail* is one of the best day hikes at Tahoe. The first half of the 5-mile climb is moderately paced until you reach smallish Cathedral Lake, ideal for a doggie dip. Then the going gets rougher as you grind your way up the front face of the 9,735-foot peak.

Once on top there won't be much that escapes your view. Lake Tahoe, Fallen Leaf Lake, the Desolation Wilderness and even the casinos across the state line in Nevada all reveal themselves on Mt. Tallac.

Mt. Tallac is in the Desolation Wilderness that requires access by permit. Permits for day hikers can be obtained at the trailhead.

Directions to Mt. Tallac (California):

Look for this trailhead approximately three miles north of South Lake Tahoe on Highway 89. The Mt. Tallac Trailhead sign is directly across from the entrance to Baldwin Beach. Turn left down a dirt road to trailhead parking.

Kiva Beach is a rare Lake Tahoe beach that welcomes dogs.

In 1950 biologists working in Lake Tahoe introduced Kokanee salmon into the ecosystem. Each fall now the fish return to Taylor Creek, guided by their acute sense of smell, to spawn in the waters of their birth. You can watch the salmon as they pass through the Stream Profile Chamber. The males have grown more and bigger teeth, developed a humpback and sprouted a long, hooked snout. They have also turned a brilliant red-orange color from their normal blueish-green and cream. The name "Kokanee"is a native word meaning "red fish." The red fish will live only a few days after they pass in front of the glass windows - they will die shortly after their mission to spawn is accomplished. You will, however, have to tether your dog while you duck into the *Stream Profile Trail*.

West Shore Trails

Cascade Falls Trail:

This is a short out-and-back trail of less than one mile that leads to memorable views of 200-foot Cascade Falls. The trail gains scarcely 100 feet of elevation and can get crowded so you will need to keep your dog under close control. The trail itself picks its way among rocks and Jeffrey pines as it clings to the mountain slope. Cascade Lake below and Lake Tahoe in the distance are in almost constant view. The final steps as you near the falls are across open granite slopes that can be slippery under paw.

Across the road from the campground is Inspiration Point, with views of Emerald Bay that have been called the most photographed in America. Below on the shore at the head of the bay is the estate of Vikingsholm. A trail leads down to the Viking castle on the beach but you will have to take it without your dog.

All the trails around Emerald Bay, including the short but demanding Eagle Falls hike, are extremely popular and recommended only for well-behaved dogs.

Directions to Cascade Falls (California):

The parking lots for the trails around Emerald Bay are directly on Highway 89.

The route to Cascade Falls picks along the side of a pine-studded mountain.

North Shore Trails

Mount Rose Wilderness:

Mount Rose is the most heavily used of the three wilderness areas around Lake Tahoe. The centerpiece trail is a 6-mile, 2,000-foot ascent to the summit of Mount Rose. This trip is for experienced canine hikers since the paw-friendly hard-packed sand trail gives way in the last two miles to rough shale that can give sharp, uncertain footing to a dog. From the top of 10,776-foot Mount Rose there are long vistas of Lake Tahoe, the Truckee Meadows and, on clear days, Pyramid Lake beyond Reno.

Other trails exploring the canyons and ridges of the high country of the Carson Range are at Mount Rose. The *Jones/Whites Creek* loop trail covers 8 miles and the 2-mile Hunter Creek explores the northern section of the wilderness.

The 3-mile *Thomas Creek* trail leads canine hikers to small lakes and lively meadows in the interior of the park.

A pleasant leg-stretcher for canine hikers at Mount Rose is the 1.3-mile *Mount Rose Meadows Interpretive Trail*. The easy loop is paved for full access but bikes and horses are not allowed. It trips through rushing streams and rough granite boulders along the way to the alpine meadow that is awash in wildflowers after the snowmelt.

Directions to Mount Rose Wilderness (Nevada):

The Mount Rose Highway, State Highway 431, runs for 15 miles to within one mile of the summit at 8,933 feet. The parking lot for the trails is on the left in Mount Rose Meadows.

Monterey Peninsula

17-Mile Drive

The Park:

Spanish explorers discovered and mapped the Monterey Peninsula in 1602 but it did not become a vacation destination until 1880 when Charles Crocker opened the Hotel Del Monte in 1880. Carriage roads were cleared for guests to enjoy the spectacular coastline or reach a secluded picnic spot. The 17-Mile Drive provides public access to the famous Pacific Ocean views, golf courses and Monterey cypress trees in the 5,000-acre Del Monte Forest.

The Walks:

17-Mile Drive is an auto road that links overlooks and prominent landmarks. The best places to get out of the car with your dog are at the picnic areas of Fanshell Beach and Spanish Bay. At Fanshell your dog can play in the surf and enjoy some pure white sand. Spanish Bay is a good place to begin an exploration of the shoreline on foot.

Just north of Spanish Bay, past the Pacific Grove Gate to 17-Mile Drive, is Asilomar State Beach. Here you can pick up a 3/4-mile walking trail on the cliffs above the coast. Dogs are allowed on the trail and the state beach. The *Recreational Trail* continues past the park and along Ocean View Boulevard as it glides in front of the Victorian town of Pacific Grove and tracks into Old Monterey. At Cannery Row in Monterey your dog can slip into the Pacific Ocean at McAbee Beach.

In Old Monterey, history buffs can extend the canine hike on the *Path of History Walking Tour* that takes in meticulously restored adobes from the late 1700s and early 1800s. Look for a sidewalk constructed of whalebone.

Directions to 17-Mile Drive (California):

There are five access gates, where an entry fee is charged, from the town of Pacific Grove in the north to Carmel in the south. Many travelers will find the entry gate directly on US Highway 1 to b the most convenient.

Website: www.pebblebeach.com/17miledrive.html

Fanshell Beach is a small pocket beach that makes an ideal stopping place during a canine hike along 17-Mile Drive.

There are only two places where the Monterey cypress grows naturally - Point Lobos, where dogs are not allowed, and Cypress Point along the 17-Mile Drive. The Crocker Grove is a quiet spot to stop and admire these hardy survivors in a 13-acre nature reserve. Nearby is the Lone Cypress that has clung to its rocky platform for over 250 years. You can walk your dog to the observation point and get a picture of this venerable California landmark.

Carmel-by-the-Sea

The Town:

The Basilica of Mission San Carlos Borromeo del Rio Carmel was the second mission built in California, founded in Monterey in 1770 and moved to its present location by Spanish missionaries a year later. Artists discovered the village in the early 1900s and strict zoning ordinances keep Carmel, only one mile square, a town of eclectic cottages and bungalows. Luckily, those strict laws don't extend to dogs and Carmel-by-the-Sea is one of the most dog-friendly towns around.

The Walks:

You will enjoy the quirky architecture walking your dog through town but he will be chomping at the leash to get to Carmel Beach City Park at the end of Ocean Avenue. Here your dog can run unleashed on soft white sand. This is the biggest beach among the craggy headlands of Monterey Peninsula. To your right will be the world-famous 18th hole of the Pebble Beach Golf Links and to your left dramatic cliffs. Straight ahead will be mesmerizing views of Monterey Bay. Dogs are also welcome on Carmel River State Beach at the east end of town.

For real canine hiking, two miles north of town on Highway 68 is Jack's Peak Regional Park. More than 10 miles of sporty trails cover the 525-acre park, including routes to the highest point on the Monterey Peninsula. From the trails you can enjoy spectacular views of both the Monterey Bay and Carmel Valley.

Directions to Carmel-by-the-Sea (California):

Carmel-by-the-Sea is located just off SR 1 on the southern end of the peninsula. Turn onto Ocean Avenue and drive into the heart of town. Turn right on Torres Street and park in the free municipal lot at 3rd Avenue and get out and explore on foot.
Website: www.carmelcalifornia.com/

You will never find a more dog-friendly beach than Carmel Beach where dogs and people mingle freely.

Big Sur - Pfeiffer Beach

The Park:

The Big Sur coastline south of the Monterey Peninsula is a must-see for any itinerary in central California. This stretch of coastline is best accessed through a series of California state parks, including Point Lobos State Reserve, once described famously as the "greatest meeting of land and water in the world." Unfortunately, dogs are not allowed on any trails here. Most other parks are not welcoming to canine hikers either. Julia Pfeiffer Burns State Park bans dogs altogether while others, Pfeiffer Big Sur State Park for example, condemn dogs to paved surfaces only.

The Walks:

Big Sur is not a complete washout for dog lovers however, thanks to Pfeiffer Beach. A short sandy trail leads to one of the most beautiful public beaches in California. The sand is wrapped in spectacular rock formations making Pfeiffer Beach a very secluded place. The rocks are sprinkled in the surf as well forming coves and making for exciting play in the waves for dogs. For the less adventurous canine swimmer, a small freshwater stream feeds into the beach. There is also room to hike along the sand to the north for restless canine hikers. And you won't be lacking for canine company at Pfeiffer Beach - most everyone who makes the drive down the long, narrow access road seems to have a dog in the back seat. This will certainly be one of your most memorable trips to the beach with your dog anywhere.

Directions to Pfeiffer Beach (California):

Pfeiffer Beach is located on Sycamore Canyon Road across from the Ranger Station on Highway 1.
Website: www.bigsurcalifornia.org/beaches.html

When travelling the Pacific Coast Highway, Pfeiffer Beach is the best beach for dog owners. The turn-off is obscured and easy to miss on the crest of a hill so be be diligent.

Redwood Coast

Redwood National and State Parks

The Park:

Development came slowly to the Redwood Coast of northern California. With no naturally deep harbors, seafaring explorers sailed on past and it wasn't until gold was discovered on Gold Bluffs Beach in 1850 that settlement began. The gold played out fast but it was hard to ignore an estimated two million acres of the world's tallest trees that dominated the landscape. Sporting bark impervious to insects and having no known diseases, coastal redwoods can live 2,000 years, grow over 350 feet tall and weigh 500 tons. Logging began in 1851 with smaller, more manageable trees but as technology improved bigger and bigger trees were taken. In the 1920s, three California state parks were established to protect the redwoods and in 1968 Redwood National Park was ushered into existence to preserve additional groves. Together the parks protect about 40,000 acres of the ancient forest.

The Walks:

Dogs are not allowed on any trails in Redwood National Park or any of the three California state parks: Jedidiah Smith Redwoods State Park, Del Norte Coast Redwoods State Park, or Prairie Creek Redwoods State Park. Your dog can experience the grandeur of the coastal redwoods only in picnic areas, overlooks and campgrounds. Dogs are allowed on two beaches: Gold Bluffs Beach north of Orick and Crescent Beach south of Crescent City. Another beach just outside the park to the south that welcomes dogs is Clam Beach.

Dogs can't hike the trails in Redwood National Park but some of the picnic areas are worth visiting.

Directions to the Redwood parks (California):

The Redwoods parks are all reached along Highway 101 except Jedidiah Smith Redwoods State Park, that is located on Howland Hill Road off Highway 101 south of Crescent City. These dense redwood groves were used by George Lucas to film chase scenes in *Return of the Jedi*.

Phone: (707) 464-6101
Website: www.nps.gov/redw/

Smith River National Recreation Area

The Park:

The closest place to get your dog on the trail under redwoods is the Smith River National Recreation Area, located adjacent to Jedediah Smith Redwoods State Park. Established in 1990, the 305,000-acre park was created around Smith River, the last free-flowing river in California without a dam. Smith River is the largest Wild & Scenic River System in the United States - more than 300 miles have been so designated.

The Walks:

The marquee trail is the *South Kelsey National Recreation Trail*, the remnants of an historic transportation link between the Pacific Ocean at Crescent City and the gold mines in the Klamath River region. This is a long linear trail that leaves between Horse and Bucks creeks and follows the South Fork of the Smith River for seven miles before beginning an ascent to 5,775-foot Baldy Peak at the 13-mile mark. Campgrounds are available on the route, which continues another 15 miles into Klamath National Forest.

Shorter day hikes with your dog are available throughout the recreation area. A walk of nearly two moderate miles on *Craig's Creek Trail* finds many redwood trees along the South Fork. The *Myrtle Creek Trail* is an interpretive hike along an old mining flume where miner Jim Slinkard once found a 47-ounce gold nugget the shape of an axe. Experienced canine hikers can tackle the *Devil's Punchbowl Trail* where switchbacks climb steeply to two postcard lakes tucked in the mountain peaks.

Directions to Smith River National Recreation Area (California):

Headquarters for the Smith River National Recreation Area is in Gasquet on U.S. Highway 199.

Phone: (707) 442-1721
Website: www.fs.fed.us/r5/sixrivers/recreation/smith-river/

Lake Earl State Wildlife Area

The Park:

Lake Earl is California's largest lagoon, probably formed 5000 years ago when expanding sand dunes plugged a shallow depression in the Smith River plain. The Tolowa Indians used the natural resources here and there is evidence of their village life in the park.

The Walks:

There are 20 miles of canine hiking scattered throughout this ancient sand dune complex that features 11 miles of coastline. There are wooded hillside trails and grassy meadows but the prime attraction in the Lake Earl State Wildlife Area are the 250 species of birds, including the rare Canada Aleutian goose, that visit the wetlands and lakes here. The *Dead Lake Loop* is the one canine hike to do at Lake Earl if you visit under a time constraint.

Directions to Lake Earl State Wildlife Area (California):

Lake Earl is located two miles north of Crescent City via Northcrest Drive off US Highway 101.

Phone: (707) 442-1721
Website: www.fs.fed.us/r5/sixrivers/recreation/smith-river/

On July 30, 1865 the sidewheeler *Brother Jonathan*, two days out of San Francisco, struck a submerged rock spire known as the Dragon's Teeth off of Point St. George in the park. Lifeboats were released but only one made it to shore with 19 survivors. The loss of 215 people is the worst maritime disaster in California history. A century later, in 1964, a tsunami generated by a great earthquake in Alaska devasted this area.

Pacific Cascades

Olympic Peninsula

The Park:

Dogs are not permitted on the trails in Olympic National Park, but there are more than one half-million acres surrounding one of America's favorite parks where your dog can trot in lush rain forests. President Grover Cleveland signed the act protecting 1,500,000 acres of the Olympic Peninsula back in 1897. When the heart of the peninsula was made a national park in 1938 the donut of land swallowing it became the national forest.

The Walks:

Some of the most diverse ecosystems in America can be found on the more than 200 miles of trail - half at lower elevations - in Olympic National Forest's five wilderness areas. Access to most of the trails is via unpaved road; motorized vehicles are prohibited in the wilderness areas.

The most unique ecosystem in the park is the Quinault Rain Forest, best explored on two loop trails off South Shore Road at Lake Quinault. The *Quinault Rain Forest Trail* penetrates deep into an old-growth forest where firs and spruce can tickle 300 feet in height. Clubmoss draping branches and thick canopies suffocate the light on the forest floor of this four-mile canine hike. In a half-mile loop the *Rain Forest Nature Trail* interprets the creation of this lush arboreal paradise. If this has only whetted your appetite for rain forests you can take the dog on a rough-and-tumble hike on the *Dry Creek Trail #872*.

You can contrast the rare forests untouched by man in the Olympic National Forest with second growth timber stands. In the Duckabush Recreation Area (22 miles north of Hoodsport) the *Interrorem Nature Trail* (.25 miles) wanders amidst amidst second-growth trees flourishing among head-high cedar stumps from early day timber harvesting. The trail is reached via the *Ranger Hole Trail* that descends sharply 100 feet to the lively waters of the Duckabush River.

Although much of the national forest land lies in the foothills of the Olympic Mountains there are also opportunities to tag a few summits here. In the Hood Canal District, Mt. Walker, Mt. Rose and Mt. Zion are all peaks that can be hiked with your dog.

Directions to Olympic National Forest (Washington):

US 101 circles the Olympic Peninsula and provides access to the national forest in the east, west and north.

Phone: (360) 956-2402
Website: www.fs.fed.us/r6/olympic/

Ross Lake National Recreation Area

The Park:

This is glacier country - the North Cascades is the most heavily glaciated area in the continental United States. The current park glacier census stands at 318 with countless more snowfields that are fed by some of the heaviest snowfalls in the world, between 400 and 700 inches in an average year. The millions of North Cascades acres have been carved up among various federal agencies since 1968 but most of the region - 93% - has been designated as the Stephen Mather Wilderness Area, named after the first director of the National Park Service.

The Walks:

Dog owners must approach the North Cascades like working a jigsaw puzzle. Dogs are banned from the North Cascades National Park North Unit and South Unit (except on the *Pacific Crest National Scenic Trail*) but are permitted in the Ross Lake National Recreation Area sandwiched in between. Dogs are also allowed in the limited-access Lake Chelan National Recreation Area to far south.

The only paved access road to the area is Washington State Route 20, the North Cascades Highway that, to the good fortune of canine hikers, runs across the dog-friendly Ross Lake NRA. Long day hikes to overnight expeditions can be found on the State Route 20 trails.

Quick leg stretchers introduce the natural and human history of the mountains at the Visitor Center in the Newhalem Area. The *River Loop* picks its way through alpine forests to a free-flowing section of the Skagit River.

Diablo Lake, with its rich turquoise waters, is the central jewel of the Ross Lake NRA and several canine hiking opportunities exist here. The *Diablo Lake Trail* on the north shore is an out-and-back affair of nearly four miles with just a modest elevation gain.

Thunder Creek, that feeds the lake with fine glacial sediment, is shadowed by a 38-mile trail but the first steps are an easy canine hike of less than than a mile to a crossing suspension bridge.

More long-distance outings are available upstream at Ross Lake, the largest of the three man-made reservoirs on the Skagit River. The *East Bank Trail* runs 17 non-strenuous miles along the shore of the lake. At Ross Dam a short walk of less than a mile leads down to the 540-foot tall dam and across the road the *Happy Creek Forest Walk* takes a short stroll through an ancient creekside forest.

Directions to Ross Lake National Recreation Area (Washington):

North Cascades access is by Washington SR 20 from east and west. Expect closures of the road between November and April.

Phone: (360) 856-5700
Website: www.nps.gov./noca

"No one appreciates the very special genius of your conversation as a dog does."
- Christopher Morley

Our 10 Favorite Dog-Friendly Adventures In Western Canada
by www.PetFriendly.ca

Rundle, a happy and hyper American Eskimo dog, and Tonka, a Pekingese who thinks he's an Eskie, love to hike with their people. Their favorite short Canadian day hikes include:

1. Little Lost Lake - Near Mount Robson Park at the Junction of Hwy 5 and 16, British Columbia.

The Little Lost Lake trail is a secluded forest hike that's perfect for a quiet picnic while the dogs splash in the lake. The trailhead is a bit difficult to spot; the sign is set back against the forest and you have to park at a pullout just off the highway on the other side of the road. The trail starts off at a moderately steep incline through dense forest, but eventually levels out for a relatively easy walk to the top. At the top of the trail you'll find a gem of a lake: quiet, peaceful, and clear, with opportunities to view wildlife.

2. Starratt Wildlife Sanctuary - Valemount, British Columbia. Trailhead off Hwy 5 by the Holiday Inn.

This is a pleasant and easy walk through the marsh and forests on a well-maintained trail, with the mountains offering a scenic backdrop. There is a wildlife viewing platform at the Holiday Inn trailhead where you can look for coyote, moose, muskrat, and a variety of birds. The trail is 6 kilometers round-trip.

3. Nose Hill Park - Calgary, Alberta. Various access points throughout north Calgary.

Nose Hill Park is Canada's largest, natural area urban park, and is a popular area for dog-walkers. Signs are located at each of the entrances to show where dogs must be leashed and where they may run off-leash. Wide-open spaces at the top of the hill give dogs plenty of room to run. In the spring and summer, providing there has been enough rainfall, there is a small "pond" at the top of the hill to the left of the 64th Avenue entrance. The Shaganappi entrance offers flat trails for those who don't feel like climbing the hill. If you're lucky and you're up at the top of the hill in the right weather conditions, you may be able to catch a view of the sunset over the city, or a crystal-clear view of the mountains in the distance.

4. Fish Creek Provincial Park - Calgary, Alberta. Various access points in south Calgary.

Dogs are permitted in most areas of Fish Creek, with the exception of the Sikome Lake area. Most trails are forested and relatively easy walks. The creek crosses here and there, giving the dogs a chance to cool off and play.

5. Bear's Hump Trail - Waterton National Park, Alberta. Trail access located behind the Visitor's Center.

Waterton National Park is a 525 square kilometer park offering crystal clear lakes, mountain scenery, and 200 kilometers of trails. The Bear's Hump trail winds its way up the mountain on a well-maintained trail that's a mere 1.4 km long (one way). However, it's also quite steep! When you make it to the top you'll be rewarded with a tranquil setting with stunning views of the lake, a birds-eye view of the historic Prince of Wales hotel, and a view of the Waterton townsite.

6. Kananaskis Country - Canadian Rockies, Alberta.

"K-Country" is a vast recreational area that offers beautiful mountain scenery, lots of opportunity for wildlife watching, and an extensive trail system. Dogs are permitted throughout Kananaskis. There are far too many great trails to mention them all! One pretty, pleasant walk is King Creek, especially in the winter. Be sure to also stop by the Mount Lorette picnic area where you'll find wonderful little nooks set into the trees, along with an easy paved pathway that weaves around a set of small ponds.

7. *East Sooke Regional Park - Sooke, on beautiful Vancouver Island in British Columbia. Follow Gillespie Rd to East Sooke Rd, then follow the signs to the park.*

East Sooke is a wilderness area that offers 50 kilometers of trails in its over 1400 hectares of natural and protected coastal landscape. The Anderson Cove entrance takes you through the forests and up to a gorgeous viewpoint on some rocky outcroppings. Keep your eyes out for the many seal that swim around the area!

8. *Roche Cove Provincial Park - Sooke, British Columbia.*

Roche Cove is part of the Galloping Goose trail system, a network of trails leading from Sooke to Sidney. The main trail at Roche Cove is a very easy walk through the trees. Dogs love to play in the huge piles of leaves that blanket the trail in the fall! There is also a trail leads down to a private and beautiful little cove, while another leads up a hill to a viewpoint. If you're lucky, you may meet a group of llamas out for a walk with their owners!

9. *Ocean Blvd - Victoria, British Columbia.*

Ocean Blvd is a "must" for dog-walkers - it's a lovely stretch of road with waterfront on both sides. You'll see lots of dogs romping through the sand and in the water! Seal, swan, and other birds are abundant.

10. *Bodega Ridge - Galiano Island, British Columbia.*

This relatively easy hike along the cliff edge and through forested areas rewards you with magnificent views of the mountains, Trincomali Channel, Vancouver Island and the Strait of Georgia. Watch for wildflowers and wildlife, particularly bald eagles and turkey vultures.

Pet Friendly Canada, operating out of Calgary, Alberta, features a wide selection of pet-friendly accommodations from across Canada. You are invited to browse the directory of hotels, cottages, B&Bs, resorts, and other lodgings that accept pets...because pets are family, too! You can reach them at www.PetFriendly.ca.

Exploring History
With Your Dog...

Chesapeake & Ohio Canal National Historic Park

The Park:

George Washington was one of the early American speculators who dreamed of the riches an inland American waterway could bring that would float goods from the West to Washington down the Potomac River. A canal that could connect the Potomac River to the Ohio River in Pittsburgh would provide a continuous water link from New Orleans to the Cheasapeake Bay. The canal, dubbed the "Great National Project" by President John Quincy Adams, was finally started on July 4, 1828. It would take 22 years to complete - actually construction just stopped since the canal route never made it out of Maryland with only 184.5 of the planned 460 miles dug - and was obsolete before it opened. Battling the young and ever-improving railroads, the Chesapeake & Ohio Canal lasted for 75 years floating cargo from Cumberland, Maryland to Georgetown. The ditch survived filling in through the efforts of Supreme Court Justice William O. Douglas who championed the canal as "a long stretch of quiet and piece."

The Walks:

At the Great Falls Tavern Visitor Center dogs are denied the extraordinary views of the powerful Great Falls of the Potomac and Mather Gorge - they are banned from the boardwalk trails on the Olmsted Island Bridges and the rock-scrambling on the *Billy Goat "A" Trail* around Bear Island. But canine hikers are welcome everywhere else and park staff even maintains a watering bowl for pets at the Visitor Center drinking fountain. The packed sand and paw-friendly towpath is one of the most scenic of its ilk - the canal section around the Great Falls opens wide and the boulder-edged water calls to mind the Canadian Rockies rather than suburban Washington.

Away from the Potomac a trail system penetrates the wooded hills above the river. These wide dirt trails make for easy dog walking through an airy, mature forest. The key route is the *Gold Mine Loop* that pushes out from behind the Visitor Center. Various short spur trails, some marked and some not, radiate off the 3.2-mile loop. The *River Trail* above the Washington Aqueduct Dam takes canine hikers along river's edge for about one mile. Even though the water can seem placid at this point, beware of unpredictable currents in the river - the Potomac River has claimed scores of lives over the years.

The prime attraction for canine hikers at the western end of the canal route is Paw Paw Tunnel at Mile 155 (from I-70 in Hancock take Route 522 south to Route 9; turn right and drive 28 miles to the town of Paw Paw). Bring a flashlight for the 15-minute dogwalk on the towpath through the 3,118-foot tunnel. It took 14 years and six million bricks to bypass the six mile stretch of the Potomac River known as Paw Paw Bends. The return trip can come via the orange-blazed *Tunnel Hill Trail*, a strenuous two-mile haul to a ridge 362 feet above the tunnel.

Directions to Chesapeake & Ohio Canal National Historic Park (Great Falls Tavern, Maryland):

The park entrance is at the junction of Falls Road (Route 189) and MacArthur Boulevard. Take Exit 39 off I-495 and continue on River Road (Route 190) West before turning left on Falls Road.

Phone: (301) 767-3714
Website: www.nps.gov/choh

During the Civil War, a Union private camped at Great Falls discovered gold-bearing quartz while tending to his chores. After the war he returned to Great Falls and began mining operations that triggered a mini-gold rush to the area. Although the Maryland Mine was active from 1867 until 1939, it yielded less than $200,000 of precious metal. The Falls Road Spur takes you to the ruins of the mine and mine diggings can be seen at several places on the trails.

Cumberland Gap National Historic Park

The Park:

Wandering animals, buffalo and deer, were the first to discover this natural break in the daunting Appalachian Mountains. These migratory mammals blazed the trail that American Indian tribes would later follow. American settlers seemed destined to be bottled up on the East Coast until April 1750 when Dr. Thomas Walker discovered the gap through the mountains. Later, Daniel Boone blazed the Wilderness Road through the Gap in 1775. Over the next 20 years, although no wagons rolled through the pass, more than 200,000 people made the journey west into the wilderness of Kentucky and beyond. The Cumberland Gap was honored as a national Historic Park in 1940 and a new tunnel through the mountains will enable the Wilderness Road to one day be restored to its 1700s appearance.

The Walks:

The Cumberland Gap National Historic Park encompasses more than 20,000 acres of rich forest lands in the mountains on the Kentucky-Virginia border. The best spot to view the gap is at Pinnacle Overlook, accessible on a 4-mile paved road. Most visitors don't make it beyond the overlook but canine hikers can take off on a wide, rolling walk at the top of mountains with good views through thin trees and from rocky perches. The *Ridge Trail* is an easy walk from the tourist parking lot or can be climbed to from a campground. It runs for 19 miles through the woods on the ridgetop; all told, there are more than 50 miles of marked trail in the park.

To walk on the Wilderness Road, try the *Tri-State Peak Trail*, a steady 1.3-mile climb around the mountain. After a narrow, rocky beginning up switchbacks, the trail goes through the historic gap before heading to the 1,990-foot summit on a wide logging road. From the pavillion on the summit are views of Virginia, Kentucky and Tennessee.

Directions to Cumberland Gap National Historic Park (Kentucky):

The Visitor Center is located on the Kentucky side of the Cumberland Gap, on US 25E.

Phone: (606) 248-2817
Website: www.nps.gov/cuga

At the base of the Tri-State Peak Trail are the remains of a 30-foot-high, charcoal-burning blast furnace that produced iron through much of the 19th century. Built of limestone slid down the mountain, the Newlee Iron Furnace was the focal point for an iron-making community here.
The furnace could produce about 3 tons of iron a day to be shipped down the Powell River to Chattanooga.

Gettysburg National Military Park

The Park:

The events at Gettysburg during the summer of 1863 are the most analyzed and dissected three days in American history and your dog is welcome to come along as you absorb what happened here when General Robert E. Lee made his only invasion of the North during the Civil War. The fields and fences and boulders look much the same as they did when more men fell in any battle ever fought in North America. The Confederate attack was repulsed but only at the cost of 51,000 killed, wounded and missing soldiers. While Lee's retreat did not end the Civil War, it virtually guaranteed that the South would never prevail in the conflict.

The battlefield swallows the town of Gettysburg although most of your walking will take place south of the village between Seminary Ridge, Warfield Ridge and Cemetery Ridge where the climatic fighting took place.

🚫 *Adjacent to the park is the 690-acre Eisenhower National Historic Site, the farm where Dwight D. Eisenhower retired after his two terms as President. It was the first home he ever owned and now reached only by shuttle bus. Your dog is also not allowed in the National Cemetery.*

Trees shattered by gunfire, like this stump on Big Round Top, are mute testimony to the fierce fighting that erupted in this quiet corner of Pennsylvania.

A short path leads through the unique rock formations of Devil's Den that were once a Confederate stronghold.

The Walks:

There is plenty to see on foot at Gettysburg and full days of hiking can be crafted on the 9-mile *Billy Yank Trail* and the 3.5-mile *Johnny Reb Trail*. The trails circle the battlefield, crossing open fields and scooting up boulder-strewn ridges. Shorter canine hikes include the one-mile *High Water Mark Trail* that interprets the final desperate race across nearly a mile of open ground by the 12,000-man "Pickett's Charge." The men who managed to breach the Union line made the deepest penetration into Northern territory of any soldiers in the war.

Another short hike twists to the summit of Big Round Top, a crucial Union position, and the top of Cemetery Ridge. Additional trails lead into the woods and across fields to many of the more than 1,400 statues and memorials that have been erected on the battlefield.

Directions to Gettysburg National Military Park (Pennsylvania):

The park is on US Route 15. From east and west, drive into Gettysburg on US Route 30, turn south on Baltimore Street (Route 97), and follow signs to Steinwehr Avenue (Business Route 15).

Phone: (717) 334-1124

Website: www.nps.gov/gett

Guilford Courthouse National Military Park

The Park:

With the Revolutionary War stalemated in the North in 1778, the British strategy to win the war shifted to the South. Georgia and South Carolina were completely under British control by 1780. Nathanael Greene, an ironmaster by trade, self-taught in the art of war and George Washington's hand-picked commander of the Southern Department, was determined to keep North Carolina out of British hands.

From his base in Virginia Greene harassed the British as their attack spread northward. Pursued by a frenetic Lord Cornwallis, Greene selected sloping ground near Guilford Courthouse to make his stand. He aligned his superior force of 4,000 men - of which scarcely one in five had ever seen battle action - in three lines to receive the British assault on March 15, 1781.

The first line, manned by inexperienced North Carolina militia, was quickly brushed aside and fled. Breaking through the second Patriot line, however, required savage fighting and by the time the redcoats reached Greene's last line, Cornwallis was becoming desperate. As the fighting raged Cornwallis directed his artillery to fire grapeshot over his own lines into the melee of friend and foe alike. The harsh directive to fire into his own troops dispersed the Americans and saved his army.

Greene retired from the field. Technically the loser, his losses had been light. Cornwallis kept the field but lost the war at Guilford Courthouse. His army limped on to Wilmington, convinced that conquering Virginia would collapse the Revolution. Greene let him go and moved southward to reconquer South Carolina and Georgia, confident that American troops assembling in Virginia would destroy Cornwallis - which they did seven months later in Yorktown.

Begun in 1887, the 220-acre park was later established in 1917 as the first battleground of the American Revolution to be preserved as a national military park.

The Walks:

The military park is a local popular dog-walking destination with level, leafy paths in a suburban environment. Nothing remains of either the small wooden courthouse or the community of March 15, 1781 but the grounds are among the most decorated of Revolutionary battlefields, graced by twenty-eight monuments. The most impressive monument is the large equestrian statue of General Greene, sculpted by Francis H. Packer. Unveiled on July 3, 1915, it bears Greene's words: "We fight, get beat, rise, and fight again."

Sidetrip: Kings Mountain National Military Park (Route 161, 12 miles northwest of York, South Carlina)

Revolutionary War buffs will want to travel southwest to the site of some of the most vicious American vs. American fighting of the war at Kings Mountain. Here some 600 "backcountry" men who had marched over 200 miles attacked Carolinians loyal to the crown. The Loyalists were under the command of "Bloody" Patrick Ferguson, the only British soldier in the battle.

Ferguson chose to defend his position on traditional high ground, a rocky outcropping surrounded by a hardwood forest. The mountain men, however, worked their way up the slopes, fighting from tree to tree on their way to the summit. The high ground in this case worked against the defenders as they were unable to get clear shots at their attackers. Sir Henry Clinton called the defeat at King's Mountain, "the first link in a chain of evils that at last ended in the total loss of America."

You can take your dog on an interpretive walking tour around Battlefield Ridge that includes the spot where Ferguson was killed, marked by a monument and covered with a traditional Scottish stone cairn.

Directions to Guilford Courthouse National Military Park (North Carolina):

The park is on New Garden Street in Greensboro, directional signs lead you in from I-85 and I-40.

Phone: (336) 288-1776
Website: www.nps.gov/guco

Harpers Ferry National Historic Park

The Park:

No place in America packs as much scenic wonder and historical importance into such a small area as Harpers Ferry National Historic Park where the Shenandoah and Potomac rivers join forces. George Washington surveyed here as a young man. Thomas Jefferson hailed the confluence as "one of the most stupendous scenes in Nature" and declared it worth a trip across the Atlantic Ocean just to see. Meriwether Lewis prepared for the Corps of Discovery in 1804 by gathering supplies of arms and military stores at Harpers Ferry. A United States Marine Colonel named Robert E. Lee captured abolitionist John Brown at Harpers Ferry when he attempted to raid the United States Arsenal and arm a slave insurrection. General Thomas "Stonewall" Jackson scored one of his greatest military victories here during the Civil War.

Congress appropriated funds for a national monument in Harpers Ferry in 1944 and 2,300 acres of Maryland, Virginia and West Virginia were interwoven into the National Historic Park in 1963.

The Walks:

Dogs are welcome in Harpers Ferry National Historic Park and hikes are available for every taste and fitness level. On the Maryland side of the Potomac River is the towpath for the Chesapeake & Ohio Canal, which was completed in 1850 as a 184.5 mile transportation link between Washington D.C. and Cumberland, Maryland. The trail is wide, flat and mostly dirt.

Beside the canal, the Maryland Heights rise dramatically 1,448 feet above the rivers. The *Stone Fort Trail* up the Heights is the area's most strenuous hike and one of the most historic. With the outbreak of the Civil War, the Union Army sought to fortify the strategic Maryland Heights with its commanding views of the waters and busy railroad lines below. The roads leading to the summit were remembered by Union soldiers as "very rocky, steep and crooked and barely wide enough for those wagons."

Wayside exhibits help hikers appreciate the effort involved in dragging guns, mortar and cannon up the mountainside. One 9-inch Dahlgren gun capable of lobbing 100-pound shells weighed 9,700 pounds. The trail leads to the remnants of the Stone Fort which straddles the crest of Maryland Heights at its highest elevation.

When you start out on a hike with your dog at Harpers Ferry it is straight up in every direction - in Maryland, Virginia or West Virginia.

Access to Lower Town in Harpers Ferry is by National Park Service shuttle bus from the visitor center. Dog owners can best access this area by driving to the Maryland Heights for parking and walking across the Potomac River. The bridge features open grating that can intimidate skittish dogs not familiar with grates.

On the other side of the town of Harpers Ferry in West Virginia, along the Shenandoah River, is Virginus Island and the ruins of a thriving industrial town that finally succumbed to flooding in 1889. The trails that weave through the ruins are flat and shady and connect to the trails in historic Lower Town, where John Brown barricaded himself in the town's fire engine house and battled Federal troops. Climbing up the steep grade out of Lower Town is a short trail to *Jefferson Rock*, where Thomas Jefferson recorded his impressions in 1783. Also available in the West Virginia section of the park is the *Bolivar Heights Trail* over wooded terrain on the site of Jackson's triumphal Civil War battle.

On the Virginia side of the Potomac River you can enjoy the heavily forested Loudon Heights. Mountainside trails here lead to the *Appalachian Trail* and there is several hours of hiking in this area of the park.

Sidetrip: (Antietam National Battlefield (SR 34/65, Sharpsburg, Maryland)

Emboldened by early successes, General Robert E. Lee decided to make his first invasion of the North in the Civil War at the crossroads town of Sharpsburg. On September 17, 1862, the bloodiest day in American history, over 23,000 men were killed or wounded as Lee was forced to withdraw.

The battlefield grounds are open to dogs and several miles of dirt trails along Antietam Creek are available. The hike leads through level farm fields (and across one major road) and visits the Sunken Road, nicknamed "Bloody Lane" when 4,000 men fell there in four hours of fighting.

The path ends at the Lower Bridge where a few hundred Georgia riflemen delayed Union troops long enough to prevent the possible anihilation of the Confederate Army. There is more canine hiking here with a rolling loop on the *Snavely Ford Trail*.

Directions to Harpers Ferry National Historic Park (West Virginia):

Harpers Ferry National Historic Park is located on Route 340, twenty miles south of I-270 in Frederick, Maryland.

Phone: (304) 535-6298
Website: www.nps.gov/hafe

A branch off the Stone Fort Trail winds down to the Overlook Cliffs, perched directly above the confluence of the Potomac and Shenandoah rivers. The best view of Harpers Ferry is from these rock outcroppings where it is easy to understand the town's importance to transportation in Colonial America, its value to the jockeying of battling armies in the Civil War and its susceptability to crippling floods. There are no protective fences and dogs should be watched carefully on the open rocks at the Overlook Cliffs.

"No animal should ever jump up on the dining room furniture unless... he can hold his own in the conversation."
- Fran Liebowitz

Morristown National Historic Park

The Park:

Morristown, a village of 250, was a center of iron supply for the American Revolution and even though it lay only 30 miles west of the main British force in New York it was protected by a series of parallel mountain ranges. It was the twin luxuries of a defensible position in close proximity to the enemy that twice brought General Washington to camp his main army here, first in 1777 and again in 1779-1780.

After the Battle of Princeton in January 3, 1777 a worn-down Colonial army swarmed the tiny town seeking shelter in the few public buildings, private homes, barns and stables then in existence. Steadily Washington rebuilt his flagging troops, overcoming desertion and insipient food shortages. His greatest foe, however, was disease. An outbreak of smallpox threatened to decimate the small army and Washington ordered the little known and, to many, horrifying procedure of innoculation. Some indeed died but most of his troops did not contract the deadly pox.

The park was created in 1933 as America's first national historic park.

The Walks:

Canine hiking at Morristown National Historic Park is found at the Jockey Hollow Encampment Area. When here, nothing could have prepared the Continental Army for the worst winter of the 18th century. Twenty-eight blizzards pounded the slopes and whipped through the wooden huts that were cut from 600 acres of hardwood forests here.

The forest is back and is open and airy with long views through the trees from the trail. Four main trails circle the Jockey Hollow Encampment. The 6.5-mile *Grand Loop Trail*, blazed in white, circles the park but doesn't visit any historical attractions without a detour. It is also the only trail that cannot be accessed from the centrally located Trail Center.

The *Aqueduct Loop Trail* and the stacked loop *Primrose Brook Trail* are two of the prettiest rambles in the park as they trace some of the many gurgling streams that once attracted the Colonial Army.

Two-room huts like this one could house as many as 15 Revolutionary War soldiers.

The long-distance *Patriot's Path* links Jockey Hollow to the New Jersey Encampment Area and neighboring park's and contributes mightily to the total of 27 well-groomed miles of Morristown trails.

All the junctions on the first-rate trails feature directional signs and park maps.

Directions to Morristown National Historic Park (New Jersey):

Morristown is located along interstate 287 in New Jersey. Traveling south on 287, exit 36. Traveling north on 287, exit 36A.

Phone: (973) 539-2085
Website: www.nps.gov/morr

Saratoga National Historic Park

The Park:

Saratoga National Historic Park preserves 3200 acres of battlefield where American Revolutionaries, behind General Horation Gates, prevented British control of the Hudson River in the Fall of 1777. In two battles three weeks apart the British suffered 1,000 casualties and General John Burgoyne, awaiting reinforcements that never arrived, was forced to surrender 6,000 men. By thwarting the British initiative to split the Colonies in half, the Americans went a long way towards gaining their independence. Saratoga is one of the most famous and influential battlefields in the world and the National Park Service maintains the ground much as it looked in 1777.

The Walks:

The *Wilkinson-National Recreation Trail* is a 4.2-mile loop across the property, much of which was farmland during the Revolution. The trail is named for the lieutenant who drew maps of the Saratoga Battlefield in 1777. Save for a single dip into the Great Ravine, this is easy canine hiking across rolling grasslands with islands of airy deciduous woods. The trail uses part of the roads British troops took to and from the two battles. Interpretive stops include British and German redoubts (outlined in red and white posts). The .6-mile *Freeman Loop* visits the sit of some of the fiercest fighting on John Freeman's farm and the British Balcarres Redoubt. If you drive the auto tour road there are additional short explorations, including a one-mile loop trail that passes the gravesite of Brigadier General Simon Fraser, the spirited core of the British troops. There is no water along the park trails and on hot days a canine canteen will be in order.

The grass trails cut through the historic Saratoga fields are easy on the paws.

Directions to Saratoga National Historic Park (New York):

Exit the Northway (I-87) at Exit 14 (from the north) or Exit 12 (from the south) and follow signs for Route 29 East to Schuylerville. Turn south on Route 4 and you will find the main entrance to the Battlefield in eight miles.

Phone: (518) 664-9821
Website: www.nps.gov/sara

Behind the Breymann Redoubt, Station C, on the Wilkinson Trail, is the unique Boot Monument. The boot in question belonged to American battle hero Benedict Arnold (before he switched sides to the British). Arnold rode through a cross-fire in front of the defensive position to secure victory and recieved a second wound in his leg. The marble boot monument does not mention the eventual traitor's name.

Valley Forge National Historic Park

The Park:

The most famous name in the American Revolution comes to us from a small iron forge built along Valley Creek in the 1740s. After a disastrous campaign in the Fall of 1777 George Washington had left Philadelphia in the hands of the British and retreated to a defensible winter campsite out of harm's way but close enough to keep an eye on the enemy in their toasty Philadelphia homes. During the winter of 1777-78, as Valley Forge grew to be the third largest city in America, hundreds of soldiers died from sickness and disease. No battles were fought here but Valley Forge, the site where the American army was born, became a symbol for the young nation.

After the Revolution, the land reverted to fields and Valley Forge was forgotten. America's interest in Valley Forge was rekindled during a Centennial in 1878 and preservation efforts eventually began with the Potts House, now known as Washington's Headquarters.

The Walks:

There are four marked trails in Valley Forge National Historical Park, plus miles of unmarked canine hikes. The *Multi-Use Trail* loops the Colonial defensive lines and Grand Parade Ground and visits George Washington's headquarters. Panoramic field vistas of the historic grounds are found all along the paved trail's six-mile length. The *Valley Creek Trail* is a flat, linear 1.2 mile walk along Valley Creek, past the original Upper Forge site.

Near the Valley Creek, beginning at the Artificer's Shops on Route 23, is the eastern terminus of the 133-mile *Horse-Shoe Trail* that ends at the *Appalachian Trail* in Hershey, Pennsylvania. In the park, the trail climbs steeply through the woods up Mount Misery, the natural southern defensive boundary of the Valley Forge camp. The historic Horse-Shoe Trail, so-named as it was built for rider and walker, quickly incorporates back roads and private property and is not worth following outside the park.

The unmarked trails in Valley Forge's Walnut Hill Section don't appear on park maps and are missed by most visitors.

Across the Schuylkill River is the 3-mile linear *Schuylkill River Trail* connecting the Pawling's Parking Area and the Betzwood Picnic Area. This wide, flat dirt trail skirts the river for its entire route and provides ample access into the broad and shallow water of the Schuylkill River for canine aquatics.

A National Park Service map provides locations for the trails and does not indicate the variety of side trails available, especially in the Walnut Hill area that connect to the Schuylkill River Trail. Only the Horseshoe Trail is blazed.

Sidetrip: The Pinnacle (3 miles north of Hamburg, Pennsylvania on Reservoir Road off Route 61 and Blue Mountain Road)

The Appalachian Trail reaches its closest point to Philadelphia an hour's ride northwest of Valley Forge. Coincidentally, the trail here leads to the most famous view on the Appalachian Trail in Pennsylvania - the Pinnacle. Although your dog will get a healthy dose of Pennsylvania's famous boot-eating jagged stone on the trail, the surface is not too severe for your dog on the 1030-foot climb to this promontory of boulders. Views from the Pinnacle sweep across neighboring Blue Mountain and down to the farms of the Cumberland Valley. Much of the hike on this 8.7-mile loop is done on old fire roads; use the blue-blazed road along the rhododendron-studded Furnace Creek to close your loop.

Directions to Valley Forge National Historic Park (Pennsylvania):

From the Pennsylvania Turnpike (I 76/I 276) get off at Exit 326 (old exit 24) - "Valley Forge." Stay right and take the Valley Forge exit just beyond tollbooth. Turn right on N. Gulph Road for approximately 1.5 miles to the park entrance on Route 23 at the top of a hill.

Phone: (610) 783-1077
Website: www.nps.gov/vafo

Adjacent to the Valley Forge National Historic Park, although not affiliated with it, nestled in the wooded hills above the Schuylkill River, is a unique, little known living memorial dedicated to the men and women who have sacrificed and, often times, given their life in service to America. The Medal of Honor Grove, conceived in 1942 and located on the grounds of the Freedoms Foundation at Valley Forge, is a 52-acre woodland memorial commemorating all those awarded our nation's highest award for valor in action against an enemy force which can be bestowed upon an individual, the Medal of Honor.

Along an attractive serpentine path each of the 50 states, Puerto Rico and the District of Columbia are represented by a one-acre plot highlighted by a seven foot-seven inch high fiberglass replica of the Washington Monument obelisk. Attached to the obelisk is a state seal, dedication plaque and a list of Medal of Honor recipients accredited to that state. To date, 25 states have replaced the standard white fiberglass obelisk with a distinctive granite or marble obelisk in their areas, all using stone native to their state. The Medal of Honor Grove can be reached from Valley Forge National Historic Park by continuing west on Route 23.

Taking Your Dog
To The Big City...

Atlanta

CITY PARK TO TAKE YOUR DOG:
GRANT PARK

The park is named for Colonel Lemuel P. Grant, a civil engineer for the Georgia Railroad who helped bring the railroad to Atlanta and earned the name "Father of Atlanta." Grant Park is near the site of the battle for Atlanta in the Civil War and defensive breastworks, constructed under the supervision of L.P. Grant, can still be seen in the 144-acre recreation area. The land for Grant Park was at one time part of Colonel Grant's extensive land holdings in young Atlanta. Dogs are welcome on the scenic trails although they are not permitted around the two prime attractions of the park: Zoo Atlanta or the Atlanta Cyclorama, the 360-degree painting of the Battle of Atlanta.

bounded by Atlanta Avenue, Sidney Street, Cherokee Street and the Boulevard

NEARBY RECREATION AREA TO ENJOY
WITH YOUR DOG:
CHATTAHOOCHEE RIVER NATIONAL RECREATION AREA

Distance from Atlanta:
less than one hour north

The Park:
Most rivers meander and change course over time but the Chattahoochee River is locked in place by the 320-mile Brevard Fault that divides the Appalachian Mountains and the Piedmont Plateau. As such, it is one of the oldest rivers in America. President Jimmy Carter created the Chattahoochee River National Recreation Area in his home state to protect 48 miles of the slow-moving waters south of Lake Lanier. Today the 4,100-acre preserve - Chattahoochee means place of flowered rocks - is one of the most popular destinations in the national park system, attracting more than three million visitors each year.

The Walks:
Two visitor centers, Paces Mill at the southern access and Island Ford near the center, service the Chattahoochee River NRA's 14 land units and more than 50 miles of trails. Much of the canine hiking on these day-use trails is easy, through meadows and wooded gorges along the river. Expect a cool swim for your dog when she plunges in - the water temperature rarely warms to more than 50 degrees.

One of the premier hikes is the *Jones Bridge Trail*, a 2.6-mile jaunt that hugs the Chattahoochee for most of its length before ascending a small ridge.

Directions to Chattahoochee River National Recreation Area (Georgia):
Paces Mill is on US 41, north of I-75. Admission to the recreation area is free but there is a nominal parking fee.
Phone: 678-538-1200
Website: www.nps.gov/chat/index.htm

The stability of the Chattahoochee River has enabled much of the history of inhabitation on its banks to remain in place. Keep an eye out for archaeological remants of the Indian tribes that lived here for hundreds of years. Among the 19th century structures that can be seen are the ruins of antebellum textile mills.

Baltimore

CITY PARK TO TAKE YOUR DOG:
DRUID HILL PARK

The city of Baltimore paid $475,000 for the Rogers family estate in 1860 to create the jewel of its park system. Colonel Nicholas Rogers designed his property to resemble a pastoral English park and the city continued the theme with picnic pavilions, grassy promenades, statues and fountains. A massive Tuscan Doric entranceway was built of Nova Scotia sandstone in 1868 at the cost of $24,000 and Druid Lake was formed in 1871 behind the largest earthen dam in America to provide drinking water. Today the historic park covers 600 acres with winding roads and grassy lawns for canine visitors.

on Druid Park Lake Drive via Pennsylvania Avenue, Eutaw Place or Mount Royal Terrace

NEARBY RECREATION AREA TO ENJOY
WITH YOUR DOG:
GUNPOWDER FALLS STATE PARK

Distance from Baltimore:
15 minutes to the north

The Park:
Gunpowder Falls State Park embraces more than 17,000 acres of property in six distinct tracts from the Maryland-Pennsylvania border to the Chesapeake Bay. There are some 100 miles of trails in the park where the fall line of the Piedmont Plateau caused rivers (known as "falls" in Maryland) to tumble and generate abundant water power for colonial mills.

The Walks:
Head first for the Hereford section where the *Gunpowder South Trail* includes bites of trail more reminiscent of Appalachia than suburban Baltimore, especially from Falls Road to Prettyboy Dam. While most of the narrow dirt trails at Hereford are easy on the paw, this waterside scramper is rock-studded.

Unlike other sections of the park the water is not the star at Sweet Air where upland farm fields, lush riparian forests and fern-encrusted hillsides are backdrops for canine hikes on the trail system along the Little Gunpowder Falls.

The best swimming for your dog is at Belair Road where trails run for eight miles beside water chutes in the river. On Long Green Run a whale-shaped rock serves as a natural diving board for playful dogs.

Hiking at Jerusalem Mill is along both sides of the Little Gunpowder Falls; downstream is the Jericho Covered Bridge, one of only six remaining covered bridges in Maryland.

Crowds are normally not a problem on the strung-out park trails but near-complete solitude is achieved in the Pleasantville section of Gunpowder Falls where the the trail follows an abandoned railbed of the Maryland and Pennsylvania Railroad, known affectionately as the Ma & Pa. It took the peripatetic railroad 77.2 twisting miles to cover its 49-mile distance.

Directions to Gunpowder Falls State Park (Maryland):
Park headquarters are located in Kingsville on Jerusalem Mill Road off US 1. This is the only place to pick up trail maps for the park; trailhead parking lots feature only a mapboard.
Phone: (410) 557-7994
Website: www.dnr.state.md.uspubliclands/centralgunpowder.html

You are never far from a good canine swimming hole at Gunpowder Falls State Park.

Boston

CITY PARK TO TAKE YOUR DOG:
BOSTON COMMON

Boston Common is the oldest public park in the country, created in 1634 as a "cow pasture and training field" for common use. Cattle grazed here for 200 years, and could look up every now and then to see the occasional public hanging that took place in the Common. The park is about 50 acres in size and is the anchor for the Emerald Necklace, a system of connected parks that visit many of Boston's neighborhoods. Dogs are welcome on Boston Common and can even run off-leash from 5-7 a.m. and 5-7 p.m.

bounded by Beacon, Charles, Boylston, Tremont and Park streets

NEARBY RECREATION AREA TO ENJOY

WITH YOUR DOG:
BLUE HILLS RESERVATION

Distance from Boston:
15 minutes south

The Park:
The first settlers came to this area 10,000 years ago and called themselves "Massachusett," meaning "people of the hills." When European explorers set sight on the forested slopes while sailing along the coastline they named the region the Blue Hills. They logged the hillsides to build hoses and barns and cleared the lowlands for crops and livestock. In 1893, the Metropolitan Parks Commission made the Blue Hills one of their first purchases for land set aside for recreation. Today, Blue Hills Reservation maintains 7,000 acres of land in the shadow of Boston for outdoor activities.

The Walks:
Some 125 miles of trails visit a variety of terrains from hills and meadows to forests and wetlands, including a unique Atlantic white cedar bog. Some of the canine hiking can be quite challenging and many of the trails are strewn with rocks. Great Blue Hill, rising 635 feet above the Neponsett Valley, is the highest of the 22 hills in the Blue Hills chain. Keep your head up for sweeping views of the metropolitan area. Also keep an eye out for the diverse wildlife in the Blue Hills Reservation that is not often associated with Boston - timber rattlesnakes, coyote and otters. Most of the trails are marked but a trail map is a wise purchase for day hikes - one is on sale at park headquarters (695 Hillside Street) or the Blue Hills Trailside Museum (1904 Canton Avenue).

Directions to Blue Hills Reservation (Massachusetts):
The Blue Hills Reservation is headquartered in Milton, 8 miles south of Boston. Take Route 93 to Exit 3, Houghton's Pond. Turn right at the stop sign onto Hillside Street. Houghton's Pond is located approximately 1/4 miles on the right; Continue 1/4 miles to the reservation headquarters on the left.
Phone: 678-538-1200
Website: www.nps.gov/chat/index.htm

> 🚫 *A natural destination for any hiker in the Boston area is Henry David Thoreau's Walden Pond. But dog owners needn't bother - the trails tramped by Thoreau through the Walden Woods are closed to dogs.*

The National Register of Historic Places lists 16 structures from Blue Hills Reservation. The most celebrated sits at the summit of Great Blue Hill - the Blue Hill Weather Observatory. Still used as a weather station, the observatory is in Eliot Tower, a stone observation post built by the Civilian Conservation Corps during the 1930s.

Charleston

CITY PARK TO TAKE YOUR DOG:
THE BATTERY/WHITE POINT GARDENS

The gardens are named for the St. Bernard-sized piles of oyster shells that covered this area where the Cooper and Ashley rivers pour into Charleston Bay. The marsh was filled in and transformed into a public recreation space beginning in 1837. The stately oaks you walk the dog under were planted in 1863. From the park you can study the positions of the forts that protected the harbor, including Fort Sumter, where the Civil War began.

behind the elevated walkway at Murray Boulevard and Battery Street

NEARBY RECREATION AREA TO ENJOY

WITH YOUR DOG:

HUNTING ISLAND STATE PARK

Distance from Charleston:
90 minutes to the south

The Park:
The 5000-acre island was once a hunting preserve, hence its name. Before that it was a stopover for sailors and pirates. Much of the park was developed as a Depression-era project and its 1120-foot fishing pier is one of the longest on the East Coast. The lighthouse in the park, built in 1859 and destroyed in the Civil War before being rebuilt with cast iron plates designed to be dismantled and moved, is the only public light in South Carolina. You can climb the 167 steps - without your dog - to the top for a commanding view of the shoreline.

The Walks:
Hunting Island State Park is one of the best places you can bring your dog. Dogs are allowed on the park trails and the ocean beach - three miles of natural sand.

The formal trails include a one-mile nature trail and a 4-mile long hiking trail. Both are easy going for you and the dog. A marsh boardwalk has been constructed over a salt water marsh overlooking Johnson Creek.

You will find an abundance of palmetto forests - the South Carolina state tree - on the island. If you remember the jungle scenes from *Forrest Gump* you will get a feel for the tropical trails on Hunting Island. The Vietnam scenes from the hit movie were filmed here.

Directions to Hunting Island State Park (South Carolina):
The park is 16 miles east of Beaufort. From Charleston, take Highway 17 (Savannah Hwy) South to Gardens Corner, then take a left on Hwy 21 to park.
Phone: (843) 838-2011
Website: www.huntingisland.com

Chicago

CITY PARK TO TAKE YOUR DOG:
GRANT PARK

Grant Park is the centerpiece of Chicago's downtown lakeshore district. Much of the park is built atop debris pushed into Lake Michigan after the Great Chicago Fire of 1871. Mail order merchandise pioneer Aaron Montgomery Ward personally defeated 46 building projects in court over 20 years to keep this space forever open. Reminiscent of French parks with lawns and paths laid out in geometric designs, your dog walk will lead over many bridges connecting areas of the park, including the *Lakefront Trail.*

on the lakefront between Randolph Street and Roosevelt Road, backed by Columbus Drive on the west

NEARBY RECREATION AREA TO ENJOY
WITH YOUR DOG:
NED BROWN PRESERVE

Distance from Chicago:
15 minutes to the northwest

The Park:
The Forest Preserve District of Cook County maintains over 67,000 acres of open space around Chicago, including some 200 miles of trails through the prairieland. The Ned Brown Preserve, created in 1965 as the third nature preserve in Illinois, protects 3,700 of those acres, including Busse Lake, the largest lake in the Forest Preserve District. This is one of the busiest parks anywhere with an estimated 2.5 million visits per year - not including dogs.

The Walks:
The main trail through the park is an 11.2-mile multi-use path that snakes through the property. All the canine hiking in the preserve is easy-going but unless you come early or late, you will dodging bikes and rollerblades and all sorts of wheeled craft.

Tucked within the preserve is the Busse Woods, a designated National Landmark with thick stands of oaks, sugar maples and basswood. Wildflowers grow in marshes that are deep glacial depressions retaining water most of the year. A two-mile nature trail of packed earth and gravel leads into this upland forest.

Directions to the Ned Brown Preserve (Illinois):
The preserve is in Rolling Meadows. From Chicago take I-90 West to Arlington Heights Road south to Higgins Road. Go west .6 mile to the park roads.
Phone: (847) 437-8330
Website: www.fpdcc.com/tier3.php?content_id=36&file=rec_36b

The American elk was once the most widely distributed member of the deer family but hunting and human settlement pushed herds to remote patches of the Rocky Mountains and the upper Northwest. The elk, the second largest of all deer, was so named by explorers for its resemblance to European elk and moose. In the preserve, at the intersection of Arlington Heights and Higgins Road, you can see an elk herd in a 14-acre enclosure.

Cincinnati

CITY PARK TO TAKE YOUR DOG:
EDEN PARK

Eden Park was created in 1859 as a reservoir for city drinking water. Today it is a passive park of quiet elegance - there are no formal trails but patches of green and groves of trees to visit with your dog. The Presidential Grove features trees planted in honor of each American president. The park's 186 acres spread across hillsides and picnic spots on Mount Adams look down on the Ohio River.

off Gilbert Avenue between Elsinore and Morris

Eden Park is a good spot to relax and watch the Ohio River flow by.

NEARBY RECREATION AREA TO ENJOY
WITH YOUR DOG:
MOUNT AIRY FOREST

Distance from Cincinnati:
10 minutes to the west

🚫 *The prettiest parts of Mount Airy Forest are in the landscaped Arboretum with its 1,600 species of trees and shrubs. Canine hikers must stay in the wilder regions of the park - no dogs allowed in the Arboretum.*

The Park:
Mount Airy Forest is the site of the first municipal reforestation project in the United States. The stripping of trees on Colerain Hill for small farms and grazing cattle in the 19th century had left the soil unproductive and vulnerable to erosion. The Cincinnati Park Board began its project in 1911 by purchasing 168 acres of land for planting new hardwoods and evergreens. Nearly a century later Mount Airy Forest is a park of almost 1500 acres, most of which remain in a natural state.

The Walks:
The hiking trail system in Mount Airy Forest, designated a National Recreational Trail, features 14 miles of walking but visiting canine hikers would do best to concentrate on *Trail E*. The trail begins in McFarlan Woods and touches on nearly every segment of the park in its ten-mile odyssey. The path can be hiked in smaller bites that are possible throughout the route. The trail is well-marked with white blazes but the trailhead - like others at Mount Airy - can be hard to spot.

The trail rolls up and down ravines but is never grueling. You'll cross plenty of trickling streams and washes cut into the hillsides for your dog to splash in, souvenirs from the early days of abuse. Look for large sinkholes that also pepper the hillsides in places. Punctuating the walks in the Mount Airy Forest are showy seasonal wildflower displays along the trails.

After your hike you can wind down with your dog in the Mt. Airy Dog Park in the Highpoint Picninc Area on Westwood Northern Boulevard between Montana Avenue and North end Road. There are two acres of fenced in ground to play here.

Directions to the Mount Airy Forest (Ohio):
Take Exit 18 off I-75 and continue onto Colerain Avenue. The park entrance is on the left hand side at 5083 Colerain Avenue.
Phone: (513) 352-4094
Website: www.cincinnati-oh.gov/cityparks/pages/-4570-/

Cleveland

CITY PARK TO TAKE YOUR DOG:
EDGEWATER PARK

Cleveland grew up on an unprotected bluff of sand and clay on top of Lake Erie. Beginning in 1865 land began to be set aside on the lakefront for parks. In 1977 the four Cleveland lakefront parks were leased to the state of Ohio. Edgewater Park is a melding of a lower and upper sections connected by a multi-use path. You'll find most paths in the park paved and many shady, with fine views of the frisky waves in Lake Erie and the Cleveland skyline.

on Lakeshore Boulevard

NEARBY RECREATION AREA TO ENJOY
WITH YOUR DOG:
CUYAHOGA VALLEY NATIONAL PARK

Distance from Cleveland:
15 minutes to the south

The Park:
To the first people who came here 12,000 years ago the Cuyahoga was the "crooked river." Its steep valley walls inhibited settlement as easterners poked into the region in the late 1700s. But a navigable water link between Lake Erie and the Ohio River was a priority in the early American Canal Age and in 1832 the Ohio & Erie Canal became a reality. Ohio boomed and settlers poured into the area. The canal was put out of business by the Great Flood of 1913 and the Cuyahoga Valley was left to recreational purposes. Once a national recreation area, the 33,000 acres of protected land along the banks of the Cuyahoga River became America's first national park in this century in 2000.

The Walks:
As befits its history as a recreation destination, Cuyahoga is a national park that permits dogs on its trails. The main trail through the park is the nearly 20 miles of the *Towpath Trail* along the route of the historic canal. Ten trailheads make it easy to hike the crushed limestone path in biscuit-size chunks. The trail is a mix of meadows and forests and the remnants of locks and villages.

Another long distance trail through the park is the *Buckeye Trail* that circles the entire state of Ohio for over 1200 miles. About 33 miles of the blue-blazed pathway wander the ravines and ridges of the valley.

Some of the best canine day hiking in the park is in the north end of the Cuyahoga Valley, in the Bradford Reservation. A five-mile all-purpose trail traverses the Tinkers Creek Gorge area, exploring Ohio's most spectacular canyon. The gorge is a National Natural Landmark, noted for its virgin hemlock forests. Short detours off the main trail include an easy walk to Bridal Veil Falls and the *Hemlock Creek Loop Trail*.

Directions to Cuyahoga Valley National Park (Ohio):
To get to Canal Visitor Center from Cleveland, exit I-77 at Rockside Road. Go 1 mile east to Canal Road; turn right. The visitor center is approximately 1.5 miles on the right.
Phone: (216) 524-1497
Website: www.nps.gov/cuva/

Columbus

CITY PARK TO TAKE YOUR DOG:
GOODALE PARK

When in downtown Columbus dog owners will want to head for Goodale Park for a romp. The 35-acre greenspace, now surrounded by high-rise sentinels, was pastoral open ground when Dr. Lincoln Goodale donated the land in 1850. Goodale was the first person to practice medicine in Columbus and the park was the town's first. You will find plenty of canine company, including organized doggie play groups, under the shade trees and near the artificial lake.

at Front Street and Goodale Boulevard

NEARBY RECREATION AREA TO ENJOY
WITH YOUR DOG:
HOCKING HILLS STATE PARK

Distance from Columbus:
one hour to the southeast

The Park:
The tribes of the Wyandot, Delaware and Shawnee knew the valley as "Hockhocking" for its bottle shape, created when glacial ice plugged the Hocking River. The sandstone is of varying hardness that has cracked and eroded into fascinating rock formations and caves. The state of Ohio began preserving this unique natural area in 1924 with a purchase of 146 acres.

The Walks:
Hocking Hills State Park is a superb destination for any dog, but is especially delightful for the canine hiker who is a few hikes beyond those days of the 10-mile treks. There are six distinct areas in the park - five for canine hiking: no dogs are permitted in the Conkles Hollow state nature preserve in the center of Hocking Hills.

The star of Hocking Hills is Old Man's Cave tucked into a heavily wooded, twisting ravine. The Old Man was Richard Rowe who moved to the area some time around 1796 to establish a trading post. Upon arriving in Hocking Hills he stayed and lived out his life here, traveling with his two dogs in search of game. Rowe is buried beneath the ledge of the main recess cave. An easy, one-mile trail works its way into and around the primeval gorge; wooden steps and bridges smooth the way. Your dog will enjoy a dip in Old Man's Creek, especially in the pool beneath the Upper Falls.

Additional attractions near Old Man's Cave are Cedar Falls and Ash Cave. Both can be accessed by car and a short walk from the parking lots. For heartier visitors, a 6-mile trail connects all three natural attractions. There is more great dog-paddling under Cedar Falls and nearby Rose Lake.

In the north sections of Hocking Hills the trails explore impressive cliff formations on trails less than one mile long. The trails are wide and graded with easy footing for your dog as you make your way from the rim to the floor at the Rock House and Cantwell Cliffs. The Rock House is a perpendicular cliff that features hollowed-out rooms at the bottom. At Cantwell Cliffs your dog will enjoy navigating through separated pillars of sandstone that have left narrow openings with colorful names like Fat Woman's Squeeze.

Directions to Hocking Hills State Park (Ohio):
Ohio SR 374 connects all six areas of Hocking Hills State Park, 10 miles west of Logan and US 33.
Phone: (740) 385-6841
Website: www.hockinghillspark.com

The gorges at Hocking Hills are draped in stately eastern hemlocks.

Dallas

CITY PARK TO TAKE YOUR DOG:
WHITE ROCK LAKE PARK

Located about five miles northeast of downtown, construction on White Rock Lake began in 1910 to provide water for a thirsty Dallas. The municipal park surrounding the lake is mostly the work of the Civilian Conservation Corps during the Depression. A complete trip around White Rock Lake on the multi-use trail will cover about 10 miles but dog owners on a time budget will want to head for the dog park at Mockingbird Point. There are two fenced-in playgrounds for big and small dogs and plenty of trees, open space and a two-tiered drinking fountain. Baseball pitching legend Nolan Ryan threw out the first dog toy when the park opened.

on Garland Road (Route 78)

NEARBY RECREATION AREA TO ENJOY
WITH YOUR DOG:
FORT RICHARDSON STATE HISTORICAL PARK

Distance from Dallas:
an hour to the northwest

The Park:
Fort Richardson, remembering General Israel B. Richardson who died at Antietam during the Civil War, was established in 1867 to protect settlers on the Texas range. During the Indian Wars of 1870-1874 it was the most heavily manned garrison in the United States but was gone by 1878. The state bought the property in 1968 and has restored seven original frontier Fort Richardson buildings.

The Walks:
The fort was built on spring-fed Lost Creek and beyond the historic area trails wind through peaceful prairie stands of pecan and oak. The *Prickly Pear Trail* explores the open plains for 1.7 miles where a deer, armadillo or roadrunner can be spotted.

Swimming dogs can take advantage of Quarry Lake and Lost Creek when flowing. A nature trail follows Lost Creek for a short half-mile stroll; the *Rumbling Spring Path* traces the stream on the opposite bank.

A trailhead for the 10-mile Lost Creek Reservoir State Trailway is located in the Fort Richardson State Park campground, where dogs are allowed. This hike-bike-equestrian trail travels to Lake Jacksboro and Lost Creek Reservoir.

Directions to Fort Richardson State Historical Site (Texas):
The park is 1/2 mile south of Jacksboro on US Highway 281.
Phone: 800-792-1112
Website: www.tpwd.state.tx.us/park/fortrich/

Dogs are not allowed inside the buildings at Fort Richardson but you can walk the property, including the expansive Parade Ground. Dominating the fort was the two-story rock hospital built with massive 18-inch thick sandstone walls. At Fort Richardson you were safer going outside the gates on an Indian campaign than walking through the hospital doors. In 11 years of operation 88 men died of disease and only 13 from Indian war wounds.

Denver

CITY PARK TO TAKE YOUR DOG:
CITY PARK

Until 1890 Colorado municipalities labored under a 40-acre limit for town parks. When new laws were passed 320 acres were purchased for City Park, today just two miles from downtown. What was once buffalo grass and sagebrush was transformed into open grassy fields and shade trees. It remains Denver's largest park and a good choice to walk the dog among fountains, monuments and ponds.

between 17th and 23rd avenues and York Street and Colorado Boulevard

NEARBY RECREATION AREA TO ENJOY
WITH YOUR DOG:
CHERRY CREEK STATE PARK

Distance from Denver:
15 minutes to the southeast

The Park:
Many people feared that Castlewood Dam was shoddily built from its beginnings in 1890 to provide irrigation for the agricultural development of Douglas County. And in August of 1933, the dam indeed collapsed sending a wall of water 1/2 mile wide and 15 feet high through Denver. This disaster resulted in the development of a comprehensive flood control program for Cherry Creek that led to the construction of the Cherry Creek Dam and reservoir in 1950. The 3,900-acre state park grew up around the project. Dogs are not allowed on the reservoir's swimming beach.

The Walks:
Since you won't be coming to this park for solitude - 1.5 million visits per year and controlled access at times - canine hikers may want to head for the dog park first. In the southern area of the park is a 60-acre off-leash playground of open grassland for dogs. A small creek provides a watery diversion.

Outside the dog park, as befits an urban park most of the 12 miles of rolling trails are paved. The *Cherry Creek Trail* slices through the park from north to south. Hardy canine hikers can explore some of the trail systems that head out of the park, including the 70-mile *Highline Canal Trail*. There is very little hiking in Cherry Creek State Park that will set your dog to panting.

Directions to Cherry Creek State Park (Colorado):
The park is in Aurora, one mile south of I-225 on Parker Road, adjacent to south Denver.
Phone: (303) 699-3860
Website: www.parks.state.co.us/default.asp?parkID=80&action=park

Detroit

CITY PARK TO TAKE YOUR DOG:
BELLE ISLE PARK

Landscape designer Frederick Law Olmsted knitted a series of individual islands together with a series of lovely bridges to create Belle Isle, the queen of Detroit city parks, in the middle of the Detroit River. Dogs can trot the paths and admire the skylines of downtown Detroit and Windsor, Ontario on the opposite shore. Great freighters and recreational sailboats ply the waters around Belle Isle. The park is home to a zoo, conservatory, and aquarium.

reached via Douglas MacArthur Bridge from Jefferson Avenue

NEARBY RECREATION AREA TO ENJOY

WITH YOUR DOG:
WATERLOO STATE RECREATION AREA

Distance from Detroit:
60 to 90 minutes west

The Park:
The Waterloo Recreation Area began in the 1930s when the federal government relocated farmers who had struggled for years to scratch a living from the sandy, gravelly soil. The farms were bought up and 12,000 acres of land designated as the Waterloo Recreation and Demonstration Area by the National Park Service. In 1943, the project was handed over to the state of Michigan and with more than 20,000 acres now set aside, Waterloo State Recreation Area is the largest park in Michigan's Lower Peninsula. The focal point of the park are the dozen or so excellent fishing lakes that lure bass fishermen to Waterloo.

The Walks:
Of the almost 50 miles of footpaths twisting through the hills in Waterloo Recreation Area, half belong to the *Waterloo Trail* as it circumnavigates Mill Lake. The trail rolls through climax hardwood forests of oak and hickory and checks in on old farm fields. For canine hikers looking for a smaller commitment there are three leg stretchers of about a mile in Hickory Hills, Dry Marsh and Woodland.

At the Gerald E. Eddy Discovery Center are 12 miles of interpretive nature trails that visit a variety of habitats from bogs to logs. In addition to the hiking trails at Waterloo, there are another 15 miles of bridle trails that can muddy up navigation at times.

Directions to Waterloo Recreation Area (Michigan):
Take Exit 147 off of I-94 and head north. There are three campgrounds in the park; the facility at Big Portage Lake is open all year.

Phone: (734) 475-8307

Website: www.ring.com/travel/dnr/sp_water.htm

The trails top out on several scenic overlooks. One, called Murder Mountain, according to legend, remembers the killing of early settlers by local Indians.

Houston

CITY PARK TO TAKE YOUR DOG:
SAM HOUSTON PARK

It was 1900 when Houston got its first park, the Kellem-Noble land backing against the Buffalo Bayou on the edge of town. Sam Houston Park was soon landscaped into a Victorian delight with an old mill, a stream, a rustic bridge, and walking paths. Since 1954 the park has been the home of The Heritage Society that preserves eight historic structures here in the menacing shadow of surrounding skyscrapers. The 19-acre park is a welcome spot to lounge with your dog in downtown Houston.

Bagby and Lamar streets

NEARBY RECREATION AREA TO ENJOY
WITH YOUR DOG:
BRAZOS BEND STATE PARK

Distance from Houston:
35 minutes to the southwest

The Park:
This area at a wide bend in the Brazos Biver is the site of Texas founder Stephen F. Austin's first colonial land grant from Mexico in 1822. Five years later the land was deeded to Abner Harris and William Barrett who used the advantageous river location to ship cotton. In the years before the state of Texas purchased the land cattle grazed here, pecans were harvested and private hunting parties prowled the woods and swamps. Brazos Bend State Park - one of the largest in Texas with 4,987 acres - opened in 1984.

The Walks:
This is easy, relaxing canine hiking. There is scarcely any elevation change over 20 miles of single-track multi-use trails and old fire roads. The footpaths are often wide and almost universally well-maintained.

An easy leg-stretcher at Brazos Bend is the *Creekfield Lake Nature Trail*, a paved half-mile trot through the wetlands. One of the most popular canine hikes in the park is the 4.5-mile *White Oak Trail* through a thick forest of willows, sycamores, cottonwood and oaks decked out in Spanish moss. The confluence of Big Creek and the Brazos River calls up the deepest of Louisiana bayous.

For a change of pace, take the dog onto the *Prairie Trail* that penetrates swamplands and upland coastal grass prairies. This is prime habitat for avian-loving canine hikers.

Directions to Brazos Bend State Park (Texas):
The park may be reached by traveling approximately 20 miles southeast of Richmond on FM 762, or by traveling south from Houston on State Highway 288 to Rosharon, then west on FM 1462.

Phone: 979/553-5101
Website: www.tpwd.state.tx.us/park/brazos/

One of the prime attractions of Brazos Bend State Park is its alligators. The park features six lakes and numerous water-filled depressions that can house an alligator. There are an estimated 250 gators over 6 feet long in the park's waters. Some of the best places to spot America's largest reptiles are on the trails along the biggest lakes - Elm Lake and 40-Acre Lake. Spring and fall are when they are most active. Although no one has ever been killed by an American alligator in Texas and a gator can go a whole year without eating, you will still want to keep your dog close in Brazos Bend State Park.

Kansas City

CITY PARK TO TAKE YOUR DOG:
LOOSE PARK

If Loose Park were a dog, it might be a poodle. The centerpiece of the 80-acre park donated by Ella Loose in 1929 is an elegant rose garden encircled by classical walkways. The manicured grounds are a far cry from October 22, 1864 when the Battle of Westport - "the Gettysburg of the West" - was fought near here. That day the greatest clash of Civil War troops west of the Mississippi River ended the Confederacy hopes in the West. Today, markers describe the battle. You can exercise your dog on a rolling path around Loose Park and in the large, grassy center of the greenspace.

Wornall Road and 51st Street

NEARBY RECREATION AREA TO ENJOY
WITH YOUR DOG:
WESTON BEND STATE PARK

Distance from Kansas City:
20 minutes to the northwest

The Park:
When Lewis and Clark reached the Weston area on July 2, 1804, the rich soils on the banks of the Missouri River had already been under cultivation by Indian tribes for hundreds of years. Fires and floods retarded the development of Weston following the Civil War and Lewis and Clark might recognize the same scenic views from park bluffs today as the same ones they saw 200 years ago.

The Walks:
The sporty canine hikes in the 1,133-acre park run up and down hills that formed on the edges of retreating glaciers. There is a cornucopia of interesting trails to choose from.

The park's multi-purpose trail is a 3-mile asphalt loop through wooded corridors. Energetic hikers will want to jump onto the dirt paths of the *Harpst Trail* when it intersects the paved trail. This one-mile loop traipses along the Missouri River bluffs until reaching the remains of the famous Harpst Orchards that once produced peaches for English royalty.

The *Missouri River Trail* takes your dog directly to the edge of the Missouri River and the *Bear Creek Trail* explores the former channel of the Missouri before a major shift in the river in 1858. Both trails are less than one mile.

Two more short trails worth checking out are the *Barn Trail* and *McCormick Trail*, both mown areas near the park office. The McCormick Trail leads to a warehouse of a distillery in continuous operation since 1858.

Directions to Weston Bend State Park (Missouri):
The park is on the west side of Highway 45 heading out of Kansas City.

Phone: (816) 640-5443
Website: www.mostateparks.com/westonbend.htm

The piers in the Missouri River were so busy shipping hemp that by 1858 Weston was considered the largest hemp port in the world. It has been tobacco, however, that has driven the area economy from then to now. The park contains five tobacco barns and an interpretive display on the history of tobacco production in the community.

Las Vegas

CITY PARK TO TAKE YOUR DOG:
SUNSET PARK

Sunset Park is a traditional urban recreational park with ballfields and playgrounds. While lacking an extensive trail system, there is fresh green grass and shade trees aplenty that will be a welcome sight for any dog visiting Las Vegas. A paved trail traces the edge of a prominent artificial pond and beyond that is a patch of undeveloped mesquite-dunes land similar to what all Las Vegas looked like before the coming of neon.

at East Sunset Road and S. Eastern Avenue

NEARBY RECREATION AREA TO ENJOY
WITH YOUR DOG:
VALLEY OF FIRE STATE PARK

Distance from Las Vegas:
45 minutes to the northeast

The Park:
The stunning red sandstone rock formations that give the Valley of Fire its name are the result of great shifting sand dunes. Two thousand years ago the Basket Maker people traveled here and left rock art reminders of their visits that can be seen today. In 1935 the Valley of Fire, now 34,000 acres, was dedicated as Nevada's first state park.

The Walks:
Dogs are welcome on all nine short interpretive trails, all easily accessed from the main park roadways. In many places the hiking is over fine red sand trails. The feature trail here is the *White Domes Loop Trail* in the far northern section of the park. The path circles through rock formations and a slot canyon on its one-mile odyssey. Look for the stone ruins of a movie set from *The Professionals* when Lee Marvin led a crew of four hard-edged adventurers on a rescue mission for a kidnapped woman. Many movies have used the Valley of Fire as a backdrop but this is the only set in the park as filmmakers are no longer allowed to abandon their sets.

The quick hikes in the Valley of Fire are especially attractive for dogs visiting in the summer when the sun's rays bouncing off the red rocks make the landscape appear on fire - and feel like it. Canine hikers visiting Las Vegas in more hospitable weather can also enjoy red rocks just west of town, heading out West Charleston Boulevard to Red Rock Canyon National Conservation Area.

A 13-mile scenic drive winds through the iron-tinged sandstone mountains and climbs about 1000 feet. Parking areas are liberally sprinkled along the route that provide access to 19 hiking trails. Many of the routes explore side canyons with only moderate elevation gains of a few hundred feet.

The most difficult of the Red Rock Canyon trails is the climb along the *Turtlehead Peak Trail*. This five-mile round trip is never too punishing as it makes its way to the 6,323-foot summit. Your purchase is sweeping views of the Calico Hills and the city of Las Vegas.

Directions to Valley of Fire State Park (Nevada):
Take I-15 north out of Las Vegas for 55 miles to the Valley of Fire Road. Head east to the park's West Entrance Station.
Phone: (702) 397-2088
Website: www.parks.nv.gov/vf.htm

Rock formations provide welcome shade for a dog hiking in the Valley of Fire.

Los Angeles

CITY PARK TO TAKE YOUR DOG:
GRIFFITH PARK

The seeds of one of the world's great city parks were sown with the arrival of Colonel Griffith Jenkins Griffith from Wales in 1865 to make a fortune in California gold mines. In 1882 Griffith came to Los Angeles and purchased 4,071 acres of an original Spanish land grant, Rancho Los Felix. In 1896 he gave more than 3,000 acres of California oaks, wild sage and manzanita to the city as a Christmas present - "a place of relaxation and rest for the masses." Today Griffith Park is the largest urban wilderness area in America, including 53 miles of trails, fire roads and bridle paths. Many of the trails feature views of the famous Hollywood sign - the 6-mile *Mt. Hollywood Trail* climbs to the top. Dog-friendly touches include a dog park adjacent to Ferraro Soccer Field and rides for dogs on the Los Angeles Live Steamers miniature train.

west of I-5 between Los Feliz Boulevard and Ventura Freeway

NEARBY RECREATION AREA TO ENJOY
WITH YOUR DOG:
SANTA MONICA MOUNTAINS NATIONAL RECREATION AREA

Distance from Los Angeles:
10 minutes west

The Park:
Santa Monica Mountain NRA is an amalgamation of 150,000 private, city, county, state and federal acres knitted into a single entity in 1978. The park stretches 46 miles from east to west, co-existing next to the most densely populated urban area in the United States - one in every 17 Americans live within an hour's drive of the Santa Monica Mountains. The Mediterranean climate in the park - hot, dry summers mixing with mild, wet winters in a coastal location - is the rarest in the world. Only four other areas in the world enjoy the same climate, the fewest acres of any ecosystem.

The Walks:
Santa Monica Mountains NRA is a paradise for canine hikers but not an unfettered one. Dogs are not allowed on state park trails so you will need to limit your explorations to national and city park lands.

An easy introduction to the park near the Visitor Center is at Rancho Sierra Vista (Satwiwa) where a loop trail slips 1.5 miles through grasslands and chaparral-covered hillsides. The loop begins and ends at the Satwiwa Native American Indian Culture Center.

Athletic dogs will want to test the many canyon trails at Zuma Canyon, Solstice Canyon, Franklin Canyon and more. Expect extended ocean views and scenic looks where the land has been folded into peaks and canyons by shifts along the San Andreas Fault.

Some of the sportiest canine hiking in the Santa Monica Mountains is at Circle K Ranch where trails ascend to Sandstone Peak, the highest point in the park at 3,111 feet. One, the *Backbone Trail*, will one day stretch 65 miles across the entire national recreation area. Dog owners may want to skip the downhill hiking on the *Grotto Trail*. After going two miles, dogs are not allowed on the final 1/8 mile to The Grotto.

Directions to Santa Monica Mountains National Recreation Area (California):
The park is confined by US 101 (the Ventura Highway) to the north and US 1 (the Pacific Coast Highway) to the south. The Visitor Center is off US 101 in Thousand Oaks.
Phone: (805) 370-2301
Website: www.nps.gov/samo/

🚫 *The park features more than 50 miles of shoreline on the Pacific Ocean but the prime swimming beaches are off-limits for dogs. Several rockier beaches in the western end - County Line Beach, Thornhill Broome and the beach at Leo Carillo State Park - are open to dog paddling.*

Miami

CITY PARK TO TAKE YOUR DOG:
BARK PARK IN AMELIA EARHART PARK

Until recently dogs were not allowed in any of Miami's parks but here and there a park is allowing dogs in now. There are quite a few dog parks in Miami, both official and unofficial.

One is a five-acre Bark Park with paved walkways, benches, shade trees, waste dispenser stations, and specially designed drinking and spray fountains for dogs and their owners at Amelia Earhart Park.

401 East 65th Street in Hialeah

NEARBY RECREATION AREA TO ENJOY
WITH YOUR DOG:
OLETA RIVER STATE PARK

Distance from Miami:
15 minutes to the north

The Park:
Historically the river, originally called Big Snake Creek, linked the Everglades with Biscayne Bay and was an important transportation route. Pineapples and vegetables were grown along its banks. The river no longer flows north to the Everglades but many of its primoridal features can still be seen in the 1,043-acre park, the largest urban park in Florida.

The Walks:
There are more than ten miles of trails in Oleta River State Park, most of which are heavily used by mountain bikers. Many of the trails run along the Biscayne Bay. Some trails are posted as "bike only" but with the lack of general canine hiking in the Miami area, this is still a good place to bring your dog.

Directions to Oleta River State Park (Florida):
The park is is located at 3400 N.E. 163rd Street, off I-95.
Phone: 305-919-1846
Website: www.floridastateparks.org/oletariver/default.asp

"And sometimes when you'd get up in the middle of the night you'd hear the reassuring thump, thump of her tail on the floor, letting you know that she was there and thinking of you."
- William Cole

Milwaukee

CITY PARK TO TAKE YOUR DOG:
GRANVILLE OFF-LEASH DOG PARK

With 640 landscaped acres, Milwaukee's Whit-nall Park is one of the largest municipal parks in America. Dogs, however, are not welcome there. Dogs can also not visit the Lake Michigan Beach in Milwaukee. The fine for having your dog in a prohibited area is $149.50, as is the fine for not having your dog leashed or not cleaning up after your dog in Milwaukee County. If you find yourself in Milwaukee with your dog, head for the Granville Dog Park, the only Milwaukee park where dogs may exercise without a leash.

located just north of Good Hope Road and west of Highway 45 along the east bank of the Menomonee River

NEARBY RECREATION AREA TO ENJOY

WITH YOUR DOG:
KETTLE MORAINE STATE FOREST

Distance from Milwaukee:
60 to 90 minutes west

The Park:
The Ice Age was so instrumental in shaping the landscape of Wisconsin that the most recent advance of the ice flows has been named the "Wisconsin Glaciation." For almost 100,000 years - until a mere 10,000 years ago - the ice spread across the state, melted, reformed and retreated again. Six major fingers of ice thrust into the land that makes Wisconsin today, scraping the land and carting boulders great distances. Hills and ridges left behind are called moraines. Where blocks of ice became detached from the main glacier, depressions formed from the melting of buried ice. These are called kettles. The Kettle Moraine west of Milwaukee is really a series of moraines formed between two great flows of ice. Some are mere pimples in the landscape; others rise to more than 300 feet above the surrounding land.

In 1937 the Wisconsin Legislature established the Kettle Moraine State Forest to protect what the glaciers created. In 1958 local citizens began agitating for an Ice Age national park and volunteers built the first trail segments of what has become the *Ice Age National Scenic Trail*. Today some 300 miles of trail have been certified along the leading edge of the great glaciers.

The Walks:
The Southern Unit of the Kettle Moraine State Forest is renowned for its trail system that permeate its 21,000 acres of land. In addition to marked hiking trails, the forest hosts more than 50 miles of horse trails, 20 miles of mountain bike trails, 30 miles of cross-country ski trails and 46 miles of snowmobile trails. A 30+-mile leg of the *Ice Age Hiking Trail* rambles through the glaciated landscape. The most apparent relics of the glaciers are the conical hills of water-worn sand called kames, piled here by streams that churned through cracks in the main ice flows. Dogs will also enjoy the many lakes left behind by the glaciers; two of the most popular are Ottawa and Whitewater lakes.

Directions to Kettle Moraine State Forest (Wisconsin):
Take Exit 282 south from I-94. Continue 14 miles to Eagle in the heart of the state forest.
Phone: (262) 626-2116
Website: www.dnr.state.wi.us/org/land/parks/specific/kmn/

Northwest of the town of Eagle is Paradise Springs, once a resort and retreat in the early 1930s. The springs poke out from the underground water table in a bowl-shaped depression that spew water at the rate of 500 gallons per minute. The water is a constant 47 degrees year round, ideal for the Brook Trout that are stocked here, the only trout native to the Kettle Moraine. The spring house near the trout pond built of native fieldstone is one of the grandest ever built in Wisconsin and was once used as a spa.

Minneapolis

CITY PARK TO TAKE YOUR DOG:
LORING PARK

Loring Park is named for Charles Loring, the "Father of the Minneapolis Park System." Loring hired Frederick Law Olmsted to bring a world-class park system to rapidly growing Minneapolis in 1883 and the first 30 acres of this park were purchased. A series of bike and walking paths wind around a lake and gardens; across the Whitney Bridge is the Minneapolis Sculpture Garden.

1382 Willow Street

NEARBY RECREATION AREA TO ENJOY
WITH YOUR DOG:
FORT SNELLING STATE PARK

Distance from Minneapolis:
10 minutes to the southeast

The Park:
The Dakota Indians considered this spot at the confluence of the Minnesota and Mississippi rivers the center of the world; European visitors recognized its strategic importance for trade and defense. On September 21, 1805 Zebulon Pike picked up 100,000 acres for $200 of trinkets, a keg of whiskey and the promise of a trading post. Colonel Josiah Snelling shaped the post into a military fort when he arrived in 1820 and so it operated as such through World War II. Fort Snelling was spared destruction when it was named as the first National Historic Landmark in Minnesota in 1960 and the park - now the state's most visited - opened two years later to conserve open space in the heart of the Twin Cities.

The Walks:
Fort Snelling State Park is packed with canine hiking opportunities - 18 miles of foot trails, 18 miles of cross-country trails and 5 miles of multi-use trails. It is a day-use park only - no camping - so you'll need to return to do it all.

This is easy, shady hiking in mature woodlands. A good place to start is the 3.2-mile hiking-only trail that circles Pike Island, site of the treaties that allowed establishment of the first European settlement in Minnesota.

The 5.8-mile gravel *Medota Trail* offers seclusion along the Minnesota River and connects to the Minnesota Valley National Wildlife Refuge. The refuge protects more than 10,000 acres of often marshy lands with 34 more miles of trails. Dogs are permitted throughout the refuge.

Directions to Fort Snelling State Park (Minnesota):
From I-94 take Highway 55 south to Highway 5 and take the Post Road exit and follow the signs.
Phone: (612) 725-2389
Website: www.dnr.state.mn.us/state_parks/fort_snelling/index.html

"If there are no dogs in Heaven, then when I die I want to go where they went."
- anonymous

Montreal

CITY PARK TO TAKE YOUR DOG:
MONT-ROYAL PARK

Another offering by the father of landscape architecture, Frederick Law Olmsted, the 1876 park is his only creation outside of the United States. It features trademark twisting paths that lead gently to the top of 765-foot Mont-Royal. The mountain, from which the city takes it name, was climbed by Jacques Cartier in 1535. At the summit are views of downtown Montreal and across the St. Lawrence River into New York's Adirondack Mountains. You can leave the wide paved trails and explore dirt paths in the upper regions of the park that pass through light woods. At the base of the mountain are plenty of grassy lawns to sprawl with your dog.

reached via Douglas MacArthur Bridge from Jefferson Avenue

There is lots of room to stretch out in Mont-Royal Park after a spirited hike.

NEARBY RECREATION AREA TO ENJOY WITH YOUR DOG:
CHEMIN DE LA PRESQU'ÎLE

Distance from Montreal:
25 minutes to the north

The Park:
Long ago, "Chemin de la Presqu'île" was the name of the horse and buggy road that linked Mascouche and Repentigny. To commemorate the road that led citizens to Repentigy lands recessed between Assomption river and the Saint-Lawrence, Jean-Marie Desrosiers decided to give the same name to the vast network of trails he created in Le Gardeur in 1978.

The Walks:
The Presqu'île Trail boasts a network of four well-marked, pleasing hiking trails ranging from a little over a mile to about 3 miles. Since the early 1990s, dogs have been welcome on the park trails and can even be walked without a leash.

The canine hiking is at an easy clip on the flat trails along the Le Gardeur section, however the hike becomes more challenging along the undulating loops that meet the Mascouche section. Small ponds provide a spot for dogs to cool off but also bring squadrons of mosquitoes. Bring plenty of insect repellent for you and your dog - the females get so hungry for a blood meal that hikers are not charged admission in summer.

Directions to Chemin de la Presqu'île (Quebec):
The park is located in Le Gardeur (Québec) and reached from Highway 40 or 640, Exit 97.
Phone: (450) 883-6060

New Orleans

CITY PARK TO TAKE YOUR DOG:
AUDUBON PARK

Frederick Law Olmsted also brought his design ideas and penchant for winding, serpentine paths to this land of Spanish Oaks and dark lagoons. In 1884-85 the park hosted the World's Industrial and Cotton Exposition and fair goers were treated to elaborate demonstrations of the new electric lighting. Today dogs can trot the dirt and paved paths through the park or play in the open, grassy spaces. A favorite spot for dog walkers is a strip of park along the Mississippi River known as "the fly."

abuts the Mississippi River between Exposition Boulevard, Walnut Street and St. Charles Avenue

NEARBY RECREATION AREA TO ENJOY
WITH YOUR DOG:
FONTAINEBLEAU STATE PARK

Distance from New Orleans:
30 minutes north and west

The Park:
This land was developed as a sugar plantation between 1829 and 1852 by Bernard de Marigny deMandeville, founder of the town of Mandeville. Bernard inherited $7,000,000 from his father in 1800 at the age af 15 and he may have been the richest man in the New World. A famous gambler, he is credited - perhaps romantically so - with introducing craps to America by adapting the European dice game of hazard. The 2,800-acre is named for a forest outside Paris that was a favorite recreation area for French kings. A paradise for water enthusiasts, the park is bordered by Lake Pontchartrain, Bayou Cane and Bayou Castine.

The Walks:
An interpretive nature trail rambles for about one mile through the marshes and woodlands of the park. It is estimated that 400 species of birds live in or visit Fontainebleau State Park. Dogs are allowed to play on the sandy beach but cannot use the *Tammany Trace* recreation path, Louisiana's only rails-to-trails conversion along Lake Pontchartrain.

Directions to Fontainebleau State Park (Louisiana):
Along the north shore of Lake Pontchartrain, the park is on US 190, southeast of the town of Mandeville.
Phone: 985-624-4443
Website: www.crt.state.la.us/crt/parks/fontaine/fontaine.htm

Does your dog have a sweet tooth? Louisiana has long been crucial to the world's supply of sugar. The first economically granular sugar was produced here and at one time more than 1,000 sugar plantations thrived in Louisiana. In a yawning oak grove along the park entrance are the brick ruins of de Mandeville's sugar mill plantation.

New York City

CITY PARK TO TAKE YOUR DOG:
CENTRAL PARK

Chances are your dog will enjoy America's most famous park in midtown Manhattan as much as you will. Dogs are not allowed everywhere (Elm Islands at the Mall, Sheep Meadow, East Green, or Strawberry Fields are among the main prohibited areas) but can go off-leash before 9 a.m. where allowed. Keep an eye out for horses and city streets that cross the park. Bring a water bowl on hot days - the only current fountain outfitted for dogs is at the entrance on East 90th Street. Architects Frederick Law Olmsted and Calvert Vaux designed the park to remain in a naturalistic setting so even in New York City you can lose yourself on woodland paths.

from 59th to 110th streets and from Fifth Avenue to Central Park West

NEARBY RECREATION AREA TO ENJOY
WITH YOUR DOG:
HARRIMAN STATE PARK

Distance from New York:
an hour to the north

The Park:
As development slowly creeped into the Hudson Highlands efforts were made to preserve the area but it was not until the State of New York tried to relocate Sing Sing Prison to Bear Mountain - so named for its resemblance to a bear in repose - that conservation forces truly mobilized. Railroad magnate E.W. Harriman and others donated land and vast sums of money to save the Highlands and in 1910 Bear Mountain-Harriman State Park was dedicated. Within five years it was hosting more than one million visitors per year.

The Walks:
There are more than 200 miles of marked hiking trails through Harriman State Park, New York's second largest, and many more in adjacent Bear Mountain State Park. Even so, the crush of visitors can be so great that designated hiker-only parking lots fill up quickly. Arrive early or face difficult access to trailheads.

Trail historians will want to hike awhile on the *Appalachian Trail* at Bear Mountain - the very first section of more than 2000 miles of America's most famous trail was built here. The canine hike to Hessian Lake on the AT is rich in Revolutionary War lore.

The Timp Hike is a popular introduction to the Hudson Highlands, starting directly on Route 9W that runs along the Hudson River opposite of Jones Point, just south of Bear Mountain. The trailhead is an unpromising break in the weeds just south of the parking lot but things pick up once your dog negotiates the awkward, rocky steps in the early stages of the journey.

The hike splits into the *Ramapo-Dunderberg Trail* (red blazes) and *Timp-Torne Trail* (blue blazes). From here, heading up the red trail, you break out to views of the Hudson River and roll up and down mountains through boulder foundations until the Timp, a peak overlooking the interior of the Highlands. Climb back down the Timp and return on the blue trail to complete a rewarding 9-mile loop.

In general, the hiking in the west region of the park is more paw-friendly. Dirt trails move through forests with little understory and long sightlines. The trails criss-cross often and there is plenty of up-and-down hiking. It is not unusual to have tagged four or five small peaks in a two-hour trip. Make sure to find a trail map before heading out.

Directions to Harriman State Park (New York):
The park is located at the intersection of the Palisades Parkway and Route 9W.

Phone: (845) 786-2701
Website: nysparks.state.ny.us/cgi-bin/cgiwrap/nysparks/
              parks.cgi?p+121

Ottawa

CITY PARK TO TAKE YOUR DOG:
PARLIAMENT HILL

Queen Victoria chose Ottawa as the capital in 1858 and the three magnificent Gothic Revival buildings that house the Canadian government were built between 1859 and 1866, although the Centre Block has been rebuilt after a spectacular fire in 1916 literally blew its green copper roof off. The splendor of the buildings carries the park - there are no showy gardens, just grassy lawns. As you walk your dog around the grounds look for 15 statues of persons who have shaped the country's heritage. At the back of Parliament Hill, overlooking the Ottawa River, is a small cat sanctuary that has been the home to stray Ottawa cats since the late 1970s.

on Wellington Street at the foot of Metcalfe Street

NEARBY RECREATION AREA TO ENJOY
WITH YOUR DOG:
GATINEAU PARK

Distance from Ottawa:
15 minutes to the northwest

The Park:
MacKenzie King, longest governing Prime Minister in Canada, first visited the Gatineau Hills in 1900 and bought a small piece of land on Kingsmere Lake. Here he would entertain guests such as Winston Churchill and Charles Lindbergh, showing off antiquities he placed in his magnificent gardens. King left the property to Canada after his death in 1950 and it spurred additional acquisitions that built the park to more than 200 square miles.

The Walks:
Much of the more than 100 miles of canine hiking is easily reached in the point of this giant wedge of a park near Ottawa. A good place to start is the MacKenzie King Estate where bucolic paths dip into mature woodlands to visit a small waterfall. Also in the southern part of the park is Lauriault Falls and a pleasant access trail less than two miles long.

Another easy exploration is on Champkin Mountain where a short, heavily-wooded trail bursts out to an observation platform at the edge of the Eardley Escarpment overlooking the Ottawa River Valley. The cliffs are more than 1000 feet above the valley floor and a hot, dry micro-climate hosts 61 endangered plants in the thick understory of the woods. The stands of red cedar are Quebec's finest.

More spirited canine hiking can be found on the Escarpment, including the challenging 5-mile *Wolf Trail*. Glaciers gripped this land 10,000 years ago and shaped the rocky landscape.

> 🚫 *All canine hiking at Gatineau must be day-hiking - dogs are not allowed in the campgrounds. This makes expeditions deep into the Laurentian Mountains problematic. Dogs are also prohibited at beaches, picnic areas and Pink Lake, King Mountain or Luskville trails.*

Directions to Gatineau Park (Quebec):
The park blankets the area north of Hull and Highways 5, 105, 148 and 366 all lead to Gatineau.
Phone: 819-827-2020
Website: www.capcan.ca/gatineau/index_e.asp

Philadelphia

CITY PARK TO TAKE YOUR DOG:
FAIRMOUNT PARK

The largest contiguous landscaped municipal park in the world with nearly 9,000 acres began with just 5 acres in 1812. It is the bucolic home to an estimated 2,500,000 trees. The backbone of the park is the *Forbidden Drive*, so named when it was closed to automobiles in the 1920s. The 7-mile paved trail travels along the Wissahickon Creek to the Schuylkill River; canine hikes can be shortened by several bridges across the Wissahickon. In addition, there are many blazed single-track trails climbing steeply out of the Wissahickon Gorge.

the Andorra Visitor Center is on Northwestern Avenue between Ridge Avenue and Germantown Avenue

NEARBY RECREATION AREA TO ENJOY
WITH YOUR DOG:
FRENCH CREEK STATE PARK

Distance from Philadelphia:
45 minutes west

The Park:
A wilderness fort once stood on the small stream flowing through these woods which was garrisoned by the French during the French and Indian War and thus "French Creek." The hillsides here were dotted with charcoal hearths through-out the 1800s, fueling the nascent American iron industry. The furnace was stoked for the last time in 1883. French Creek State Park was originally developed by the federal government during the Depression as a National Park Service Demonstration Area and in 1946, the area was transferred to the Commonwealth of Pennsylvania.

The Walks:
Approximately 40 miles of trails visit every corner of French Creek's 7,339 acres. There are nine featured hikes of between one and four hours' duration. The marquee walk is the *Boone Trail*, a six-mile loop connecting all the major attractions of the park. The *Mill Creek Trail* is a back-country hike that visits Millers Point, a pile of large boulders where you and the dog can easily scramble to the top.

As the area was repeatedly timbered in the past there is little understory in today's woods and the trails are almost universally wide and easy to walk. Two lakes, the 21-acre cold water Scotts Run Lake and the 63-acre Hopewell Lake, will be irresistible to water-loving dogs.

Directions to French Creek State Park (Pennsylvania):
From the Pennsylvania Turnpike take Exit 22, the Morgantown Interchange. Go east on Route 23 to Route 345 North and the south entrance of the park.

Phone: 610-582-9680
Website: www.dcnr.state.pa.us/stateparks/parks/w-clay.htm

Considered by some as the "Orienteering Capital of North America," French Creek has developed a permanent self-guided course for the practioners of the art of map and compass. You can even challenge your dog's nose in a wayfinding contest.

Phoenix

CITY PARK TO TAKE YOUR DOG:
ENCANTO PARK

In the heart of downtown Phoenix is this oasis for people and dogs, named for the Spanish word for "enchanted." Acquisition of the 222 acres began in 1934 through donations and land buys. You can walk your dog around the palm-studded lagoon where the sternwheeler "Encanto Queen" plies the gentle waters.

15th Avenue and Encanto Boulevard

NEARBY RECREATION AREA TO ENJOY
WITH YOUR DOG:
SOUTH MOUNTAIN PARK

Distance from Phoenix:
southern Phoenix

The Park:
South Mountain Park is actually three mountain ranges - the Ma Ha Tauk, Gila and Guadalupe - where prospectors probed for riches in the early 1900s. The city of Phoenix acquired 13,000 acres of land in 1924 for just $17,000 from the federal government and the park was on its way to becoming the largest municipal park in America. The National Park Service also did the bulk of the development work when the Civilian Conservation Corps carved out trails and picnic areas and built many of the park facilities.

The Walks:
This is pure Sonoran desert hiking - open, rocky and hot. Canine hikers are advised to stick to South Mountain's shorter trails and there are plenty to choose from of less than two miles. Bring more water than you'll think you need and pay close attention to your dog's paw pads. The rocks and packed dirt can get blisteringly hot.

Once common-sense precautions in the desert are accounted for, the going at South Mountain is suitable for most any dog. The highest point you can reach on foot is 2,330-foot Dobbins Lookout and steep climbs are spread out on the park trails.

The *National Trail* cuts through the spine of the park for more than 14 miles and can be used for loops. It moves though chiseled rocks and crags amidst a desert environment of more than 300 species of plants.

Expect to adopt a pack mentality when taking your dog to South Mountain Park - more than three million hikers sample its trails each year.

Directions to South Mountain Park (Arizona):
Go south on Central Avenue to the park entrance.
Phone: 602-495-0222
Website: www.ci.phoenix.az.us/PARKS/hikesoth.html

Pittsburgh

CITY PARK TO TAKE YOUR DOG:
SCHENLEY PARK

Mary Croghan Schenley was a 14-year old heiress when she ran off with a British sea captain in 1842 to great scandal. She fought a long battle in the courts to keep her inheritance and when she won she donated 300 acres to Pittsburgh on the conditions that the land be called Schenley Park and that it never be sold. The resulting open space is a classically designed 19th century park with formal gathering places and pastoral landscapes.

Schenley Avenue next to the University of Pittsburgh

The high ground in Schenley Park with picnic pavilions and open space is a great place for a game of fetch.

NEARBY RECREATION AREA TO ENJOY
WITH YOUR DOG:
HARTWOOD ACRES

Distance from Pittsburgh:
30 minutes northeast

The Park:
Hartwood Manor, named for a 16th century English country estate, was developed by Mary Flinn Lawrence. In 1969 she offered the estate to Allegeny County as a park after her death and all of a sudden the county had a ready-made crown jewel for its park system.

The Walks:
When you come to Hartwood Acres, you come to walk. There are no recreation or sport facilities on its 629 acres. The manor house, horse stable and outdoor sculptures are still in place to admire before heading out on the rolling dirt trails through the wooded countryside. A spider-web of short and long trails and immaculate horse trails conspire to provide delightful canine hiking in Hartwood Acres.

Directions to Hartwood Acres (Pennsylvania):
From the Pennsylvania Turnpike north of Pittsburgh take Exit 4 (Butler Valley) and go south on Route 8 for two miles. Turn left on Wildwood Road and right on Middle Road for about 1.5 miles until the entrance to Hartwood Acres (on the left).
Phone: 412-767-9200
Website: www.county.allegheny.pa.us/parks/

"If you pick up a starving dog and make him prosperous, he will not bite you; that is the principal difference between a dog and a man."
- Mark Twain

St. Louis

CITY PARK TO TAKE YOUR DOG:
FOREST PARK

This large 1370-acre urban park was four miles from the city center when it opened on June 24, 1876 - the day before Custer's Last Stand at the Battle of Little Bighorn. Designed by Maximillian G. Kern, Forest Park superintendent and landscape gardener, the landscape is decorated with several lakes and Kennedy Forest. The park hosted the 1904 World's Fair and in 1912 tennis was introduced to the Forest Park by Parks Commissioner Dwight Davis, donor of the sport's most famous trophy. A multi-use 7.5-mile asphalt path tours the historic park.

bounded by Lindell, Skinker and Kings boulevards and Oakland Avenue

NEARBY RECREATION AREA TO ENJOY
WITH YOUR DOG:
ROUTE 66 STATE PARK

Distance from Saint Louis:

30 minutes to the south

The Park:

At one time Route 66, "America's Main Street," ran through the wooded bluffs of the Meramec River valley. Designed in 1926, the federal road helped link vast stretches of remote lands between Chicago and Los Angeles. The resort community of Times Beach once welcomed visitors here. The town was abandoned in 1980 after waste oil sprayed on the streets to keep dust down proved to be toxic. When the clean-up was complete the 409-acre park was created in 1999 to showcase the beauty of the valley and preserve some of the history of John Steinbeck's "Mother Road."

The Walks:

The canine hiking is light and easy on the seven-plus miles of trails that circle the park. The trail system links with surrounding systems for extended outings along the Meramec River. Expect to share the trails with bikes and horses on these wide, level paths.

The country park abounds in wildlife such as deer and turkey and you can even walk the dog along a stretch of historic Route 66 that remains in the park.

Directions to Route 66 State Park (Missouri):

Take I-55 South to I-44 West and exit at Lewis Road (Exit 266). Go past West Tyson County Park entrance to a stop sign on Lewis Road. Cross Lewis Road to the Visitor Center.

Phone: (636) 938-7198

Website: www.mostateparks.com/route66/trails.htm

Salt Lake City

CITY PARK TO TAKE YOUR DOG:
LIBERTY PARK

Liberty Park, with fountains and formal pathways, is a traditional park with 100 acres set aside for walking and relaxing. The Main Walk is a spacious, lighted promenade under spreading cottonwood trees; narrow off-shoots include strolls like the Pine Walk. In the south end is the Tracy Aviary with more than 1,000 birds on display from around the world.

500 to 700 East Street and 900 to 1300 South Street

NEARBY RECREATION AREA TO ENJOY
WITH YOUR DOG:
ANTELOPE ISLAND STATE PARK

Distance from Salt Lake City:
30 minutes to the northwest

The Park:
Only the Dead Sea holds saltier water than the Great Salt Lake, the biggest lake in the American West. The salinity can be as high as 27% - eight times saltier than ocean water. Antelope Island is the largest of the Great Salt Lake's 10 islands. The ancestral antelopes for which John Fremont and Kit Carson named the island in 1843 disappeared but were reintroduced to the 28,022-acre park in 1993. But the animal stars of the park are the bison, first shipped here in 1893 and now 600 strong. Sheep also grazed here for decades, supporting the busiest sheering operation west of the Mississippi River. The first state lands on the island were purchased in 1969 and the entire island became a state park in 1987.

The Walks:
At the heart of the 20-mile hiking system on Antelope Island is the *White Rock Bay Loop*, over 9 miles of long ascents and descents from the shoreline. Like most of the canine hiking in the park, the trail is open all the way and gets hot in the summer. There is no fresh water available so bring plenty to keep your dog refreshed. The trail is often paw-friendly sand.

A quicker way to see the island is the *Buffalo Trail*, a one-mile round trip that features benches to stop and gaze around the native vegatation of the Great Basin. For extended views get on the *Mountain View Trail* that provides hours of easy canine hiking.

Everyone will want to include a quarter-mile trail to Beacon Knob on the day hiking agenda. This trail high point serves up panoramas of the Wasatch Front Range across the water. To get close to the Great Salt Lake the *Lakeside Trail* is a 3-mile out-and-back shadow on the shore.

Directions to Antelope Island State Park (Utah):
The park is 7 miles west of Layton at Exit 355 off I-15.

Phone: 801-773-2941
Website: www.utah.com/stateparks/antelope_island.htm

🚫 *A popular hike on Antelope Island is to the summit of 6,596-foot Frary Peak, named for George and Alice who homesteaded here. The entire Wasatch Front Range comes into view at the top but your dog will never see it. No dogs are allowed on Frary.*

Visiting the Great Salt Lake, you can be overwhelmed by the stench of the air - the result of billions of decaying organisms that have died after being washed from freshwater streams into the briny water. The smell is confined mostly to the eastern shore (where the micro-biotic slaughter occurs), however, and, canine hikers can usually expect fresh, salty air on Antelope Island.

San Diego

CITY PARK TO TAKE YOUR DOG:

BALBOA PARK

The land for this world-famous park was set aside in 1868. In 1910 a contest named the developing park in honor of Vasco Nunez de Balboa, the first European to see the Pacific Ocean. Dogs are allowed on trails throughout the 1400-acre park and there are also a pair of 24-hour dog parks: a large grassy area on Balboa Drive at El Prado, on the south side of Cabrillo Bridge, and at Morley Field on the east side of the park northwest of the tennis courts. Grape Street Park is designated as a dog-off-leash area during the following times: Monday-Friday, 7:30-10:00 a.m. and 4:00-9:00 p.m.; Saturday, Sunday and holidays, 9:00-11:00 a.m. and 4:00-9:00 p.m.

Park Boulevard off I-5

NEARBY RECREATION AREA TO ENJOY

WITH YOUR DOG:

MISSION TRAILS REGIONAL PARK

Distance from San Diego:
15 minutes to the northeast

The Park:
Dating back as far as 8,000 B.C., this was the land of the the mighty Kumeyaay Nation with 18 communities spanning California and Mexico, 12 in San Diego County alone. Established only in 1974 on the site of Old Mission Dam, the park's nearly 6,000 natural acres recalls the land at the time of the first Spanish settlement in San Diego Bay in 1542.

The Walks:
Dogs are welcome on the more than 40 miles of hard-packed trails here across open chaparral and sage scrub. For short openers at Mission Trails consider the *Oak Grove Loop* and *Visitor Center Loop* at the Visitor and Interpretive Center. Other easy canine hikes include the *Grassland Loop* in East Fortuna and the *Father Junipero Serra Trail* that visits all the habitats of the park including wetlands feeding Mission Canyon and oak woodlands.

The star at Mission Trails is Cowles Mountain where several trails lead to the highest point in San Diego - 1,591 feet. The 360-degree views can be had with round trips ranging from three to five miles on the trail. A short detour to the northwest leads to 1379-foot Pyles Peak.

Directions to Mission Trails Regional Park (California):
The park is located off Mission Gorge Road at the corners of Father Junipero Serra Trail and Echo Dell Road.

Phone: (619) 668-3275
Website: www.mtrp.org/

In San Diego during the Winter Solstice, wake the dog up early and head for the slopes of Cowles Mountain. The Kumeyaay once painstakingly arranged stones in an ancient observatory on the mountain so that at sunrise the sun appeared to be an orb balanced on a peak. The original stone arrangement has been recreated so that at dawn on the days surrounding the solstice a peak splits the rising sun.

San Francisco

CITY PARK TO TAKE YOUR DOG:
GOLDEN GATE PARK

San Francisco's first great city park began to take shape shortly after the end of the Civil War. First park superintendent William Hammond Hall laid out the grounds with winding paths to discourage speeding horses and shield strollers from the wind. In 1887 Hall ceded his duties to landscape gardener John McLaren and over the next 50 years the Scotsman would mold Golden Gate Park into one of the world's most admired urban greenscapes. He built nine artificial lakes and miles of roads, bridle paths and foot trails. Golden Gate Park boasts more than one million trees and plants from lands around the globe. Over the years the park has hosted every conceivable form of recreation from golf to archery to polo to San Francisco 49er football. The park encompasses more than 1,000 acres and stretches from the Pacific Ocean halfway across the city - more than three miles.

bounded by Fulton Street to the north and Lincoln Way to the south from the Pacific Ocean to Stanyan Street

Sometimes you have to know when to stop hiking and accept a ride.

NEARBY RECREATION AREA TO ENJOY
WITH YOUR DOG:
GOLDEN GATE NATIONAL RECREATION AREA

Distance from San Francisco:
  in city to 30 minutes north

The Park:
  In 1972 a menagerie of government properties around the San Francisco Bay that included forts, a prison, an airfield, beaches and forests came together as the Golden Gate National Recreation Area, becoming one of the world's largest urban national parks. In the park are such popular destinations as Alcatraz, the Presidio and the Cliff House at Lands End. Today the park administers 75,388 acres of land - including 28 miles of shoreline - on more than 20 separate parcels.

The Walks:
  You will not be lacking things to do with your dog in the Golden Gate National Recreation Area. One of the best places for dog owners to head is Fort Funston on the Pacific Ocean at the southern extreme of the park in the city (off Skyline Boulevard - Route 35). There are trails to romp along among the cliffs and plenty of unrestricted access to the beach. Look for hang gliders soaring above the cliffs. Except for areas of bird nesting and small China Beach, dogs are permitted on the sand in the city of San Francisco all the way north from Fort Funston to the San Francisco Bay.
  Across the bay there is first-rate canine hiking in the Marin Headlands and the Oakwood Valley on designated trails. Elevations in the wooded hills climb to over 1000 feet. Dogs are not permitted in the Muir Woods or the Tennessee Valley, the two most significant prohibitions against dogs in the Golden Gate National Recreation Area.

Directions to Golden Gate National Recreation Area (California):
  The park is located in the western edge of San Francisco along the Great Highway. The parcels of land can be accessed from US Route 1.
Phone: (415) 561-4700
Website: www.nps.gov/goga/index.htm

A Canine Hike With A View

Connecting the Golden Gate National Recreation Area on both sides of the San Francisco Bay is one of the world's most famous bridges - the Golden Gate Bridge. You can walk your dog across the familiar orange bridge, maybe the most photographed man-made structure in the world. The hike is more than 1.5 miles one-way and an estimated 3800 people make the walk each weekday with foot traffic doubling on the weekends.

You will pass under the world's two highest bridge towers, 220 feet above the water. Views from the bridge on a clear day can extend 20 miles out to sea, although the pedestrian walkway is on the east (city) side.

This is not a hike for a skittery dog - you are only feet from speeding traffic, it is noisy and the bridge does sway. A new 4'6" Public Safety Railing has recently been installed to provide a better buffer for bridge hikers. The south terminus of the hike in San Francisco is in Fort Point and the Golden Gate Promenade extends the hike another 3.5 miles along the bay.

A live webcam provides continuous pictures of the bridge at goldengatebridge.org so you can check on visibility before making a special trip to the bridge with your dog.

Seattle

CITY PARK TO TAKE YOUR DOG:
SEWARD PARK

Development of this once-remote park on Bailey Peninsula named after Secretary of State William Seward came slowly after the property was bought in 1911. But when Lake Washington was lowered the park began to take shape into a keystone of Seattle's park system. A paved loop travels 2.4 miles around the peninsula and nine numbered trails explore the guts of the park that features Seattle's largest old growth forest. These sporty hikes take place under towering Douglas firs, red cedars and western hemlocks.

5902 Lake Washington Boulevard South

NEARBY RECREATION AREA TO ENJOY
WITH YOUR DOG:
MOUNT SI

Distance from Seattle:
45 minutes to the east

The Park:
Frances North, a state legislator, was instrumental in having more than 1000 acres of land set aside for conservation in 1987. Today nearly 9000 acres are protected. The mountain, named for settler Josiah Merritt known familiarly as "Uncle Si," is familiar to television fans as the backdrop of the cult series *Twin Peaks*.

The Walks:
The walk up Mount Si is steep but any dog can make it - and at times it can seem as if every dog in Seattle is trying. Mount Si is often snow-free when trails around it are closed and the trail gets very crowded. The 200-car parking lot at the trailhead is not always adequate for everyone heading for the summit - from strollers to mountaineers on training runs.

Most of this canine hike is in the trees, although they begin to fall away at the end of the 3400-foot elevation gain. From rocky ledges above the Snoqualmie River Valley you can often see Seattle and Puget Sound beyond.

At about 2100 feet the trail levels off at the Snag Flats with a nearby stream for your dog. In a bit over two more miles the 4-mile hike ends for most canine hikers at Haystack Basin. The final quarter-mile push up the Haystack can be tricky.

Directions to Mount Si (Washington):
You can reach the Mount Si trailhead off Exit 31 of I-90. Go east on North Bend Way and make a left onto Mount Si Road.
Phone: (360) 825-1631
Website: www.dnr.wa.gov/

"My dog is worrid about the economy because Alpo is up to 99 cents a can. That's almost $7.00 in dog money."
- Joe Weinstein

Toronto

City Park to take your dog:
High Park

Many of High Park's 400 acres were donated by George Howard, Toronto's first formally trained architect, in 1873. Well-maintained walking paths connect manicured gardens on the west side to forest land on the east side. A highlight of the park is Grenadier Pond, supposedly named for British soldiers who fell through its ice rushing to defend the city from American attack in the War of 1812. High Park also sports 24-hour off-leash areas at Dog Hill northeast of the Grenadier Restaurant and west of the Dream Site.

Bloor Street West and Parkside Drive

Nearby Recreation Area to enjoy

with your dog:
Bronte Creek Provincial Park

Distance from Toronto:
20 minutes to the south

The Park:
Although this wide stream travels 32 miles to the mouth of Lake Ontario, it was known as Twelve Mile Creek by settlers who came to operate mills along its many rapids and water-falls. The village of Bronte, named for the large estate granted Admiral Lord Horatio Nelson for his naval victory in the Battle of Trafalgar, grew up on the stream and became a major port for shipping wheat in the mid 1800s. The creek took the same name in the 1930s.

The Walks:
Much of the lands here devoted to agriculture have reverted back to deciduous forests that provide a quiet, pastoral backdrop to canine hiking in Bronte Creek. A selection of short trails explore the best example of prairie vegetation in greater Toronto.

Canine hikers will want to head first to the *Leash Free Path* to let your dog run through tall grass for nearly a mile. All the hiking is non-strenuous on the valley rims along Bronte Creek and the only trail that is not barrier-free is the stacked loop *Half Moon Valley Trail*. Staircases smooth out any steep segments 80 feet above the busy waters.

The longest trail in the park - still not two miles long - is the *Ravine Trail*. Here a dark coniferous forest guards overlooks of the Bronte Creek ravine. Make your way down to the stream for playful canine aquatics.

Directions to Bronte Creek Provincial Park (Ontario):
From the Q.E.W. take Exit 109, Burloak Drive and turn right. The Day Use Area will be on the right hand side.
Phone: (905) 827-6911
Website: www.ontarioparks.com/english/bron.html

"Ever consider what they must think of us? I mean, here we come back from the grocery store with the most amazing haul - chicken, pork, half a cow... they must think we're the greatest hunters on earth."
- Anne Tyler

Vancouver

CITY PARK TO TAKE YOUR DOG:
STANLEY PARK

Frederick Arthur Stanley was the sixth Governor-General of Canada, presiding over a completely uneventful five-year term beginning in 1888. He had the good fortune, however, to be immortalized by two tangential occurances during his service. One, he authorized the equivalent of $48 to purchase a trophy for a hockey tournament that became the National Hockey League's Stanley Cup and two, he was in office when one of North America's most spectacular urban parks opened in Vancouver. More than 50 miles of roads and paths twist under majestic cedars, hemlocks and firs. The dogwalk along the 5.5-mile seawall around the entire peninsula is one of the most popular activities in town. Started in the 1920s to halt erosion, the stone wall took six decades to completely finish. At nearly three dozen Vancouver parks, including Stanley Park, dogs are allowed off-leash from 6:00 a.m. to 10:00 a.m and 5:00 p.m. to 10:00 p.m.

West Georgia Street, Route 99/1A, on a peninsula north of town on English Bay

NEARBY RECREATION AREA TO ENJOY
WITH YOUR DOG:
CYPRESS PROVINCIAL PARK

Distance from Vancouver:
15 minutes northeast of downtown

The Park:
The lure of the North Shore Mountains looking down on Vancouver brought hikers and skiers by boat until the opening of the Lions Gate Bridge in 1939. This new easy access threatened the old growth forests when clear-cut logging began under the guise of cutting ski trails. Preservation forces aligned to save the trees, including namesake stands of yellow cypress, and the park was created in 1975.

The Walks:
Alpine canine hiking is convenient to Cypress Parkway on three mountains: Black Mountain, Mount Strachan and Hollyburn Mountain. The *Hollyburn Mountain Trail* is a hardy ascent of about four miles round trip to the summit and the *Black Mountain Loop Trail* visits sub-alpine meadows and glacial lakes ideal for a doggie dip. The full circuit will take about two hours.

Less strenuous fare can be found around the mountain bases. The *Yew Lake Trail* is a 30-minute canine hike from the main Cypress Mountain visitor center, on fully accessible terrain through wetlands and meadows.

Experienced hikers can tackle the *Howe Crest Sound Trail* but maybe not with your dog. Small cliffs are negotiated with ropes and you will encounter narrow trail chutes. The rugged 18-mile trail tops several mountains and is best attempted by canine hikers in small, well-researched bites.

Directions to Cypress Provincial Park (British Columbia):
Take Exit #8 off the Upper Levels Highway in West Vancouver, and follow the road up the mountain.

Phone: (604) 929-1291
Website: www.britishcolumbia.com/ParksAndTrails/Parks/details/?ID=103

Washington D.C.

CITY PARK TO TAKE YOUR DOG:
NATIONAL MALL

In the words of Calvin Coolidge, "any man who does not like dogs and want them does not deserve to be in the White House." Across the street, on the National Mall, dogs are not only welcome but often celebrated. The finals of the canine frisbee disc championships have traditionally been held on the National Mall. The patchy grass squares make a fun place to play with your dog or the Mall can be the setting for a people-watching canine hike of almost two miles from the Capitol Steps to the feet of Abraham Lincoln.

from the Lincoln Memorial to the United States Capitol

CITY PARK TO TAKE YOUR DOG:
ROCK CREEK PARK

Distance from Washington D.C:
northwest part of the city

The Park:
Although technically a national park, Rock Creek Park is more like a city park administered by the National Park Service. How many other national parks boast of ballfields and 30 picnic sites? It was the Army Corps of Engineers that first proposed the creation of Rock Creek Park when they considered moving the White House out of the mosquito-infested lowlands of downtown Washington after the Civil War. In 1890 Congress carved 1,754 acres from the Rock Creek Valley to establish the park.

The Walks:
Two main parallel hiking trails, run the length of the park from north to south on either side of Rock Creek. The wiser choice for canine hikers is the *Valley Trail* (blue blazes) on the east side. In contrast with its twin, the *Western Ridge Trail* (green blazes), there are fewer picnic areas and less competition for the trail. Each is a rooty and rocky frolic up and down the slopes above Rock Creek, a superb canine swimming hole. Numerous spur trails and bridle paths connect the two major arteries that connect at the north and south to create a loop about ten miles long.

Directions to Rock Creek Park:
Rock Creek Park abut the western edge of 16th Street, Route 29, running north to south. The main road through the park, Beach Drive, can be picked up from the north on the East West Highway, Route 410.
Phone: (202) 895-6070
Website: www.nps.gov/rocr/

The nation's capital was protected with a ring of 68 forts during the Civil War and Rock Creek Park administers several military sites. Your dog can visit the remnants of Fort De Russy, an earthworks fortification returned to its natural state just east of the Western Ridge Trail on a bridle path at Oregon Avenue and Military Road. Also near Military Road, three blocks east of the main park on 13th Street, is Fort Stevens. It was here the only fighting of the Civil War took place within the limits of Washington D.C. Union defenders repulsed a Confederate attack from General Jubal Early on July 11-12, 1864. Abraham Lincoln rode up from the White House and stood on a parapet watching the battle - the only time in United States history that an American president was under fire by enemy guns while in office. A dramatized plaque marks the spot today in the partially reconstructed fort. Your dog will probably be more interested in playing fetch on the grassy grounds.

Winnipeg

CITY PARK TO TAKE YOUR DOG:

ASSINBOINE PARK

Winnipeg's first suburban park was opened on Victoria Day 1909 and incorporated in an amalgamated Winnipeg in 1972. It is designed in the English Landscape Style with Tudor-inspired buildings, large open meadows and lawns backed by borders of native Manitoba plants. Nearby, off Grant Avenue, is the spacious Assinboine Forest with popular walking on the one-mile *Saginay Trail* that leads to a scenic pond.

junction of Park Boulevard and Wellington Crescent at 2355 Corydon Avenue

NEARBY RECREATION AREA TO ENJOY

WITH YOUR DOG:

WHITESHELL PROVINCIAL PARK

Distance from Winnipeg:

one hour to the east

The Park:

The park rests on the western edge of the Canadian or Precambrian Shield, the oldest geological formation in the world. Rocks here have been worn down from 10,000-foot mountains over 500 million years. The Canada Pacific Railway roared through lower Manitoba in 1877 and a mini-gold rush near the small town of Keewatin brought in more people. Vacationers began favoring the area in the 1920s and in 1961 Whiteshell, composed of 672,734 acres over four districts, was granted provincial park status.

The Walks:

Some of the best canine hiking and swimming at Whiteshell is around the more than 200 lakes in the park. West Hawk Lake, one of Manitoba's deepest canine swimming pools, was formed by a meteor some 100 million years ago.

A good place to experience the thin soils and rock outcroppings of the Precambrian Shield is at Jessica Lake where a series of sporty looping trails roll across the exposed granite. Take care - the rocky going can be tough on your dog's paws.

If you really become enamored of Shield country you can plan a multi-day canine hike on the *Mantario Trail.* Pick up the 36-mile hike at Big Whiteshell Lake.

Directions to Whiteshell Provincial Park (Manitoba):

The park can be accessed by Highway 1E.

Phone (Falcon Lake District):   (204) 349-2201
Website: www.whiteshell.mb.ca/

The Anishinabe and other First Nations people believed the Creator lowered the first man from the sky to ground here. Small white seashells found in the area - the ones that give the park its name - were held to be sacred. Also believed to be sacred are the Bannock Point Petroforms - rocks and boulders laid out to resemble snakes and turtles and abstract shapes. Their meaning is open to interpretation and petroform sites are still used for ceremonial purposes.

Five Towns Your
Dog Will Love...

Jacksonville, Oregon

The Town:

Gold was discovered in Oregon's Jackson Creek in 1851 but it brought neither fame nor fortune to the prospector, a lone miner remembered today only as "Mr. Sykes." Gold fever ignited soon enough and within two years there were thousands of men tediously pulling flakes and nuggets from area creek beds. Jacksonville's first brick buildings were in place by 1853 as the town thrived. It even became the county seat but when the Oregon & California Railroad headed for nearby Medford in 1887 and bypassed Jacksonville the good times ground to a halt. Jacksonville residents built their own railroad four years later but the struggling line was dismantled and sold in 1925. During the Depression struggling residents dug deeper into the hills around town to extract a few dollars of gold to survive. Not much happened in town after that. So little changed, in fact, that the entire downtown was designated a National Historic Landmark in 1966.

The Walks:

In 1989, Jacksonville residents formed the Jacksonville Woodlands Association to preserve and protect the quiet forests on the slopes surrounding the town. Most explorations of the Jacksonville Woodlands will start in town along the *Zigler Trail*, a flat one-mile journey along the Jackson Creek where gold was discovered in 1851. A detailed brochure tells the fascinating story and makes for a prolonged walk with the dog. Strollers will want to turn around at the footbridge and retrace your pawprints but adventurous canine hikers will turn left and climb the ridges and canyons above the town. The three-mile *Rich Gulch Trail* leads to a panoramic view of the town and countryside.

On the east end of town, behind the country Gothic house built by apprentice carpenter-turned-pioneer banker Cornelius Beekman in 1873, you will find the *Beekman Canyon Loop*. The trail begins and ends in a small arboretum that displays eight distinct bio-habitats found in the region. The trail climbs somewhat steeply through light woods before descending back into the Beekman Garden.

After hiking through the peaceful Jacksonville Woodlands, be sure to take your dog on a walk through town. More than 80 original brick and wooden buildings from the 1800s are listed on the National Register of Historic Places. You can continue just outside of town into the Jacksonville Cemetery that has been in use for over 150 years. Dogs are as welcome in Jacksonville today as they were in the mining camps of yesteryear - there is a water bowl placed for dogs outside the Visitor Information kiosk.

Sidetrip: Rogue River National Forest (Exit 6 off I-5 towards Mount Ashland Ski Area)

High on the western slopes of the Cascade Mountains, tiny streams fill with snow melt and trickle along until coming together to form the Rogue River and begin its wild 235-mile journey to the Pacific. The Rogue is one of eight rivers in the United States designated as wild and scenic and the national forest surrounds its headwaters.

The *Pacific Crest Trail* passes through the forest and one of the best places for your dog to experience this legendary long distance trail is at Mount Ashland Meadows. An easy, practically level, dirt trail slices through five flower-studded subalpine meadows. This is a 3.4-mile linear trail through the meadowscape so you can decide when you've had your fill of purple larkspur, lavender, blue lupine and purple aster before turning around.

> 🚫 *Part of the Rogue River National Forest includes Crater Lake, America's deepest and bluest lake. Dogs are not permitted on the trails in this national park and only one trail leads to the water so your dog won't be able to experience its crystal waters.*

Directions to Jacksonville:

Jacksonville is located on Route 238 off of I-5 out of Grants Pass to the north or Medford from the south.

Phone: (541) 899-8118
Website: www.jacksonvilleoregon.org/

Ketchum, Idaho

The Town:

In 1879 a tall, wiry prospector named David Ketchum built a small shelter along the Trail Creek to use as his base of operations in the area. He didn't stay long. By 1880, when mining operations began to be permanently established, Ketchum was long gone, rumored to be in Arizona, or perhaps dead in a saloon standoff. The new town called itself Leadville but the United States Post Office turned down the name because Leadvilles were as common as dashed dreams in the West by that time. The settlers decided to name their town after pioneering David Ketchum, whose rudimentary shelter still stood down by Trail Creek.

For more than a decade Ketchum boomed but the collapse of the silver market in 1894 opened a gash in the town's economy that drained 90 percent of its population. The town recovered some with an infusion of sheep ranching but by the 1930s there were fewer than 300 people living in Ketchum.

In 1935 Austrian Count Felix Schaffgotsch was hired by Union Pacific Railroad Chairman W. Averell Harriman to scout the American West for the best site to build a destination ski resort like the tony resorts in the European Alps. Schaffgotsch scoured the mountain regions of the West and rejected such places as Aspen, Jackson Hole and Yosemite. He was prepared to return to New York and report his failure when a railroad representative from Idaho asked him to check out Ketchum. Within three days, the Count wired Harriman: "Among the many attractive spots I have visited, this combines more delightful features of any place I have seen in the United States, Switzerland, or Austria for a winter sports resort." Eleven months later Sun Valley Resort opened to international acclaim and Ketchum's future viability was assured.

The Walks:

Ketchum features over 40 miles of trails located within a 5-mile radius of town. The marquee walk is the 5-mile *Bald Mountain Trail*, at the end of 3d Avenue at River Run Plaza on the edge of town. The trail crosses numerous ski trails up 3400 feet to an elevation above the tree line at 9151 feet. Not only are dogs allowed on the Bald Mountain Trail, but halfway up the mountain, in a glade of giant fir trees, is a drinking fountain with a perpetually-filled dog drinking bowl built right into the trail. About the only place dogs are not allowed is on the ski lifts.

Other trails around Ketchum include hikes around Corral Creek in the Sun Valley resort and additional alpine walks north of town on Highway 75 at Fox Creek and Adams Gulch. These dirt and grass trails are afire with wildflowers through the summer months.

Further up Highway 75, just seven miles from Ketchum is the Sawtooth National Recreation Area, with 756,000 acres of public land. A highlight in the Sawtooths, with more than 40 peaks higher than 10,000 feet, are more than 300 high mountain lakes. Several of the lakes, including Baker Lake and the Norton Lakes are within two miles of a trailhead.

The *Harriman Trail* is a 31-kilometer corridor in three segments that is open to hiking, biking and cross-country-skiing that starts at the Sawtooth headquarters. The trail climaxes in Galena, overlooking the headwaters of the Salmon River.

Directions to Ketchum:

Ketchum is north of I-80 on Highway 75. The Visitor Center on Main Street (Highway 75) features abundant material on the various hiking options in the area.

Phone: (208) 726-3841
Website: www.ci.ketchum.id.us/

Ernest Hemingway spent his final years in Ketchum and he is remembered with a memorial on a shaded bank of *Trail Creek* in Sun Valley. Nearby, in the Ketchum Cemetery on the northen edge of town on Route 75, is Hemingway's unadorned grave. Guarded by a sentry of trees, the marker is flush with the ground and offers no more than a name and dates for the life of America's most celebrated writer of the 20th century. Hemingway's four dogs - Black, Negrita, Neron, and Linda - are buried in a neat patio at his home in Cuba.

Moab, Utah

The Town:

Most of us have seen the spectacular scenery around Moab without realizing it - the landscape has often been used as the setting for Hollywood westerns. Before that, popular Western novelist Zane Grey stoked the imaginations of readers with action placed in Moab. Real people started coming to the Colorado River town in the 1950s when uranium was discovered nearby. Even though the mines have since played out, the town has never returned to its sleepy agricultural days. Today Moab is an outdoors mecca at the foot of the La Salle Mountains. Moab is the gateway to southeastern Utah's canyon country and the national parks at Canyonlands and Arches. In these parks dogs are not allowed in the backcountry, on trails or on rivers within the park. Still, there are plenty of other opportunities here that make Moab a prime destination for canine hikers.

The Walks:

Legend has it that cowboys once herded wild mustangs onto to the top of this mesa - 2000 feet above the Colorado River - and blocked off their escape across a narrow neck of land with branches and brush, thus creating a natural corral. Once the horses in the corral were forgotten about and died of thirst while looking at the unaccessible Colorado River below. In 1959 more than 5,000 acres, most of which are on the mesa top, were designated Dead Horse Point State Park (nine miles north of Moab on US 191; turn west on SR 313, then go 22 miles to the Visitor Center).

While your dog will never trot the trails of Canyonlands National Park and look straight down 1000 feet at the confluence of the Green and Colorado rivers, she can get the same kind of experience next door in Dead Horse Point State Park. Two loops, connected by the Visitor Center, skirt the edges of the rim of the rock peninsula. Numerous short spur trails poke out to promontories overlooking the canyonlands (most are unfenced and provide no protection for over-curious canines). This is sparse desert land on top of the mesa and during a hot summer day there is little shade and no natural drinking water on the trails for thirsty dogs. All told there are ten miles of paved and primitive trail at Dead Horse Point, most on hard, rocky paths.

Dogs will welcome little bits of shade atop the open Dead Horse Point mesa in summer.

To the east of Moab on Scenic Route 128 is the Colorado Riverway Recreation Area with distinctly different canine adventures in store. Director John Ford began shooting Hollywood westerns on location here in 1949 he went searching for a new desert location for his upcoming *Wagon Master* to star Ben Johnson and Ward Bond. He arrived in Moab where he was shown the Professor Valley and the Fisher Towers on the Colorado River. Ford indeed made *Wagon Master* here and more than 50 feature films would

A half-mile spur on the western side of the Dead Horse Point mesa leads to an overlook of Shafer Canyon. Across the canyon you can see an open plain that was used to film the famous final scene in the movie *Thelma & Louise* when Susan Sarandon drives a Thunderbird convertible over a cliff. Although there are wrecked automobiles in Shafer Canyon, they were placed there by the Bureau of Land Management to shore up the river bank. The wreckage from the movie was airlifted out of the canyon by helicopter.

be shot on location around Moab in the next 50 years. To John Wayne, this area always defined the West.

Your dog won't be able to draw a full conclusion to agree or disagree with the Duke - the canine hike at Fisher Towers ends when a ladder climb scales an awkward rock before the end of the trail. Upstream, the packed-sand *Negro Bill Canyon Trail* climbs gently up a scenic canyon, crossing and tracing a clear-flowing stream for two miles to reach the Morning Glory Natural Bridge. Your dog won't be able to walk under the magnificent natural arches in Arches National Park but he can play under the sixth longest natural rock span in the United States. The pool under the bridge makes an ideal doggie swimming pool but be careful of the flourishing poison ivy growing nearby.

Directions to Moab:

Moab is in northeast Utah at the interesction of US 191 and Scenic Route 128.

Phone: (208) 726-3841
Website: www.moab.net

Redding, California

The Town:

The California & Oregon Railroad built a temporary supply center here in 1872 and named it Redding after B.B. Redding, its railroad land agent. The settlement took hold and in 1874 the California State Legislature changed the town's name to Reading, in recognition of Pierson B. Reading, an early gold miner and rancher in the region. But the new "Reading" could not displace the original in the minds of the fledgling residents and when the town incorporated in 1887 it was "Redding."

Redding has aggressively developed recreational trails, including two that have received a National Recreation Trail designation. In September 2000 the city hosted the biannual National Trails Symposium and the National Trails Association has recently moved its headquarters to Redding.

The Walks:

The feature trail in Redding is the *Sacramento River Trail*, a 12-foot wide paved path that rolls along both sides of California's largest river, the lively Sacramento. You will encounter a steep uphill every now and then in the course of the nearly 10 miles of trail but overall this is easy canine hiking. The main loop runs from the Diestlehorst Bridge to the Ribbon Bridge and covers about six miles.

Also along the Sacramento River, running north out of town, is the *Sacramento River Rail Trail*. When the Southern Pacific Railroad opened this route in 1888 it was billed as "the road of a thousand wonders." A 500-foot long tunnel keeps the gravel trail moving on the gentle 1% grade of the old rail line for its entire 9-mile route. The cold waters of the adjoing Sacramento River can be swift so dogs without wetsuits should be careful.

There is more challenging hiking fare on the west side of the Sacramento River at the *Westside/ Mary Lake Trails* where elevations range from 750 feet to 1250 feet. The Westside Trails, Redding's only system of improved dirt trails, grind up invigorating slopes to sweeping views of the city. The cruise around Mary Lake is an easy stroll for a dog of less than one mile on a paved surface with plenty of places for a doggie dip along the way. There are dog scoop dispensers, trashcans and water fountains along the path.

Nearby is the *Blue Gravel Trail*, a paved 2.4-mile out-and-back affair that features a modest 200-foot elevation gain. This is where the City of Redding once operated a gold mine in Blue Gravel canyon, the only town in California ever to do so. Dogs are welcome here - the drinking fountain near the center of the trail features a dog bowl. Your dog will also enjoy the trees and bushes that provide a bit of shade during triple-digit summers. Across town, the privately developed *Lema Ranch Trail System* does not allow dogs.

The Sacramento River Trail is an ideal hike for studying bridge architecture. Classical arch bridges transport vehicular traffic across the Sacramento and the Diestlehorst Bridge is a prototypical 19th century pier-and-girder bridge. The Ribbon Bridge is the first of its kind in the nation - a 13-foot wide, 420-foot long concrete stess-ribbon structure. The Sundial Bridge at Turtle Bay is the first American project for the celebrated Spanish bridge architect, Santiago Calatrava. The focal point of his design is a 218-foot curved tower on the north bank of the river that doubles as support for the bridge's suspension cables and as the world's largest sundial. The bridge sports a glass decking that enhances the natural light and enables unobstructed views of the mountains at the horizon and the salmon at play below.

Sidetrip: Shasta Lake National Recreation Area (Shasta Dam Boulevard off I-5)

When construction began in 1938, the Shasta Dam was one of the most ambitious construction projects ever conceived. When completed in 1945, the water spilling over the Shasta Dam created the largest artificial waterfall ever seen - three times higher than the drop at Niagara Falls. Shasta Lake, fed by three rivers, is the largest lake in California.

The recreation area at Shasta Lake features more than 30 miles of paw-friendly dirt trails in three arms of the lake. Most are located in the McCloud Arm, including several less than one mile for canine hikers who like to bag many trails in an outing. The *Bailey Cove Trail* is a stand-out here as it loops for 2.9 miles around a peninsula in the lake. A longer scenic hike around a peninsula is the 7-mile *Clikapudi Trail*. This popular trail is shared with equestrians, joggers and mountain bikers.

Directions to Redding:

From the north or south, Redding is located directly on I-5. From the east or west, Routes 44 and 299 lead into the town.
Website: www.ci.redding.ca.us/

The waves can get frisky in Shasta Lake behind the mammoth Shasta Dam.

Steamboat Springs, Colorado

The Town:

James Crawford is the father of Steamboat Springs, having settled in a cabin on Soda Creek in 1874. Instead of becoming "Crawfordville," legend has it the town was named for the rhythmic chugging of a hot spring that disgorged mineral water 15 feet into the air. The medicinal springs brought the first settlers to the valley and later the town became an international ski jumping mecca with the arrival of Norwegian champion Carl Howelsen in 1913. Today outdoor enthusiasts don't wait for the snow to fall to make their way to Steamboat Springs.

The Walks:

In town, the *Yampa River Trail* system links Steamboat Springs with the surrounding mountain area. The trails provide easy dog walking along the Yampa River and through city parks. More than 150 hot springs gurgle around Steamboat Springs. The *Hot Springs Walking Tour* visits seven historic springs around town, including Heart Springs. The origin and history of each spring is detailed on interpretive signs. Look for the descriptive brochure in the Chamber Info Center (1255 South Lincoln/Highway 40).

To get out of town head for the *Spring Creek Trail*, an 8-mile round-trip that begins at the corner of Amethyst Drive and East Spring Street. The route is an easy canine hike on a well-graded trail that meanders up to the Spring Creek Reservoir and Dry Lake Campground.

Just north of town is Fish Creek Falls, a 283-foot plunging waterfall that is the town's leading visitor attraction. Canine hikers will know it as the starting point for the *Fish Creek National Recreation Trail*. Long wooded inclines at the beginning of the trail give way to a steep, rocky climb before leveling off in alpine meadows on the 5-mile journey to Long Lake. Continuing past Long Lake, you shortly reach the Continental Divide. The elevation gain on this out-and-back trail, Forest Service Trail #1102, rises from 7400 to more than 10,000 feet and and patches of snow in shady spots will delight your dog even in summer.

Directions to Steamboat Springs:

Steamboat Springs is located northwest of Denver, on US 40.

Phone: (970) 879-0880
Website: www.steamboat-chamber.com/

Your Dog At
The Beach...

DOGS ON ATLANTIC OCEAN BEACHES

MAINE

Maine is known for its rocky coastline, especially in the northern stretches, but the many coves offer small sandy beaches in places. Maine is in the middle-of the pack for dog-friendliness on its beaches. Dogs are not allowed on state beaches and you will have to wait until the off-season to take advantage of most of the town beaches.

Downeast/Acadia:

Bar Harbor	Acadia National Park	207-288-3338	NO DOGS ON SAND BEACH
Boothbay Harbor	Barrett Park	207-633-2353	LEASHED DOGS ALLOWED ON BEACH
	Grimes Cove Beach	207-633-2353	LEASHED DOGS ALLOWED ON BEACH
Castine	Back Shore Beach	207-326-4502	DOGS ALLOWED ON BEACH UNDER VOICE CONTROL OR ON A LEASH
Dennysville	Cobscook Bay State Park	207-726-4412	NO DOGS ON BEACH
Eastport	Shackford Head State Park	207-941-4014	NO DOGS ON BEACH
Lamoine	Lamoine Beach	207-667-2242	LEASHED DOGS ALLOWED ON BEACH
Lubec	Quoddy Head State Park	207-941-4014	DOGS ALLOWED ON CARRYING PLACE COVE BEACH OUTSIDE PARK
Rogue Bluffs	Rogue Bluffs State Park	207-255-3475	NO DOGS ALLOWED ON BEACH
Seal Harbor	Town Beach	207-276-5531	DOGS ALLOWED ON BEACH OCTOBER 15 TO MAY 15
Stockton Springs	Sandy Point Beach	207-567-3404	DOGS ALLOWED ON BEACH

Midcoast:

Brunswick	Thomas Point Beach	207-725-6009	DOGS ALLOWED ON THE BEACH EXCEPT DURING EVENTS
Georgetown	Reid State Park	207-371-2303	NO DOGS ALLOWED ON BEACH
Owls Head	Birch Point State Park	207-941-4014	NO DOGS ALLOWED ON BEACH
Phippsburg	Popham Beach State Park	207-389-1335	NO DOGS ALLOWED ON BEACH
	Town Beach	207-389-1835	DOGS ALLOWED ON BEACH
Richmond	Peacock Beach State Park	207-582-2813	NO DOGS ON BEACH

Greater Portland:

Cape Elizabeth	Crescent Beach State Park	207-799-5871	NO DOGS ON BEACH
Portland	East End Beach	207-874-8793	CAN BE UNDER VOICE CONTROL FROM DAY AFTER LABOR DAY TO DAY BEFORE MEMORIAL DAY; NO DOGS IN SUMMER

Scarborough	Ferry Beach State Park	207-283-0067	NO DOGS ON BEACH
	Higgins Beach	207-883-7778	*DOGS ALLOWED ON BEACH EXCEPT MID-DAY DURING THE SUMMER*
	Pine Point Beach	207-883-7778	*DOGS ALLOWED ON BEACH EXCEPT MID-DAY DURING THE SUMMER*
	Scarborough Beach State Park	207-883-2416	NO DOGS ON BEACH
	Western Beach	207-883-7778	*DOGS ALLOWED ON BEACH EXCEPT MID-DAY DURING THE SUMMER*
South Portland	Willard Beach	207-767-3201	*DOGS ALLOWED ON BEACH FROM OCTOBER THROUGH APRIL AND MAY THROUGH SEPTEMBER BETWEEN 6 AM AND 9 AM*

Southern Coast:

Biddeford	Beach Avenue	207-284-9307	*LEASHED DOGS ALLOWED ON BEACH EXCEPT DURING THE HOURS BETWEEN 9 AM AND 8 PM FROM MAY 25 TO SEPTEMBER 15*
	Biddeford Pool	207-284-9307	*LEASHED DOGS ALLOWED ON BEACH EXCEPT DURING THE HOURS BETWEEN 9 AM AND 8 PM FROM MAY 25 TO SEPTEMBER 15*
	Fortunes Rocks Beach	207-284-9307	*LEASHED DOGS ALLOWED ON BEACH EXCEPT DURING THE HOURS BETWEEN 9 AM AND 8 PM FROM MAY 25 TO SEPTEMBER 15*
	Hills Beach	207-284-9307	*LEASHED DOGS ALLOWED ON BEACH EXCEPT DURING THE HOURS BETWEEN 9 AM AND 8 PM FROM MAY 25 TO SEPTEMBER 15*
	Rotary Beach Park	207-284-9307	*LEASHED DOGS ALLOWED ON BEACH EXCEPT DURING THE HOURS BETWEEN 9 AM AND 8 PM FROM MAY 25 TO SEPTEMBER 15*
Kennebunk	Gooch's Beach	207-967-4243	*FROM THE DAY FOLLOWING LABOR DAY UNTIL JUNE 15 DOGS ALLOWED ANYTIME; OTHERWISE DOGS NOT ALLOWED ON BEACH BEWTEEN 9 AM AND 5 PM*
	Middle Beach	207-967-4243	*FROM THE DAY FOLLOWING LABOR DAY UNTIL JUNE 15 DOGS ALLOWED ANYTIME; OTHERWISE DOGS NOT ALLOWED ON BEACH BEWTEEN 9 AM AND 5 PM*
	Mother's Beach	207-967-4243	*FROM THE DAY FOLLOWING LABOR DAY UNTIL JUNE 15 DOGS ALLOWED ANYTIME; OTHERWISE DOGS NOT ALLOWED ON BEACH BEWTEEN 9 AM AND 5 PM*
	Parson's Beach	207-985-2102	*FROM THE DAY FOLLOWING LABOR DAY UNTIL JUNE 15 DOGS ALLOWED ANYTIME; OTHERWISE DOGS NOT ALLOWED ON BEACH BEWTEEN 9 AM AND 5 PM*
Kennebunkport	Arundel Beach	207-967-4243	*FROM THE DAY FOLLOWING LABOR DAY UNTIL JUNE 15 DOGS ALLOWED ANYTIME; OTHERWISE DOGS NOT ALLOWED ON BEACH BEWTEEN 9 AM AND 5 PM*
	Cleaves Cove Beach	207-967-4243	*FROM THE DAY FOLLOWING LABOR DAY UNTIL JUNE 15 DOGS ALLOWED ANYTIME; OTHERWISE DOGS NOT ALLOWED ON BEACH BEWTEEN 9 AM AND 5 PM*

Kennebunkport	Colony Beach	207-967-4243	*FROM THE DAY FOLLOWING LABOR DAY UNTIL JUNE 15 DOGS ALLOWED ANYTIME; OTHERWISE DOGS NOT ALLOWED ON BEACH BEWTEEN 9 AM AND 5 PM*
	Goose Rocks Beach	207-967-4243	*FROM THE DAY FOLLOWING LABOR DAY UNTIL JUNE 15 DOGS ALLOWED ANYTIME; OTHERWISE DOGS NOT ALLOWED ON BEACH BEWTEEN 9 AM AND 5 PM*
Kittery	Fort Foster Park	207-439-0452	*DOGS ALLOWED ON BEACH*
	Seapoint Beach	207-439-0452	*DOGS ALLOWED BEFORE 10 AM AND AFTER 5 PM*
Ogunquit	Foot Bridge Beach	207-646-5139	*NO DOGS MAY 1 TO OCTOBER 15*
	Moody Beach	207-646-5139	*NO DOGS MAY 1 TO OCTOBER 15*
	Ogunquit Beach	207-646-5139	*NO DOGS MAY 1 TO OCTOBER 15*
Old Orchard Beach	Town Beach	207-934-2500	*DOGS ARE ALLOWED ON THE BEACH ANYTIME EXCEPT MEMORIAL DAY TO LABOR DAY FROM 10 AM TO 5 PM*
Saco	Bayview Beach	207-284-4831	*LEASHED DOGS ALLOWED ON BEACH*
Wells	Drakes Island Beach	207-646-5113	*FROM 6/16 TO 9/15 NO DOGS ALLOWED ON BEACH FROM 8 AM TO 6 PM; BEFORE 8 AM AND AFTER 6 PM UNDER CHARGE OF RESPONSIBLE PERSON; ANYTIME FROM 9/16 TO 6/15*
	Wells Beach	207-646-5113	*FROM 6/16 TO 9/15 NO DOGS ALLOWED ON BEACH FROM 8 AM TO 6 PM; BEFORE 8 AM AND AFTER 6 PM UNDER CHARGE OF RESPONSIBLE PERSON; ANYTIME FROM 9/16 TO 6/15*

Coves along the Maine coast create sandy beaches ideal for dogs like this one in York.

York	Cape Neddick Beach	207-363-1000	*YES! DOGS ALLOWED ON BEACH*
	Harbor Beach	207-363-1000	*IN SUMMER NO DOGS ALLOWED ON BEACH FROM 8 AM TO 6 PM; ANYTIME OFF-SEASON*
	Long Sands Beach	207-363-1000	*IN SUMMER NO DOGS ALLOWED ON BEACH FROM 8 AM TO 6 PM; ANYTIME OFF-SEASON*
	Short Sands Beach	207-363-1000	*IN SUMMER NO DOGS ALLOWED ON BEACH FROM 8 AM TO 6 PM; ANYTIME OFF-SEASON*

NEW HAMPSHIRE

If you are taking the dog to New Hampshire, head for the mountains. The Granite State does not give dog owners much reason to stop when driving along its 18 miles of Atlantic Ocean shoreline.

Hampton	Hampton Beach	603-926-8718	NO DOGS ALLOWED ON BEACH
	Hampton Beach State Park	603-926-3784	NO DOGS ALLOWED ON BEACH
	North Beach	603-926-8718	NO DOGS ALLOWED ON BEACH
New Castle	Grand Island Common	603-431-6710	*NO DOGS ON BEACH FROM MAY 15 TO SEPTEMBER 15*
North Hampton	North Hampton State Beach	603-436-1552	NO DOGS ALLOWED ON BEACH
Rye	Foss Beach	603-964-6281	*DOGS ALLOWED ON BEACH FROM OCTOBER 1 TO THE SATURDAY BEFORE MEMORIAL DAY AND BEFORE 8 AM AND AFTER 6 PM OTHERWISE*
	Jenness State Beach	603-436-1552	NO DOGS ALLOWED ON BEACH
	Wallis Sands State Beach	603-436-9404	NO DOGS ALLOWED ON BEACH
Seabrook	Seabrook Beach	603-474-3871	NO DOGS ALLOWED ON BEACH

MASSACHUSETTS

Massachusetts is the best northeastern state to take the dog to the beach in summer. The resort islands are particularly dog-friendly and several spots on Cape Cod will permit dogs in non-swimming areas. The beaches around Boston are generally restrictive until the off-season.

North Shore:

Beverly	Brackenberry Beach	978-921-6067	*NO DOGS ON BEACH MEMORIAL DAY TO LABOR DAY*
	Dane Street Beach	978-921-6067	*NO DOGS ON BEACH MEMORIAL DAY TO LABOR DAY*
	Independence Park	978-921-6067	*NO DOGS ON BEACH MEMORIAL DAY TO LABOR DAY*
	Lynch Park Beach	978-921-6067	*NO DOGS ON BEACH MEMORIAL DAY TO LABOR DAY*
	Pleasant View Beach	978-921-6067	*NO DOGS ON BEACH MEMORIAL DAY TO LABOR DAY*
	Woodbury Beach	978-921-6067	*NO DOGS ON BEACH MEMORIAL DAY TO LABOR DAY*
Danvers	Sandy Beach	978-777-0001	*LEASHED DOGS ALLOWED ON BEACH*

Gloucester	Cressey's Beach	800-649-6839	*NO DOGS ON BEACH MEMORIAL DAY TO LABOR DAY*
	Good Harbor Beach	800-649-6839	*NO DOGS ON BEACH MEMORIAL DAY TO LABOR DAY*
	Half Moon Beach	800-649-6839	*NO DOGS ON BEACH MEMORIAL DAY TO LABOR DAY*
	Niles Beach	800-649-6839	*NO DOGS ON BEACH MEMORIAL DAY TO LABOR DAY*
	Stage Fort Beach	800-649-6839	*NO DOGS ON BEACH MEMORIAL DAY TO LABOR DAY*
	Wingaersheek Beach	800-649-6839	*NO DOGS ON BEACH MEMORIAL DAY TO LABOR DAY*
Ipswich	Crane Beach	978-356-4351	*NO DOGS ON BEACH IN SUMMER AND NEVER IN DUNES*
Lynn	Lynn Beach	781-598-4000	*NO DOGS ON BEACH MEMORIAL DAY TO LABOR DAY*
	Lynn Shores Reservation	617-727-1397	*NO DOGS ON BEACH IN SWIMMING AREAS*
	Pavilion Beach	781-598-4000	*NO DOGS ON BEACH MEMORIAL DAY TO LABOR DAY*
Manchester	Black & White Beaches	978-526-2000	*NO DOGS ON BEACH MAY 1 TO OCTOBER 1*
	Singing Beach	978-526-2000	*NO DOGS ON BEACH MAY 1 TO OCTOBER 1*
Marblehead	Devereux Beach	781-631-0000	*NO DOGS ON BEACH MAY TO SEPTEMBER*
	Grace Oliver Beach	781-631-0000	*NO DOGS ON BEACH MAY TO SEPTEMBER*
Nahant	Forty Steps Beach	617-581-0018	*NO DOGS ON BEACH MAY TO OCTOBER*
	Long Beach	617-581-0018	*NO DOGS ON BEACH MAY TO OCTOBER*
	Short Beach	617-581-0018	*NO DOGS ON BEACH MAY TO OCTOBER*
	Tudor Beach	617-581-0018	*NO DOGS ON BEACH MAY TO OCTOBER*
Newburyport	Plum Island Beach	978-465-5753	*NO DOGS ON BEACH APRIL 1 TO OCTOBER*
Revere	Revere Beach	617-727-8856	NO DOGS ON BEACH
Rockport	Back and Front Beaches	978-546-6894	*NO DOGS ON BEACH JUNE 1 TO SEPTEMBER 15*
	Cape Hedge	978-546-6894	*NO DOGS ON BEACH JUNE 1 TO SEPTEMBER 15*
	Halibut Point	978-546-6894	*DOGS ALLOWED ON BEACH*
	Old Garden Beach	978-546-6894	*NO DOGS ON BEACH JUNE 1 TO SEPTEMBER 15*
	Pebble Beach	978-546-6894	*NO DOGS ON BEACH JUNE 1 TO SEPTEMBER 15*
Salem	Collins Cove	978-745-0241	*LEASHED DOGS ALLOWED ON BEACH*
	Willows Beach	978-745-0241	*LEASHED DOGS ALLOWED ON BEACH*
	Winter Island	978-745-0241	NO DOGS ON BEACH
Salisbury	Salisbury State Reservation	978-462-4481	*DOGS ALLOWED ON BEACH FROM THE DAY AFTER COLUMBUS DAY TO THE DAY BEFORE PATRIOT'S DAY*
	Salisbury Town Beach	978-465-3581	*NO DOGS ALLOWED ON BEACH IN SUMMER*

Swampscott	Fishermen's Beach	781-596-8854	*DOGS ALLOWED ON BEACH OCTOBER 1 TO MAY 20*
	King's Beach	781-596-8854	*DOGS ALLOWED ON BEACH OCTOBER 1 TO MAY 20*
	Phillips Beach	781-596-8854	*DOGS ALLOWED ON BEACH OCTOBER 1 TO MAY 20*
	Preston Beach	781-596-8854	*DOGS ALLOWED ON BEACH OCTOBER 1 TO MAY 20*
	Whale's Beach	781-596-8854	*DOGS ALLOWED ON BEACH OCTOBER 1 TO MAY 20*

South Shore:

Boston Harbor Islands National Park		617-223-8666	NO DOGS ALLOWED ON BEACH
Boston	Dorchester Shores Reservation	617-727-6034	NO DOGS ON BEACH IN SWIMMING AREA
Hull	Nantasket Beach Reservation	617-727-8856	NO DOGS ON BEACH IN SWIMMING AREA
Plymouth	Duxbury Beach	508-830-4095	*LEASHED DOGS ALLOWED ON BEACH*
	Nelson Beach	508-830-4095	*LEASHED DOGS ALLOWED ON BEACH*
	Plymouth's Long Beach	508-830-4095	*LEASHED DOGS ALLOWED ON BEACH*
Quincy	Quincy Shore Reservation	617-727-5293	NO DOGS ON BEACH IN SWIMMING AREA
Scituate	Egypt Beach	781-545-8704	*NO DOGS ON BEACH 10 AM TO 6 PM FROM JUNE 15 TO SEPTEMBER 15*
	Humarock Beach	781-545-8704	*NO DOGS ON BEACH 10 AM TO 6 PM FROM JUNE 15 TO SEPTEMBER 15*
	Minot Beach	781-545-8704	*NO DOGS ON BEACH 10 AM TO 6 PM FROM JUNE 15 TO SEPTEMBER 15*
	Peggotty Beach	781-545-8704	*NO DOGS ON BEACH 10 AM TO 6 PM FROM JUNE 15 TO SEPTEMBER 15*
	Sand Hills Beach	781-545-8704	*NO DOGS ON BEACH 10 AM TO 6 PM FROM JUNE 15 TO SEPTEMBER 15*

Cape Cod:

Cape Cod National Seashore		508-487-1256	*DOGS ALLOWED ON BEACH ANYTIME BUT NOT IN LIFEGUARDED SWIMMING AREAS, NATURE TRAILS, HIKING TRAILS OR BIRD NESTING AREAS*
Barnstable	Craigville Beach	877-492-6647	*DOGS ALLOWED ON BEACH SEPTEMBER 15 TO MAY 15*
	Kalmus Park Beach	877-492-6647	*DOGS ALLOWED ON BEACH SEPTEMBER 15 TO MAY 15*
	Orrin Keyes Beach	877-492-6647	*DOGS ALLOWED ON BEACH SEPTEMBER 15 TO MAY 15*
	Sandy Neck Beach	877-492-6647	*DOGS ALLOWED ON BEACH SEPTEMBER 15 TO MAY 15*
	Veterans Beach	877-492-6647	*DOGS ALLOWED ON BEACH SEPTEMBER 15 TO MAY 15*
Bourne	Monument Beach	508-759-6000	NO DOGS ALLOWED ON BEACH
Brewster	Breakwater Beach	508-896-3500	*DOGS ALLOWED ON BEACH OCTOBER 1 TO MEMORIAL DAY*
	Paine's Creek Beach	508-896-3500	*DOGS ALLOWED ON BEACH OCTOBER 1 TO MEMORIAL DAY*
	Robbins Hill Beach	508-896-3500	*DOGS ALLOWED ON BEACH OCTOBER 1 TO MEMORIAL DAY*

Chatham	Cockle Cove Beach	508-945-5199	*DOGS ALLOWED ON THE BEACH SEPTEMBER 16 TO MAY 14*
	Forest Beach	508-945-5199	*DOGS ALLOWED ON THE BEACH SEPTEMBER 16 TO MAY 14*
	Hardings Beach	508-945-5199	*DOGS ALLOWED ON THE BEACH SEPTEMBER 16 TO MAY 14*
	Ridgevale Beach	508-945-5199	*DOGS ALLOWED ON THE BEACH SEPTEMBER 16 TO MAY 14*
Dennis	Chapin Memorial Beach	508-394-8300	*DOGS ALLOWED ON BEACH LABOR DAY TO MEMORIAL DAY*
	Corporation Road Beach	508-394-8300	*DOGS ALLOWED ON BEACH LABOR DAY TO MEMORIAL DAY*
	Glendon Road Beach	508-394-8300	*DOGS ALLOWED ON BEACH LABOR DAY TO MEMORIAL DAY*
	Haigis Beach	508-394-8300	*DOGS ALLOWED ON BEACH LABOR DAY TO MEMORIAL DAY*
	Horsefoot Path Beach	508-394-8300	*DOGS ALLOWED ON BEACH LABOR DAY TO MEMORIAL DAY*
	Howes Street Beach	508-394-8300	*DOGS ALLOWED ON BEACH LABOR DAY TO MEMORIAL DAY*
	Inman Road Beach	508-394-8300	*DOGS ALLOWED ON BEACH LABOR DAY TO MEMORIAL DAY*
	Mayflower Beach	508-394-8300	*DOGS ALLOWED ON BEACH LABOR DAY TO MEMORIAL DAY*
	Raycroft Parking Beach	508-394-8300	*DOGS ALLOWED ON BEACH LABOR DAY TO MEMORIAL DAY*
	Sea Street Beach	508-394-8300	*DOGS ALLOWED ON BEACH LABOR DAY TO MEMORIAL DAY*
	South Village Road Beach	508-394-8300	*DOGS ALLOWED ON BEACH LABOR DAY TO MEMORIAL DAY*
	West Dennis Beach	508-394-8300	*DOGS ALLOWED ON BEACH LABOR DAY TO MEMORIAL DAY*
Eastham	Campground Beach	508-240-7211	*DOGS ALLOWED ON BEACH LABOR DAY TO FLAG DAY*
	Coast Guard Beach	508-240-7211	*DOGS ALLOWED ON BEACH LABOR DAY TO FLAG DAY*
	Cooks Brook Beach	508-240-7211	*DOGS ALLOWED ON BEACH LABOR DAY TO FLAG DAY*
	First Encounter Beach	508-240-7211	*DOGS ALLOWED ON BEACH LABOR DAY TO FLAG DAY*
	Nauset Light Beach	508-240-7211	*DOGS ALLOWED ON BEACH LABOR DAY TO FLAG DAY*
	Sunken Meadow Beach	508-240-7211	*DOGS ALLOWED ON BEACH LABOR DAY TO FLAG DAY*
	Thumpertown Beach	508-240-7211	*DOGS ALLOWED ON BEACH LABOR DAY TO FLAG DAY*
Falmouth	Bristol Beach	800-526-8532	*DOGS ALLOWED ON BEACH ALL YEAR EXCEPT DURING "BEACH HOURS"*
	Chapoquoit Beach	800-526-8532	*DOGS ALLOWED ON BEACH ALL YEAR EXCEPT DURING "BEACH HOURS"*
	Falmouth Heights Beach	800-526-8532	*DOGS ALLOWED ON BEACH ALL YEAR EXCEPT DURING "BEACH HOURS"*
	Megansett Beach	800-526-8532	*DOGS ALLOWED ON BEACH ALL YEAR EXCEPT DURING "BEACH HOURS"*
	Menauhant Beach	800-526-8532	*DOGS ALLOWED ON BEACH ALL YEAR EXCEPT DURING "BEACH HOURS"*
	Old Silver Beach	800-526-8532	*DOGS ALLOWED ON BEACH ALL YEAR EXCEPT DURING "BEACH HOURS"*
	Stoney Beach	800-526-8532	*DOGS ALLOWED ON BEACH ALL YEAR EXCEPT DURING "BEACH HOURS"*

Falmouth	Surf Drive Beach	800-526-8532	*DOGS ALLOWED ON BEACH ALL YEAR EXCEPT DURING "BEACH HOURS"*
	Trunk River Beach	800-526-8532	*DOGS ALLOWED ON BEACH ALL YEAR EXCEPT DURING "BEACH HOURS"*
	Wood Heck Beach	800-526-8532	*DOGS ALLOWED ON BEACH ALL YEAR EXCEPT DURING "BEACH HOURS"*
Harwich	Bank Street Beach	800-442-7942	*DOGS ALLOWED ON BEACH OCTOBER 1 TO MAY 14*
	Jenkins Beach	800-442-7942	*DOGS ALLOWED ON BEACH OCTOBER 1 TO MAY 14*
	Merkle Beach	800-442-7942	*DOGS ALLOWED ON BEACH OCTOBER 1 TO MAY 14*
	Pleasant Road Beach	800-442-7942	*DOGS ALLOWED ON BEACH OCTOBER 1 TO MAY 14*
	Red River Beach	800-442-7942	*DOGS ALLOWED ON BEACH OCTOBER 1 TO MAY 14*
Mashpee	South Cape Beach	508-477-0792	NO DOGS ALLOWED ON BEACH
Orleans	Nauset Beach	800-865-1386	*DOGS ALLOWED ON BEACH LABOR DAY TO MEMORIAL DAY*
	Pleasant Bay Beach	800-865-1386	*DOGS ALLOWED ON BEACH LABOR DAY TO MEMORIAL DAY*
	Rock Harbor Beach	800-865-1386	*DOGS ALLOWED ON BEACH LABOR DAY TO MEMORIAL DAY*
	Skaket Beach	800-865-1386	*DOGS ALLOWED ON BEACH LABOR DAY TO MEMORIAL DAY*
Provincetown	Herring Cove	508-487-3424	*DOGS ALLOWED ON BEACH EXCEPT IN SWIMMING AREAS*
	Race Point	508-487-3424	*DOGS ALLOWED ON BEACH EXCEPT IN SWIMMING AREAS*
	Town Beach	508-487-3424	*DOGS ALLOWED ON BEACH EXCEPT IN SWIMMING AREAS*
Sandwich	East Sandwich Beach	508-759-6000	*YES! DOGS ALLOWED ON BEACH*
	Scusset Beach	508-759-6000	*YES! DOGS ALLOWED ON BEACH*
	Town Neck Beach	508-759-6000	*YES! DOGS ALLOWED ON BEACH*
Truro	Ballston Beach	508-487-1288	*DOGS ALLOWED ON BEACH ALL YEAR EXCEPT JULY AND AUGUST BETWEEN 9 AM AND 5 PM*
	Coast Guard Beach	508-487-1288	*DOGS ALLOWED ON BEACH ALL YEAR EXCEPT JULY AND AUGUST BETWEEN 9 AM AND 5 PM*
	Corn Hill Beach	508-487-1288	*DOGS ALLOWED ON BEACH ALL YEAR EXCEPT JULY AND AUGUST BETWEEN 9 AM AND 5 PM*
	Fisher Beach	508-487-1288	*DOGS ALLOWED ON BEACH ALL YEAR EXCEPT JULY AND AUGUST BETWEEN 9 AM AND 5 PM*
	Great Hollow Beach	508-487-1288	*DOGS ALLOWED ON BEACH ALL YEAR EXCEPT JULY AND AUGUST BETWEEN 9 AM AND 5 PM*
	Head of Meadow Beach	508-487-1288	*DOGS ALLOWED ON BEACH ALL YEAR EXCEPT JULY AND AUGUST BETWEEN 9 AM AND 5 PM*
	Longnook Beach	508-487-1288	*DOGS ALLOWED ON BEACH ALL YEAR EXCEPT JULY AND AUGUST BETWEEN 9 AM AND 5 PM*
	Ryder Beach	508-487-1288	*DOGS ALLOWED ON BEACH ALL YEAR EXCEPT JULY AND AUGUST BETWEEN 9 AM AND 5 PM*

Wareham	Briarwood Beach	508-291-3140	*LEASHED DOGS ALLOWED ON BEACH BETWEEN 5:01 PM and 7:59 AM*
	Hamilton Beach	508-291-3140	*LEASHED DOGS ALLOWED ON BEACH BETWEEN 5:01 PM and 7:59 AM*
	Little Harbor Beach	508-291-3140	*LEASHED DOGS ALLOWED ON BEACH BETWEEN 5:01 PM and 7:59 AM*
	Long Beach	508-291-3140	*LEASHED DOGS ALLOWED ON BEACH BETWEEN 5:01 PM and 7:59 AM*
	Parkwood Beach	508-291-3140	*LEASHED DOGS ALLOWED ON BEACH BETWEEN 5:01 PM and 7:59 AM*
	Pinehurst Beach	508-291-3140	*LEASHED DOGS ALLOWED ON BEACH BETWEEN 5:01 PM and 7:59 AM*
	Swifts Beach	508-291-3140	*LEASHED DOGS ALLOWED ON BEACH BETWEEN 5:01 PM and 7:59 AM*
Wellfleet	Cahoon Hollow Beach	508-349-9818	*DOGS ALLOWED ON BEACH BEFORE 9 AM AND AFTER 5 PM FROM SATURDAY PRIOR TO JULY 1 THROUGH LABOR DAY AND ANYTIME OTHERWISE; KEEP DOGS AWAY FROM BATHERS*
	Marconi Beach	508-349-9818	*DOGS ALLOWED ON BEACH OUTSIDE SWIMMING AREAS*
	White Crest Beach	508-349-9818	*DOGS ALLOWED ON BEACH BEFORE 9 AM AND AFTER 5 PM FROM SATURDAY PRIOR TO JULY 1 THROUGH LABOR DAY AND ANYTIME OTHERWISE; KEEP DOGS AWAY FROM BATHERS*
Yarmouth	Bass Hole Beach	508-398-2231	NO DOGS ALLOWED ON BEACH
	Bay View Beach	508-398-2231	NO DOGS ALLOWED ON BEACH
	Eagle View Beach	508-398-2231	NO DOGS ALLOWED ON BEACH
	Parkers River Beach	508-398-2231	NO DOGS ALLOWED ON BEACH
	Seagull Beach	508-398-2231	NO DOGS ALLOWED ON BEACH
	Seaview Beach	508-398-2231	NO DOGS ALLOWED ON BEACH
The Islands:	Windmill Beach	508-398-2231	NO DOGS ALLOWED ON BEACH

Martha's Vineyard

Aquinnah	Lobsterstown Beach	508-645-2300	NO DOGS ALLOWED ON BEACH
	Moshup (Gay Head) Beach	508-645-2300	NO DOGS ALLOWED ON BEACH
	Philbin Beach	508-645-2300	NO DOGS ALLOWED ON BEACH
Edgartown	East Beach	508-627-1000	*DOGS ALLOWED ON BEACH IN OFF-SEASON*
	Katama Beach	508-627-1000	*DOGS ALLOWED ON BEACH IN OFF-SEASON*
	Norton Point Beach	508-627-1000	*DOGS ARE ALLOWED ON BEACH AT ALL TIMES EXCEPT BETWEEN MAY 15 AND SEPTEMBER 15 FROM THE HOURS OF 8 AM TO 6 PM; MUST ALSO KEEP DOGS 100 YARDS FROM POSTED BIRD NESTING AREAS*
	Lighthouse Beach	508-627-1000	*DOGS ALLOWED ON BEACH IN OFF-SEASON*
	South Beach	508-627-1000	*DOGS ALLOWED ON BEACH IN OFF-SEASON*
Menemsha	Menemsha Public Beach	508-693-0085	*DOGS ALLOWED ON BEACH IN OFF-SEASON*

Oak Bluffs	Eastville Point Beach	508-693-5511	DOGS ARE ALLOWED ON BEACH AT ALL TIMES EXCEPT BETWEEN MAY 15 AND SEPTEMBER 15 FROM THE HOURS OF 8 AM TO 6 PM; MUST ALSO KEEP DOGS 100 YARDS FROM POSTED BIRD NESTING AREAS
	Joseph Sylvia Sate Beach	508-693-5511	DOGS ARE ALLOWED ON BEACH AT ALL TIMES EXCEPT BETWEEN MAY 15 AND SEPTEMBER 15 FROM THE HOURS OF 8 AM TO 6 PM; MUST ALSO KEEP DOGS 100 YARDS FROM POSTED BIRD NESTING AREAS
	Town Beach	508-693-5511	DOGS ARE ALLOWED ON BEACH AT ALL TIMES EXCEPT BETWEEN MAY 15 AND SEPTEMBER 15 FROM THE HOURS OF 8 AM TO 6 PM; MUST ALSO KEEP DOGS 100 YARDS FROM POSTED BIRD NESTING AREAS
Vineyard Haven	Owen Park Beach	508-696-4200	DOGS ALLOWED ON BEACH IN OFF-SEASON
Nantucket Island			
	Brandt Point Beach	508-228-1700	NANTUCKET IS A VERY DOG-FRIENDLY ISLAND; GENERALLY DOGS NOT ALLOWED IN SWIMMING AREAS OF THE BEACHES AND HOURS ARE RESTRICTED DURING MID-DAY IN THE BUSY SUMMER SEASON; DOGS ARE ALSO WELCOME ON THE SHUTTLE BUSES TO BEACHES
	Children's Beach	508-228-1700	
	Cisco Beach	508-228-1700	
	Dionis Beach	508-228-1700	
	Francis Street Beach	508-228-1700	
	Jetties Beach	508-228-1700	
	Madaket Beach	508-228-1700	
	Miacomet Beach	508-228-1700	
	Siasconet Beach	508-228-1700	
	Surfside Beach	508-228-1700	

South Coast:

Dartmouth	Apponagansett Beach	508-910-1812	NO DOGS ALLOWED ON THE BEACH
	Demarest Lloyd State Park	508-636-8816	NO DOGS ALLOWED ON THE BEACH
	Jones Park	508-910-1812	NO DOGS ALLOWED ON THE BEACH
	Round Hill	508-910-1812	RESIDENTS ONLY BEACH
Fairhaven	Fort Phoenix State Reservation	508-992-4524	DOGS NOT ALLOWED IN THE SWIMMING AREAS
	West Island Town Beach	508-979-4025	DOGS ALLOWED ON BEACH
Marion	Silver Shell Beach	508-748-3502	NO DOGS ALLOWED ON THE BEACH
Mattapoisett	Town Beach (Aucott Road)	508-758-4103	DOGS ALLOWED ON THE BEACH
	Town Beach (Water Street)	508-758-4103	DOGS ALLOWED ON THE BEACH
New Bedford	East Beach	508-979-1450	NO DOGS ALLOWED ON BEACH
	West Beach	508-979-1450	NO DOGS ALLOWED ON BEACH
Westport	Cherry & Webb Beach	508-616-1000	DOGS ALLOWED ON BEACH FROM NOVEMBER 1 TO APRIL 1
	East Beach	508-616-1000	DOGS ALLOWED ON BEACH FROM NOVEMBER 1 TO APRIL 1
	Horseneck Beach State Reservation		NO DOGS ALLOWED IN THE SWIMMING AREAS

RHODE ISLAND

On most beaches in the Ocean State you will have to wait for the off-season to get the dog on the sand. If you are in Rhode Island in the summer, get out to Block Island where dogs are welcome on the beach all year-round.

Block Island	All beaches	401-466-2474	*LEASHED DOGS ALLOWED THROUGHOUT THE YEAR*
Charlestown	East Beach	401-322-8910	NO DOGS ALLOWED ON THE BEACH
Middletown	Navy Beach	401-847-5511	*DOGS ALLOWED ON BEACH FROM LABOR DAY TO MEMORIAL DAY*
	Sachusest Beach (Second Beach)	401-847-5511	*DOGS ALLOWED ON BEACH FROM LABOR DAY TO MEMORIAL DAY*
Narrangansett	Roger Wheeler State Beach	401-789-8374	*DOGS ALLOWED ON BEACH FROM OCTOBER 1 TO MARCH 31*
	Salty Brine State Beach	401-789-8374	*DOGS ALLOWED ON BEACH FROM OCTOBER 1 TO MARCH 31*
Newport	Bailey's Beach	401-846-9600	*DOGS ALLOWED ON BEACH FROM LABOR DAY TO MEMORIAL DAY*
	Easton's Beach (First Beach)	401-846-9600	*DOGS ALLOWED ON BEACH FROM LABOR DAY TO MEMORIAL DAY*
	Gooseberry Beach	401-846-9600	*DOGS ALLOWED ON BEACH FROM LABOR DAY TO MEMORIAL DAY*
Scarborough	North Beach	401-789-2324	NO DOGS ALLOWED ON BEACH
	South Beach	401-782-1319	NO DOGS ALLOWED ON BEACH
South Kingston	East Matunick State Beach	401-789-8374	*DOGS ALLOWED ON BEACH FROM OCTOBER 1 TO MARCH 31*
Westerly	Misquamicut State Beach	401-322-8910	*DOGS ALLOWED ON BEACH FROM OCTOBER 1 TO MARCH 31*

Active dogs are never at a loss for things to do at the beach.

CONNECTICUT

The sandy beaches of the Nutmeg State on Long Island Sound are not known for being dog-friendly. But many aren't that friendly to people either, with restricted access being common.

Clinton	Town Beach	203-669-6901	NO DOGS ALLOWED ON BEACH
East Haven	Town Beach	203-468-3367	*DOGS ALLOWED ON BEACH FROM LABOR DAY TO MEMORIAL DAY*
East Lyme	Rocky Neck State Park	860-739-5471	DOGS NOT ALLOWED ON BEACH BUT ARE ALLOWED ON TRAILS
Fairfield	Jennings Beach	203-256-3000	*DOGS ALLOWED ON BEACH FROM OCTOBER 1 TO APRIL 1*
	Penfield Beach	203-256-3000	*DOGS ALLOWED ON BEACH FROM OCTOBER 1 TO APRIL 1*
	Richards Beach	203-256-3000	*DOGS ALLOWED ON BEACH FROM OCTOBER 1 TO APRIL 1*
	Sasco Beach	203-256-3000	*DOGS ALLOWED ON BEACH FROM OCTOBER 1 TO APRIL 1*
	Southport Beach	203-256-3000	*DOGS ALLOWED ON BEACH FROM OCTOBER 1 TO APRIL 1*
Groton	Bluff Point Park	860-536-5680	*DOGS ALLOWED ON BEACH*
	Esker Point Beach	860-536-5680	*DOGS ALLOWED ON BEACH EXCEPT DURING NIGHTS WITH CONCERTS*
	Main Street Beach	860-536-5680	*DOGS ALLOWED ON BEACH*
Madison	East Wharf Beach	203-245-5623	NO DOGS ALLOWED ON BEACH
	Hammonasset Beach State Park	203-245-1817	NO DOGS ALLOWED ON BEACH; GRASSY FIELDS ONLY
	Surf Club Beach	203-245-5623	NO DOGS ALLOWED ON BEACH
	West Wharf Beach	203-245-5623	NO DOGS ALLOWED ON BEACH
Milford	Gulf Beach	203-783-3201	NO DOGS ALLOWED ON BEACH
	Silver Sands State Beach	203-735-4311	NO DOGS ALLOWED ON BEACH
	Walnut Beach	203-783-3201	NO DOGS ALLOWED ON BEACH
New Haven	Lighthouse Point Park	203-946-8790	NO DOGS ALLOWED ON BEACH BUT ARE PERMITTED IN GRASSY AREAS
New London	Ocean Beach Park	800-510-7263	NO DOGS ALLOWED ON BEACH
Old Lyme	Sound View Beach	860-434-1605	NO DOGS ALLOWED ON BEACH
Old Saybrook	Harvey's Beach	860-395-3123	NO DOGS ALLOWED ON BEACH
	Town Beach	860-395-3123	NO DOGS ALLOWED ON BEACH
Stamford	Cove Island Park	203-977-4054	*LEASHED DOGS ALLOWED ON BEACH*
	Cummings Park	203-977-4054	*LEASHED DOGS ALLOWED ON BEACH*
Stonington	Dubois Beach	860-535-5060	NO DOGS ALLOWED ON BEACH
Stratford	Long Beach	203-385-4020	NO DOGS ALLOWED ON BEACH
	Russian Beach	203-385-4020	NO DOGS ALLOWED ON BEACH
	Short Beach Park	203-385-4020	NO DOGS ALLOWED ON BEACH

West Haven	Altschuler Beach	203-937-3651	NO DOGS ALLOWED ON BEACH
	Bradley Point Park	203-937-3651	NO DOGS ALLOWED ON BEACH
	Dawson Beach	203-937-3651	NO DOGS ALLOWED ON BEACH
	Morse Beach	203-937-3651	NO DOGS ALLOWED ON BEACH
	Oak Street Beach	203-937-3651	NO DOGS ALLOWED ON BEACH
	Peck Beach	203-937-3651	NO DOGS ALLOWED ON BEACH
	Seabluff Beach	203-937-3651	NO DOGS ALLOWED ON BEACH
Westport	Burying Hill Beach	203-341-1038	*DOGS ALLOWED ON BEACH NOVEMBER 1 TO APRIL 30*
	Canal Beach	203-341-1038	*DOGS ALLOWED ON BEACH NOVEMBER 1 TO APRIL 30*
	Compo Beach	203-341-1038	*DOGS ALLOWED ON BEACH NOVEMBER 1 TO APRIL 30*
	Old Mill Beach	203-341-1038	*DOGS ALLOWED ON BEACH NOVEMBER 1 TO APRIL 30*
	Sherwood Island State Park	203-226-6983	*LEASHED DOGS ALLOWED IN PARK OCTOBER 1 TO APRIL 14*

NEW YORK

The further east you go out on Long Island the more dog-friendly New York becomes but whether on the north shore or south shore you can find a place to get the dog to the sea.

Nassau County - North Shore:

Bayville	Creek Beach	516-628-1439	BEACH FOR RESIDENTS ONLY
Port Washington	Bar Beach Park	516-883-6566	NO DOGS ALLOWED ON BEACH
	Hempstead Harbor Beach Park	516-766-1029	NO DOGS ALLOWED ON BEACH
	Manorhaven Beach Park	516-883-6566	NO DOGS ALLOWED ON BEACH

Nassau County - South Shore:

| Lido | Nassau Beach Park | 516-571-7700 | *DOGS ALLOWED ON BEACH EXCEPT WHEN BIRDS ARE NESTING* |
| Wantaugh | Wantaugh | 516-785-1600 | NO DOGS ALLOWED ON BEACH |

Suffolk County - North Shore:

Centerport	Centerport Beach	516-754-9537	NO DOGS ALLOWED ON BEACH
	Fleets Cove Beach	516-351-9481	NO DOGS ALLOWED ON BEACH
	Seniors Beach (seniors only)	516-754-9537	NO DOGS ALLOWED ON BEACH
Eatons Neck	Asharoken Beach	631-261-7574	NO DOGS ALLOWED ON BEACH
Huntington	Crescent Beach	516-423-0014	NO DOGS ALLOWED ON BEACH
	Gold Star Battalion Beach	516-351-9289	NO DOGS ALLOWED ON BEACH
	West Neck Beach	516-351-9565	NO DOGS ALLOWED ON BEACH
Kings Park	Sunken Meadow State Park	631-269-4333	NO DOGS ALLOWED ON BEACH
Lloyd Harbor	Caumesett State Park	516-423-1770	NO DOGS ALLOWED ON BEACH

Suffolk County - Eastern Forks:

Amagansett	Alberts Landing Beach	631-324-4143	LOCAL RESIDENTS ONLY IN SEASON
	Atlantic Avenue Beach	631-324-4143	*DOGS ALLOWED ON BEACH IN OFF SEASON*
	Indian Wells Beach	631-324-4143	LOCAL RESIDENTS ONLY IN SEASON
Bridgehampton	Mecox Beach	631-283-6011	LOCAL RESIDENTS ONLY IN SEASON
	W. Scott Cameron Beach	631-283-6011	LOCAL RESIDENTS ONLY IN SEASON
East Hampton	Town Beaches	631-324-4140	*NO DOGS ALLOWED ON BEACH BETWEEN THE HOURS OF 10 AM AND 6 PM BETWEEN MAY 15 AND SEPTEMBER 15*
Montauk	Ditch Plains Beach	631-668-5081	*DOGS ALLOWED ON BEACH - NO LEASH LAWS*
	Fort Pond Beach	631-668-5081	*DOGS ALLOWED ON BEACH - NO LEASH LAWS*
	Gin Beach	631-668-5081	*DOGS ALLOWED ON BEACH - NO LEASH LAWS*
	Hither Hills State Park	631-668-2461	NO DOGS ALLOWED IN BATHING AREAS
	Kirk Park Beach	631-668-5081	*DOGS ALLOWED ON BEACH - NO LEASH LAWS*
	Montauk Point State Park	631-668-2461	NO DOGS ALLOWED IN BATHING AREAS
	Shadmoor State Park	631-669-1000	NO DOGS ALLOWED IN BATHING AREAS
	Theodore Roosevelt County Park	631-852-7879	*LEASHED DOGS ALLOWED ON BEACH*
Orient	Orient Beach State Park	631-323-2440	NO DOGS ALLOWED ON BEACH
Sag Harbor	Havens Beach	631-725-0011	*NO DOGS ALLOWED ON BEACH FROM THE THURSDAY PRECEDING MEMORIAL DAY THROUGH AND INCLUDING THE TUESDAY FOLLOWING LABOR DAY*
Southampton	Cooper's Beach	631-283-0247	*LEASHED DOGS ALLOWED ON BEACH*
	Flying Point Beach	631-283-6000	*LEASHED DOGS ALLOWED ON BEACH*
	Meschutt Beach County Park	631-852-8205	*LEASHED DOGS ALLOWED ON BEACH*
	Ponquoque Beach	631-283-6011	*DOGS ALLOWED ON BEACH FROM SEPTEMBER 15 TO MARCH 15 BUT NOT WITHIN 50 FEET OF NESTING BIRDS*
	Shinnecock Inlet County Park	631-852-8899	*LEASHED DOGS ALLOWED ON BEACH*
	Tiana Beach	631-283-6011	*DOGS ALLOWED ON BEACH FROM SEPTEMBER 15 TO MARCH 15 BUT NOT WITHIN 50 FEET OF NESTING BIRDS*
Southold	Goose Creek Beach	631-765-5182	NO DOGS ALLOWED ON TOWN BEACHES
	Kenny's Beach	631-765-5182	NO DOGS ALLOWED ON TOWN BEACHES
	McCabe's Beach	631-765-5182	NO DOGS ALLOWED ON TOWN BEACHES
	New Suffolk Beach	631-765-5182	NO DOGS ALLOWED ON TOWN BEACHES
	Town Beach	631-765-5182	NO DOGS ALLOWED ON TOWN BEACHES

Suffolk County - South Shore:

Fire Island National Seashore		631-289-4810	*DOGS ALLOWED ON LIGHTHOUSE BEACH BUT NOT IN SWIMMING AREAS*
Brookhaven	Blue Point Beach	516-451-6000	NO DOGS ALLOWED ON BEACH
East Islip	Heckscher State Park	631-581-2100	NO DOGS ALLOWED IN BATHING AREAS

Fire Island	Robert Moses State Park	631-669-0449	*DOGS ALLOWED ON FIELD 5*
	Smith Point County Park	631-852-1313	*LEASHED DOGS ALLOWED ON BEACH*
Patchogue	Sand Spit Beach	631-475-4300	NO DOGS ALLOWED ON BEACH
Westhampton	Cupsogue Beach	631-854-4949	NO DOGS ALLOWED ON BEACH
	Lashley Beach	631-288-1654	NO DOGS ALLOWED ON BEACH
	Pike's Beach	631-288-1654	NO DOGS ALLOWED ON BEACH
	Rogers Beach	631-288-1654	NO DOGS ALLOWED ON BEACH
	Westhampton Beach	631-288-1654	NO DOGS ALLOWED ON BEACH

New York City Area:

Brooklyn	Coney Island	718-372-5159	NO DOGS ALLOWED ON THE BEACH
Gateway National Recreation Area - Fort Tilden		718-318-4300	*LEASHED DOGS ALLOWED ON BEACH AND BAYSIDE BEACHES*
Gateway National Recreation Area - Riis Park		718-318-4300	NO DOGS ALLOWED ON BEACH OR BOARDWALK

NEW JERSEY

In-season, the New Jersey shore isn't especially welcoming to canine hikers. After Labor Day, however, some of America's best sand beaches start to open wide for dogs.

Gateway National Recreation Area - Riis Park		732-872-5970	*DOGS ALLOWED ON BEACH FROM LABOR DAY TO MARCH 15*
Asbury Park	Town Beach	732-775-2100	*DOGS ALLOWED ON BEACH IN OFF-SEASON*
Atlantic City	Town Beach	888-228-4748	DOGS ARE NOT ALLOWED ON THE BEACHES OR BOARDWALK
Avalon	Town Beach	609-967-3066	*DOGS ARE NOT ALLOWED ON THE BEACH, BOARDWALK OR DUNES BETWEEN MARCH 1 AND SEPTEMBER 30*

Avon -By-The-Sea	Town Beach	732-502-4510	*DOGS ALLOWED ON THE BEACH FROM NOVEMBER 1 TO APRIL1 BUT NEVER ON BOARDWALK*
Barnegat Light	Town Beach	609-494-9196	*DOGS ALLOWED ON THE BEACHES FROM OCTOBER 1 TO MAY 1*
Beach Haven	Town Beach	609-492-0111	NO DOGS ALLOWED ON BEACH
Belmar	Town Beach	732-681-3700	NO DOGS ALLOWED ON BEACH
Bradley Beach	Town Beach	732-776-2999	*DOGS ALLOWED FROM OCTOBER 15 TO APRIL 15*
Brigantine Beach	Town Beach	609-266-5233	*DOGS ALLOWED ON BEACH FROM 14TH STREET NORTH TO THE NORTHERNMOST JETTY*
Cape May	Sunset Beach	609-884-5508 609-884-5508	*DOGS ALLOWED ON BEACH* DOGS NOT ALLOWED ON BEACH, BOARDWALK OR OUTDOOR SHOPPING AREAS
Cape May Point	Town Beach	609-884-5508	NO DOGS ALLOWED ON BEACH
Lavallette	Town Beach	732-793-2566	NO DOGS ALLOWED ON BEACH BUT CAN GO ON BOARDWALK FROM AFTER LABOR DAY UNTIL THE START OF SWIMMING SEASON IN LATE JUNE
Mantoloking	Lyman Street Beach	732-899-6600	*DOGS ALLOWED ON BEACH OCTOBER 1 TO MAY 15*
	Town Beach	732-899-6600	*LEASHED DOGS ALLOWED ON BEACH OCTOBER 1 TO MAY 15 ANYTIME AND SUNRISE TO 8 AM AND 6 PM TO SUNSET OTHERWISE*
North Wildwood	Town Beach	609-729-4000	*DOGS ALLOWED ON BEACH FROM SEPTEMBER 15 TO MAY 15*
Ocean City	Town Beach	609-399-6111	*DOGS ARE NEVER ALLOWED ON THE BOARDWALK BUT CAN BE LEASHED ON THE BEACH FROM OCTOBER 1 TO APRIL 30*
Ocean Grove	Town Beach	732-774-1391	*DOGS ALLOWED ON BEACH AND BOARDWALK FROM OCTOBER 1 TO MAY 1*
Point Pleasant Beach	Town Beach	732-892-5813	*DOGS ALLOWED ON BEACH ANYTIME FROM SEPTEMBER 15 TO JUNE 15 AND BEFORE 8 AM AND AFTER 6 PM OTHERWISE*
Sea Isle City	Town Beach	609-263-0050	NO DOGS ALLOWED ON BEACH, BEACH APPROACHES OR PROMENADE AT ANY TIME
Seaside Park	Island Beach State Park	732-793-0506	*DOGS ALLOWED ON NON-RECREATIONAL BEACHES BUT NOT ON TRAILS*
Ship Bottom	Town Beach		*DOGS ALLOWED ON BEACH AFTER OCTOBER 1*
Spring Lake	Town Beach	732-449-0800	*DOGS ALLOWED ON BEACH IN OFF-SEASON*

Stone Harbor	Town Beach		DOGS ALLOWED ON BEACH OCTOBER 1 TO MARCH 1
Strathmere	Town Beach		DOGS ALLOWED ON THE BEACH IN MORNINGS AND EVENINGS IN SEASON
Surf City	Town Beach		NO DOGS ALLOWED ON BEACH
Wildwood	Town Beach	609-729-4000	NO DOGS ALLOWED ON BEACH OR BOARDWALK
Wildwood Crest	Town Beach	609-729-4000	NO DOGS ALLOWED ON BEACH

DELAWARE

Off-season, Delaware's quiet, sandy beaches area paradise for dogs. Don't bother to make a special trip for the sparse Delaware Bay beaches.

Bethany Beach	Town Beach	302-539-8011	DOGS ALLOWED ON BEACH AND BOARDWALK FROM OCTOBER 1 TO APRIL 1
Delaware Seashore State Park		302-227-2800	DOGS ALLOWED ON BEACH FROM OCTOBER 1 TO MAY 1
Dewey Beach	Town Beach	302-227-6363	DOGS ARE ALLOWED ON BEACH ALL YEAR BUT IN SEASON NOT BETWEEN 9:30 AM AND 5:30 PM
Fenwick Island	Fenwick Island State Park	302-539-9060	DOGS ALLOWED ON BEACH FROM OCTOBER 1 TO MAY 1
Lewes	Cape Henlopen State Park	302-645-8983	DOGS ALLOWED ON BEACH FROM OCTOBER 1 TO MAY 1
Rehoboth	Town Beach	302-227-6181	DOGS ALLOWED ON BEACH AND BOARDWALK FROM NOVEMBER 1 TO APRIL 1

MARYLAND

Sandy beaches on the Chesapeake Bay that welcome dogs are few and far between but once you reach the Atlantic Ocean the sands get friendlier. Stay clear of the Maryland state parks.

Atlantic Ocean:

Assateague Island National Seashore		410-641-1441	DOGS ALLOWED ON BEACH BUT NOT ON TRAILS
Berlin	Assateague State Park	410-641-2120	NO DOGS ALLOWED ON BEACH
Ocean City	Town Beach	410-250-0125	DOGS ALLOWED ON BEACH AND BOARDWALK OCTOBER 1 TO APRIL 30

Chesapeake Bay:

Annapolis	Sandy Point State Park	410-974-2149	NO DOGS ALLOWED ON BEACH
Chase	Gunpowder Falls State Park-Hammerman	410-592-2897	NO DOGS ALLOWED ON BEACH
Chesapeake Beach	Bayfront Park	410-257-2230	*DOGS ALLOWED ON BEACH*
	Breezy Point Public Beach	410-535-1600	*DOGS ALLOWED ON BEACH*
Dameron	Elms Public Beach	301-475-4572	*DOGS ALLOWED ON BEACH*
Edgemere	North Point State Park	410-592-2897	*DOGS ALLOWED ON BEACH*
Essex	Rocky Point Park	410-887-3780	NO DOGS ALLOWED ON BEACH
Lusby	Calvert Cliffs State Park	800-784-5380	NO DOGS ALLOWED ON BEACH
	Flag Ponds Nature Park	410-586-1477	*DOGS ALLOWED ON BEACH*
North Beach	North Beach Public Beach	410-257-9610	NO DOGS ALLOWED ON BEACH
Pinehurst	Downs Memorial Park	410-222-6230	*DOG BEACH IN PARK*
Scotland	Point Lookout State Park	301-872-5688	*DOGS ALLOWED ON BEACH NORTH OF CAUSEWAY*

VIRGINIA

Virginia makes plenty of allowances for dogs on its beaches, even its popular sand and surf spots.

Chincoteague	National Wildlife Refuge	757-336-6122	NO DOGS ALLOWED IN REFUGE BUT CAN GO LEASHED ON BEACH IN NATIONAL SEASHORE
Gloucester Point	Gloucester Point Beach	804-642-9474	*LEASHED DOGS ALLOWED IN PARK*
Mathews	Bethel Beach	804-725-4229	*LEASHED DOGS ALLOWED ON BEACH*
Virginia Beach	Back Bay National Wildlife Refuge	757-721-2412	*DOGS ALLOWED ON BEACH OCTOBER 1 TO MARCH 31*
	False Cape State Park	757-426-7128	*DOGS ALLOWED BY BOAT OR BEACH TRAIL NOVEMBER TO MARCH; BOAT ONLY APRIL TO SEPTEMBER AND NOT IN SWIMMING AREAS*
	First Landing State Park	757-412-2300	*DOGS ALLOWED ON BEACH*
	Little Island Park (Sandbridge)	757-426-7200	*DOGS ALLOWED ON BEACH BUT NOT IN SWIMMING AREAS*
	North End-41st to 80th Street	800-822-3224	*DOGS ALLOWED ON BEACH THE DAY AFTER LABOR DAY TO THE FRIDAY BEFORE MEMORIAL DAY; IN SUMMER DOGS ALLOWED ON RESIDENTIAL BEACHES ABOVE 42ND STREET BEFORE 10 AM AND AFTER 6 PM*
	Oceanfront-1st to 40th Street ("The Strip")	800-822-3224	*DOGS ALLOWED ON BEACH THE DAY AFTER LABOR DAY TO THE FRIDAY BEFORE MEMORIAL DAY; IN SUMMER DOGS ALLOWED ON RESIDENTIAL BEACHES ABOVE 42ND STREET BEFORE 10 AM AND AFTER 6 PM*

NORTH CAROLINA

By any definition, the public beaches of the barrier islands of North Carolina are among the most dog-friendly aorund.

Outer Banks:

Cape Hatteras National Seashore		252-473-2111	DOGS ALLOWED ON BEACH YEAR-ROUND ON 6-FOOT LEASH
Corolla	Town Beach	877-2877482	DOGS ALLOWED ON BEACH UNDER VOICE CONTROL
Duck	Town Beach	252-255-1234	UNLEASHED DOGS ALLOWED ON BEACH
Kill Devil Hills	Town Beach	252-449-5300	DOGS ALLOWED ON BEACH FROM MID-SEPTEMBER TO MID-MAY
Kitty Hawk	Town Beach	252-261-3552	DOGS ALLOWED UNLEASHED SEPTEMBER 1 TO JUNE 1 AND BEFORE 10 AM AND AFTER 6 PM OTHERWISE; LEASHED DOGS ALLOWED ON BEACH 10 AM TO 6 PM JUNE 1 TO SEPTEMBER 1
Nags Head	Town Beach	252-441-5508	DOGS ALLOWED ON BEACH YEAR ROUND ON 10-FOOT LEASH
Southern Shores	Town Beach		LEASHED DOGS ALLOWED ON BEACH SEPTEMBER 15 TO MAY 15

Crystal Coast:

Cape Lookout National Seashore		252-728-2250	DOGS ALLOWED ON BEACH YEAR-ROUND ON 6-FOOT LEASH
Atlantic Beach	Town Beach	252-726-2121	LEASHED DOGS ALLOWED ON BEACH EXCEPT IN THE CIRCLE AND BEACH AREA IN FRONT OF CIRCLE FROM EASTER TO LABOR DAY
Emerald Isle	Town Beach	252-354-3424	LEASHED DOGS ALLOWED ON BEACH
Ocracoke Island	Village Beach	252-928-6711	DOGS ALLOWED ON BEACH YEAR-ROUND ON 6-FOOT LEASH

Cape Fear:

Carolina Beach	Town Beach	910-458-8434	UNLEASHED DOGS ALLOWED ON NORTH SIDE OF ISLAND
Holden Beach	Town Beach	910-842-6488	LEASHED DOGS ALLOWED ON BEACH LABOR DAY TO MEMORIAL DAY AND DURING THE SUMMER BEFORE 9 AM AND AFTER 5 PM
Kure Beach	Fort Fisher State Recreation Area	910-458-5798	DOGS ALLOWED ON BEACH IN NON-SWIMMING AREAS
Oak Island	Long Beach	910-278-5811	LEASHED DOGS ALLOWED ON BEACH

Ocean Isle Beach	Town Beach	910-579-2166	*LEASHED DOGS ALLOWED ON BEACH LABOR DAY TO MEMORIAL DAY AND FROM JUNE 1 TO AUGUST 31 BEFORE 9 AM AND AFTER 6 PM*
Sunset Beach	Town Beach	910-579-2151	*LEASHED DOGS ALLOWED ON BEACH LABOR DAY TO MEMORIAL DAY AND DURING THE SUMMER BEFORE 8 AM AND AFTER 6 PM*
Topsail Beach	Town Beach	910-328-5841	*LEASHED DOGS ALLOWED MAY 15 THROUGH SEPTEMBER 30 AND UNDER VOICE CONTROL AT OTHER TIMES*
Wrightsville Beach	Town Beach	910-256-7910	*LEASHED DOGS ALLOWED ON BEACH FROM OCTOBER 1 TO APRIL 1*

SOUTH CAROLINA

Get away from the people and commercial beaches and there is plenty of dog-friendly sand in the Palmetto State.

Beaufort	Hunting Island State Park	843-838-2011	*DOGS ALLOWED ON BEACH*
Edisto Beach	Edisto Beach State Park	843-869-2756	*LEASHED DOGS ALLOWED ON BEACH*
Folly Beach	Town Beach	843-588-2426	*DOGS ALLOWED ON BEACH IN EVENING IN SUMMER AND ENTIRE DAY OTHERWISE*
Garden City Beach	Town Beach	843-546-8436	*DOGS ALLOWED ON BEACH UNDER VOICE COMMAND*
Georgetown	Huntington Beach State Park Town Beach	843-237-4440 843-546-8436	*LEASHED DOGS ALLOWED ON BEACH DOGS ALLOWED ON BEACH UNDER VOICE COMMAND*
Hilton Head Island	Driessden's Beach Park Folly Field Beach	843-785-3673 843-785-3673	*LEASHED DOGS ALLOWED ON BEACH LEASHED DOGS ALLOWED ON BEACH*
Isle of Palms	Town Beach	843-886-3863	*DOGS ALLOWED ON BEACH UNDER VOICE CONTROL FROM 5 AM TO 8 AM WITH OWNER HOLDING LEASH; LEASHED DOGS ALLOWED ON BEACH OTHER HOURS*
Kiawah Island	Beachwalker Park	843-768-2395	*LEASHED DOGS ALLOWED FROM MARCH 15 TO OCTOBER 31 AND UNDER VOICE CONTROL REST OF YEAR*
Litchfield Beach	Town Beach	843-546-8436	*DOGS ALLOWED ON BEACH UNDER VOICE COMMAND*
Myrtle Beach	21st Ave N to 13th Ave S Rest of Town Beach	800-356-3016 800-356-3016	*NO DOGS ALLOWED ON BEACH DOGS ALLOWED ON BEACH SEPTEMBER 15 TO MAY 15 ANYTIME AND OTHERWISE BEFORE 9 AM AND AFTER 5 PM*
North Myrtle Beach	Town Beach	843-280-5570	*DOGS ALLOWED ON BEACH SEPTEMBER 15 TO MAY 15 ANYTIME AND OTHERWISE BEFORE 9 AM AND AFTER 5 PM*

Pawleys Island	Town Beach	843-237-1698	*LEASHED DOGS ALLOWED ON BEACH MAY TO OCTOBER; UNDER VOICE CONTROL OTHER TIMES*
Sullivans Island	Town Beach	843-958-4000	*DOGS ALLOWED ON BEACH UNDER VOICE CONTROL FROM 5 AM TO 8 AM WITH OWNER HOLDING LEASH; LEASH DOGS ALLOWED ON BEACH OTHER HOURS*
Surfside Beach	Town Beach	843-913-6111	*DOGS ALLOWED ON BEACH SEPTEMBER 16 TO MAY 14*

GEORGIA

The beaches on Georgia's barrier islands are mostly under control of resorts and the Golden Isles are most welcoming to dogs. Savannah's beach at Tybee Island is closed to dogs.

Cumberland Island National Seashore		818-817-3421	*LEASHED DOGS ALLOWED ON BEACH BUT CAN BE REACHED BY PRIVATE BOAT ONLY*
Jekyll Island	Oceanfront Beach	912-635-3636	*NO DOGS ALLOWED ON BEACH IN SEASON FROM 9 AM TO 4:30 PM; OTHERWISE LEASHED DOGS ALLOWED*
Sea Island	Oceanfront Beach	912-265-0620	*NO DOGS ALLOWED ON BEACH IN SEASON FROM 9 AM TO 4:30 PM; OTHERWISE LEASHED DOGS ALLOWED*
St. Simons Island	Oceanfront Beach		*NO DOGS ALLOWED ON BEACH IN SEASON FROM 9 AM TO 4:30 PM; OTHERWISE LEASHED DOGS ALLOWED*
Tybee Island	Town Beach	800-868-2322	NO DOGS ALLOWED ON BEACH

Sticks aren't always easy to come by on barrier islands.

FLORIDA

Florida ranks among the most dog-unfriendly of states. Entire counties and regions ban dogs from the beach. There are so many prohibitions already against dogs on Florida beaches that when they change, it is typically in favor of dogs. For the Atlantic beaches the northeast part of the state around Jacksonville offers some of the best beaches for dogs in the state but heading south below Daytona, dogs are almost universally banned from the sand.

First Coast:

Amelia Island	Burney Beach Park	904-277-1221	*LEASHED DOGS ALLOWED ON BEACH*
	Fernadina Beach	904-321-5700	*LEASHED DOGS ALLOWED ON BEACH*
	Fort Clinch State Park	904-277-7274	NO DOGS ALLOWED ON BEACH
	Peter's Point Beach	904-277-1221	*LEASHED DOGS ALLOWED ON BEACH*
	Scott Road Beach	904-277-1221	*LEASHED DOGS ALLOWED ON BEACH*
Jacksonville Area	Atlantic Beach	904-798-9111	*LEASHED DOGS ALLOWED ON BEACH*
	Big Talbot Island State Park	904-251-2320	NO DOGS ALLOWED ON BEACH
	Fort George State Cultural Site	904-251-2320	NO DOGS ALLOWED ON BEACH
	Huguenot Memorial Park	904-251-3335	*DOGS ALLOWED ON BEACH*
	Jacksonville Beach	904-798-9111	*DOGS ALLOWED ON BEACH EXCEPT 8 AM TO 5 PM FROM NOVEMBER TO MARCH AND 9 AM TO 7 PM APRIL TO OCTOBER*
	Kathryn Abbey Hanna Park	904-249-4700	*DOGS ALLOWED ON BEACH*
	Little Talbot Island State Park	904-251-2320	NO DOGS ALLOWED ON BEACH
	Neptune Beach	904-798-9111	*DOGS ALLOWED ON BEACH BEFORE 9 AM AND AFTER 5 PM*
	North Beach	904-798-9111	NO DOGS ALLOWED ON BEACH
	Ponte Vedra Beach	904-798-9111	*DOGS ALLOWED ON BEACH UP TO HIGHWATER LINE*
	South Ponte Vedra Beach	904-798-9111	*DOGS ALLOWED ON BEACH UP TO HIGHWATER LINE*
	Vilano Beach	904-798-9111	*DOGS ALLOWED ON BEACH*
St. Augustine Area	Anastasia State Park	904-825-1007	NO DOGS ALLOWED ON BEACH
	Beverly Beach	904-439-6888	*DOGS ALLOWED ON BEACH*
	Crescent Beach	904-825-1007	*LEASHED DOGS ALLOWED ON BEACH*
	New Smyrna Beach	904-424-2100	*DOGS ALLOWED ON THE BEACH IN DESIGNATED AREAS*
	St. Augustine Beach	904-825-1007	*LEASHED DOGS ALLOWED ON BEACH*

Space Coast:

Canaveral National Seashore		321-267-1110	NO DOGS ALLOWED ON BEACH OR BEYOND PARKING LOT
Daytona Area	Dahlia Park	386-322-5000	NO DOGS ALLOWED ON BEACH
	Daytona Beach	386-947-3010	NO DOGS ALLOWED ON BEACH
	Flagler Beach	386-517-2000	*DOGS ALLOWED ON BEACH BETWEEN 10TH STREET N AND 10TH STREET S*
	Gamble Rogers State Park	386-517-2086	NO DOGS ALLOWED ON BEACH
	Smyrna Dune Park	396-424-2935	*DOGS ALLOWED ON BEACH BUT MUST BE LEASHED AT ALL TIMES, INCLUDING IN THE WATER*
	South Daytona Beach	386-322-3000	NO DOGS ALLOWED ON BEACH
	Tomoka State Park	386-677-0311	NO DOGS ALLOWED ON BEACH

Melbourne Area	Cocoa Beach	321-868-3333	NO DOGS ALLOWED ON BEACH
	Indialantic Beach	800-872-1969	NO DOGS ALLOWED ON BEACH
	Melbourne Beach	321-724-5860	NO DOGS ALLOWED ON BEACH
	Satellite Beach	321-773-4407	NO DOGS ALLOWED ON BEACH BUT DOG PARK IN TOWN NEAR LIBRARY
	Sebastian Inlet State Park	321-984-4852	NO DOGS ALLOWED ON OCEAN BEACH BUT DOGS ALLOWED ON INLET SIDE
Sebastian Area	Ambler Sands Beach	772-589-9223	NO DOGS ALLOWED ON BEACH
	Golden Sands Beach	772-589-9223	NO DOGS ALLOWED ON BEACH
	Sea Grape Trail Beach	772-589-9223	NO DOGS ALLOWED ON BEACH
	Treasure Shores Park	772-589-9223	NO DOGS ALLOWED ON BEACH
	Turtle Trail Beach	772-589-9223	NO DOGS ALLOWED ON BEACH
	Wabes Beach Park	772-589-9223	NO DOGS ALLOWED ON BEACH

Treasure Coast:

Fort Pierce	Fort Pierce Inlet State Park	561-468-3985	NO DOGS ALLOWED ON OCEAN BEACH BUT DOGS ALLOWED ON INLET SIDE
	Pepper Beach State Park	561-468-3985	NO DOGS ALLOWED ON BEACH
Highland Beach	Town Beach	561-278-4540	*LEASHED DOGS ALLOWED ON BEACH*
Hutchinson Island	Alex's Beach	732-334-3444	NO DOGS ALLOWED ON BEACH
	Bathtub Reef Park	732-334-3444	NO DOGS ALLOWED ON BEACH
	Bob Graham Beach	732-334-3444	NO DOGS ALLOWED ON BEACH
	Chastain Beach	732-334-3444	NO DOGS ALLOWED ON BEACH
	Fletcher Beach	732-334-3444	NO DOGS ALLOWED ON BEACH
	Glasscock Beach	732-334-3444	NO DOGS ALLOWED ON BEACH
	Sea Turtle/Jensen Beach Park	732-334-3444	NO DOGS ALLOWED ON BEACH
	Stuart Beach	732-334-3444	NO DOGS ALLOWED ON BEACH
	Tiger Shores Beach	732-334-3444	NO DOGS ALLOWED ON BEACH
	Virginia Forrest Beach	732-334-3444	NO DOGS ALLOWED ON BEACH
	Waveland Beach	732-334-3444	NO DOGS ALLOWED ON BEACH
Juno Beach	Juno Beach	561-626-4122	NO DOGS ALLOWED ON BEACH
	Loggerhead Park	561-626-4122	NO DOGS ALLOWED ON BEACH
	Ocean Cay Park	561-626-4122	NO DOGS ALLOWED ON BEACH
Jupiter	Hobe Sound National Wildlife Refuge	561-546-6141	*DOGS ALLOWED ON BEACH*
	Carlin Park	561-746-5134	*DOGS ALLOWED ON BEACH UNDER VOICE CONTROL IN NON-GUARDED AREAS*
	Dubois Park	561-746-5134	*DOGS ALLOWED ON BEACH UNDER VOICE CONTROL IN NON-GUARDED AREAS*
	Jupiter Beach	561-746-5134	*DOGS ALLOWED ON BEACH UNDER VOICE CONTROL IN NON-GUARDED AREAS*
Orchid	Town Beach	561-567-3491	NO DOGS ALLOWED ON BEACH
Tequesta	Coral Cove Beach	561-746-7111	NO DOGS ALLOWED ON BEACH
Vero Beach	Town Beach	561-567-3491	*DOGS ALLOWED ON UNPROTECTED BEACHES*

Gold Coast:

Boca Raton	Red Reef Park	561-393-7806	NO DOGS ALLOWED ON BEACH
	South Beach Park	561-393-7806	NO DOGS ALLOWED ON BEACH
	South Inlet Park	561-966-6600	NO DOGS ALLOWED ON BEACH
	Spanish Reef Park	561-393-7806	NO DOGS ALLOWED ON BEACH
Boynton Beach	Boynton Public Beach	561-375-6226	NO DOGS ALLOWED ON BEACH
	Gulf Stream County Park	561-966-6600	NO DOGS ALLOWED ON BEACH
Dania	John U. Lloyd Beach State Park	954-923-2833	NO DOGS ALLOWED ON BEACH
Delray Beach	Anchor Park	561-243-7250	NO DOGS ALLOWED ON BEACH
	Atlantic Dunes Park Beach	561-243-7250	NO DOGS ALLOWED ON BEACH
	Delray Municipal	561-243-7352	*DOGS ALLOWED ON SIDEWALK AND GRASSY AREA WEST OF THE DUNE LINE ON THE EAST SIDE OF A-1A*
	Sandoway Park	561-243-7250	NO DOGS ALLOWED ON BEACH
Fort Lauderdale	D.C. Alexander Park	954-761-5346	NO DOGS ALLOWED ON BEACH
	Fort Lauderdale Dog Beach	954-828-7275	*100-YARD STRIP OF BEACH AT SUNRISE AND A1A ON SATURDAYS AND SUNDAYS FROM 3-6 PM; ONE DAY PASS AND SUNDAYS FROM 3-6 PM; ONE DAY PASS REQUIRED*
	Fort Lauderdale Beach-North	954-828-7275	NO DOGS ALLOWED ON BEACH
	Harbor Beach	954-761-5346	NO DOGS ALLOWED ON BEACH
	Hugh Taylor Birch State Park	954-564-4521	NO DOGS ALLOWED ON BEACH
	Vista Park	954-761-5346	NO DOGS ALLOWED ON BEACH
Hallandale	Hallandale Beach	954-457-1456	NO DOGS ALLOWED ON BEACH
Hillsboro Inlet	Deerfield Beach	954-480-4429	NO DOGS ALLOWED ON BEACH
	Friedt Park	954-776-0576	NO DOGS ALLOWED ON BEACH
	Hillsboro Beach	954-776-0576	NO DOGS ALLOWED ON BEACH
	Lauderdale-by-the-Sea Beach	954-776-0576	NO DOGS ALLOWED ON BEACH
	North Ocean Park	954-786-4111	NO DOGS ALLOWED ON BEACH
	Pompano Beach Public Beach	954-941-2940	NO DOGS ALLOWED ON BEACH
Hollywood	Hollywood Public Beach	954-921-3423	NO DOGS ALLOWED ON BEACH
	North Hollywood Beach	954-921-3423	NO DOGS ALLOWED ON BEACH
Homestead	Biscayne National Park	305-230-7275	*LEASHED DOGS ALLOWED AT CONVOY MAINLAND AND IN DEVELOPED AREAS OF ELLIOTT KEY BUT NO BEACHES OR OTHER ISLANDS*
Key Biscayne	Bill Baggs Cape Florida State Park	305-361-5811	NO DOGS ALLOWED ON BEACH
	Crandon Park Beach	305-361-7385	NO DOGS ALLOWED ON BEACH
Lake Worth Area	Lake Worth Beach	561-533-7367	NO DOGS ALLOWED ON BEACH
	Lantana Municipal Beach Park	561-540-5735	NO DOGS ALLOWED ON BEACH
	Manalapan Beach	561-233-3000	NO DOGS ALLOWED ON BEACH
	Phipps Ocean Park	561-533-7367	NO DOGS ALLOWED ON BEACH
	Richard G. Kreusler Park	561-533-7367	NO DOGS ALLOWED ON BEACH
Miami	Rickenbacker Causeway and Beach	305-250-5360	*DOGS ALLOWED ON BEACH HERE AND NOWHERE ELSE IN MIAMI*

Miami Beach	Bal Harbor Beach	305-866-4633	NO DOGS ALLOWED ON BEACH
	Collins Park	305-673-7400	NO DOGS ALLOWED ON BEACH
	Golden Beach	305-884-1101	NO DOGS ALLOWED ON BEACH
	Haulover Beach	305-944-3040	NO DOGS ALLOWED ON BEACH
	Indian Beach Park	305-673-7400	NO DOGS ALLOWED ON BEACH
	Lummus Park	305-673-7400	NO DOGS ALLOWED ON BEACH
	North Shore Park	305-673-7400	NO DOGS ALLOWED ON BEACH
	Oleta River State Park	305-673-7400	NO DOGS ALLOWED ON BEACH
	Pier Park	305-673-7400	NO DOGS ALLOWED ON BEACH
	65th Street Park	305-673-7400	NO DOGS ALLOWED ON BEACH
	South Beach	305-673-7400	NO DOGS ALLOWED ON BEACH
	South Pointe Park	305-673-7400	NO DOGS ALLOWED ON BEACH
Singer Island	John D. MacArthur Beach State Park	561-624-6950	NO DOGS ALLOWED ON BEACH
South Miami	Matheson Hammock County Park	305-665-5475	NO DOGS ALLOWED ON BEACH

DOGS ON GULF OF MEXICO BEACHES

FLORIDA

The Gulf Coast beaches in the Florida Panhandle and western coast offer precious little for dog owners. Head for Franklin County, though, where dogs are allowed on all the public beaches - and the only county in Florida to allow dogs to run free.

The Keys:

Bahia Key	Bahia Honda State Park	305-872-2353	NO DOGS ALLOWED ON BEACH
	Little Duck Key County Park	305-872-2353	*DOGS ALLOWED ON BEACH*
Key Largo	John Pennekamp State Park	305-451-1202	NO DOGS ALLOWED ON BEACH
Key West	Clarence Higgs Beach	305-292-8227	NO DOGS ALLOWED ON BEACH
	Dog Beach	305-292-8227	*DOGS ALLOWED ON BEACH AT WADDELL & VERNON AVENUES*
	Fort Zachary Taylor Historic State Park	305-292-6713	NO DOGS ALLOWED ON BEACH OR FORT
	Smathers Beach	305-292-8227	NO DOGS ALLOWED ON BEACH
Long Key	Long Key State Park	305-664-4815	NO DOGS ALLOWED ON BEACH
Lower Matecumbe	Anne's Beach	305-292-4560	*DOGS ALLOWED ON BEACH*
Marathon	Sombrero Beach	305-292-4560	*DOGS ALLOWED ON BEACH*
Tavernier	Harry Harris Park	305-852-7161	NO DOGS ALLOWED IN SWIMMING AREAS

Suncoast:

Fort Myers Area	Algiers Beach	941-472-1080	*DOGS ALLOWED ON SANIBEL ISLAND BEACHES*
	Bonita Beach	239-992-5011	NO DOGS ALLOWED ON BEACH
	Bowman's Beach	941-472-1080	*DOGS ALLOWED ON SANIBEL ISLAND BEACHES*
	Captiva Beach	941-472-1080	NO DOGS ALLOWED ON CAPTIVA ISLANDBEACHES
	Cayo Costa State Park	941-964-0375	NO DOGS ALLOWED ON BEACH
	Fort Myers Beach Park	239-463-4588	NO DOGS ALLOWED ON BEACH
	Gasparilla Island State Park	941-964-0375	NO DOGS ALLOWED ON BEACH
	Lighthouse Pier and Park	941-472-1080	*DOGS ALLOWED ON SANIBEL ISLAND BEACHES*
	Lovers Key Carl E. Johnson State Park	239-463-4588	NO DOGS ALLOWED ON BEACH
	New Pass Beach	239-992-5011	NO DOGS ALLOWED ON BEACH
	Sanibel Beach	941-472-1080	*DOGS ALLOWED ON SANIBEL ISLAND BEACHES*
	Turner Beach	941-472-1080	NO DOGS ALLOWED ON CAPTIVA ISLANDBEACHES
Naples Area	Barefoot Beach State Park	239-597-6196	NO DOGS ALLOWED ON BEACH
	Clam Pass Beach	239-213-1015	NO DOGS ALLOWED ON BEACH
	Delnor-Wiggins Pass State Park	239-597-6196	NO DOGS ALLOWED ON BEACH
	Lely Barefoot Beach	239-213-1015	NO DOGS ALLOWED ON BEACH
	Lowdermilk Park Beach	239-434-4698	NO DOGS ALLOWED ON BEACH
	Naples Municipal Beach	239-213-1015	NO DOGS ALLOWED ON BEACH
	South Marco Beach	239-213-1015	NO DOGS ALLOWED ON BEACH
	Tigertail Beach	239-389-5000	NO DOGS ALLOWED ON BEACH
	Vanderbilt Beach	239-597-6196	NO DOGS ALLOWED ON BEACH
Sarasota Area	Bayfront Park	941-742-5923	NO DOGS ALLOWED ON BEACH
	Blind Pass Beach	941-627-1628	NO DOGS ALLOWED ON BEACH
	Bradenton Beach	941-742-5923	NO DOGS ALLOWED ON BEACH
	Brohard Park Beach	941-488-2236	*DOGS ALLOWED ON BEACH UNDER VOICE CONTROL BEHIND WASTE WATER PLANT*
	Chadwick Park at Englewood Beach	941-627-1628	NO DOGS ALLOWED ON THE BEACH
	Coquina Beach	941-742-5926	NO DOGS ALLOWED ON THE BEACH
	Cortez Beach	941-742-5926	NO DOGS ALLOWED ON THE BEACH
	Don Pedro Island State Park	941-964-0375	NO DOGS ALLOWED ON THE BEACH
	Englewood Beach	941-627-1628	NO DOGS ALLOWED ON THE BEACH
	Greek Island	941-742-5923	NO DOGS ALLOWED ON THE BEACH
	Holmes Beach	941-742-5923	NO DOGS ALLOWED ON THE BEACH
	Lido Beach	941-861-5000	NO DOGS ALLOWED ON THE BEACH
	Manasota Beach	941-627-1628	NO DOGS ALLOWED ON THE BEACH
	Manatee County Beach	941-742-5923	NO DOGS ALLOWED ON THE BEACH
	Nokomis Beach	941-861-5000	NO DOGS ALLOWED ON THE BEACH
	North Jetty Park	941-861-5000	NO DOGS ALLOWED ON THE BEACH
	Palmer Point South	941-861-5000	NO DOGS ALLOWED ON THE BEACH
	Port Charlotte Beach Park	941-627-1628	NO DOGS ALLOWED ON THE BEACH
	Siesta Key Beach	941-861-5000	NO DOGS ALLOWED ON THE BEACH
	South Lido Beach	941-861-5000	NO DOGS ALLOWED ON THE BEACH
	Stump Pass Beach	941-964-0375	NO DOGS ALLOWED ON THE BEACH
	Turtle Beach	941-861-5000	NO DOGS ALLOWED ON THE BEACH
	Venice Municipal Beach	941-488-2236	NO DOGS ALLOWED ON THE BEACH

Tampa Bay/ St. Petersburg Area	Anclote Key State Park	727-469-5942	NO DOGS ALLOWED ON BEACH
	Ben Davis Municipal Beach	813-931-2121	NO DOGS ALLOWED ON BEACH
	Caladesi Island State Park	727-469-5918	NO DOGS ALLOWED ON BEACH
	Clearwater Beach Island	727-464-3347	NO DOGS ALLOWED ON BEACH
	Clearwater Beach Park	727-464-3347	NO DOGS ALLOWED ON BEACH
	Davis Island	813-931-2121	*DOGS ALLOWED ON SOUTH END OF BEACH*
	E.G. Simmons Park	813-671-7655	NO DOGS ALLOWED ON SWIMMING BEACH
	Fort DeSoto County Park	727-582-2267	*NO DOGS ALLOWED ON BEACH BUT PAST PARK LIMIT THERE IS BEACH ACCESS ON PINELLAS BAYWAY*
	Fred Howard Park	727-943-4081	NO DOGS ALLOWED ON BEACH
	Gandy Boulevard Dog Park	727-461-6963	*DOGS ALLOWED ON THIS BAY BEACH*
	Honeymoon Island State Park	727-469-5942	*NO DOGS ALLOWED ON SWIMMING BEACH BUT ARE ALLOWED AT SOUTH BEACH ON LEASH (LEASH MUST REMAIN ON DOG IN WATER BUT NEED NOT BE HELD)*
	Indian Rocks Beach	727-588-4852	NO DOGS ALLOWED ON BEACH
	Indian Shores	727-549-6165	NO DOGS ALLOWED ON BEACH
	John Pass Beach	727-391-6111	NO DOGS ALLOWED ON BEACH
	Madeira Beach	727-549-6165	NO DOGS ALLOWED ON BEACH
	Mandalay Park	727-464-3347	NO DOGS ALLOWED ON BEACH
	Pass-a-Grille Beach	727-367-2735	NO DOGS ALLOWED ON BEACH
	Redington Shores County Park	727-549-6165	NO DOGS ALLOWED ON BEACH
	Sand Key Park	727-588-4852	NO DOGS ALLOWED ON BEACH
	St. Petersburg Beach	727-866-2484	NO DOGS ALLOWED ON BEACH
	Treasure Island	727-549-6165	NO DOGS ALLOWED ON BEACH

Emerald Coast:

Gulf Islands National Seashore		850-934-2600	NO DOGS ALLOWED ON BEACH
Fort Walton Area	Destin Beach	850-837-4540	NO DOGS ALLOWED ON BEACH
	Grayton Beach State Park	850-231-4210	NO DOGS ALLOWED ON BEACH
	Henderson Beach State Park	850-837-7550	NO DOGS ALLOWED ON BEACH
	John C. Beasley Park	850-651-7515	NO DOGS ALLOWED ON BEACH
	Okaloosa Island Pier	850-651-7515	NO DOGS ALLOWED ON BEACH
	Ross Marler Park	850-651-7515	NO DOGS ALLOWED ON BEACH
	Silver Beach	850-267-0683	NO DOGS ALLOWED ON BEACH
Panama City Area	Carrabelle Beach	850-697-2585	*DOGS ALLOWED ON BEACH*
	Dr. Julian G. Bruce Beach	850-653-9419	*DOGS ALLOWED ON BEACH*
	Mexico Beach	850-235-1159	NO DOGS ALLOWED ON BEACH
	Panama City Beach	850-233-5045	NO DOGS ALLOWED ON BEACH
	Saint Andrews State Park	850-233-5140	NO DOGS ALLOWED ON GULF BEACH BUT ON GRAND LAGOON BEACH
	St. George Island State Park	850-927-2111	*LEASHED DOGS ALLOWED ON BEACH*
	St. Joseph Peninsula State Park	850-227-1327	NO DOGS ALLOWED ON BEACH OR ANY PARK WATERS
	St. Vincent National Wildlife Refuge	850-953-9893	NO DOGS ALLOWED ON ISLAND
Pensacola Area	Big Lagoon State Park	850-492-1595	NO DOGS ALLOWED ON BEACH
	Casino Beach	850-983-1866	NO DOGS ALLOWED ON BEACH
	East Park	850-983-1866	NO DOGS ALLOWED ON BEACH
	Fort Pickens	850-492-1595	NO DOGS ALLOWED ON BEACH
	Johnson Beach	850-983-1866	NO DOGS ALLOWED ON BEACH
	Langdon Beach	850-492-1595	NO DOGS ALLOWED ON BEACH
	Navarre Beach	850-983-1866	NO DOGS ALLOWED ON BEACH
	Opal Beach	850-492-1595	NO DOGS ALLOWED ON BEACH
	Pensacola Beach	850-983-1866	NO DOGS ALLOWED ON BEACH
	Perdido Key State Park	850-492-1595	NO DOGS ALLOWED ON BEACH BUT CAN GO ON TRAILS

ALABAMA

For dog owners, Alabama may as well not even have the few beaches it does on the Gulf of Mexico.

Daphne	Municipal Pier	251-621-3703	NO DOGS ALLOWED ON BEACH
Dauphin Island	Public Beach	251-861-6992	NO DOGS ALLOWED ON BEACH
Fairhope	Municipal Beach	251-928-2136	*DOGS ALLOWED ON BEACH*
Gulf Shores	Gulf State Park	251-948-7275	NO DOGS ALLOWED ON BEACH
	Town Beach	251-974-1510	NO DOGS ALLOWED ON BEACH
Orange Beach	Town Beach	251-981-6979	NO DOGS ALLOWED ON BEACH

MISSISSIPPI

For dog owners, stay on the western coast in Hancock County; dogs aren't allowed around the populated Biloxi beaches.

Gulf Islands National Seashore		228-875-9057	NO DOGS ALLOWED ON BEACH
Bay St. Louis	Town Beach	228-467-9092	*LEASHED DOGS ALLOWED ON BEACH*
Biloxi	Town Beach	228-896-6699	NO DOGS ALLOWED ON BEACH
Ocean Springs	Davis Bayou Beach	228-875-4424	*DOGS ALLOWED ON BEACH*
Waveland	Waveland Public Beach	228-463-9222	*LEASHED DOGS ALLOWED ON BEACH*

LOUISIANA

People don't seek out Louisiana for its sandy beaches; most of the coastline is made up of bayous. Grand Isle State Park is the only state park with access to the Gulf of Mexico.

| Port Fourchon | Fourchon Beach | 985-632-6701 | *THERE ARE NO RESTRICTIONS ON DOGS ON THIS BEACH* |
| Grand Isle | Grand Isle State Park | 985-787-2559 | *LEASHED DOGS ALLOWED IN NON-SWIMMING AREAS* |

TEXAS

Padre Island is America's longest barrier island; there is plenty of room for dogs on its 113 miles of sand. Galveston Island serves up another 32 miles of mostly dog-friendly beach.

Padre Island National Seashore

361-949-8173   *DOGS ARE ALLOWED ANYWHERE EXCEPT ON THE DECK AT MALAQUITE BEACH AND IN FRONT OF THE VISITOR CENTER AT THE SWIMMING*

Bolivar	Town Beach	409-684-5940	*DOGS ALLOWED ON ISLAND BEACHES*
Crystal Beach	Town Beach	409-684-5940	*DOGS ALLOWED ON ISLAND BEACHES*
Galveston	East Beach	409-762-3278	*LEASHED DOGS ALLOWED ON BEACH*
	Galveston Island State Park	409-737-1222	*LEASHED DOGS ALLOWED ON BEACH*
	Stewart Beach Park	888-425-4753	*LEASHED DOGS ALLOWED ON BEACH*
Port Arsanas	Mustang Island State Park	361-749-4111	*LEASHED DOGS ALLOWED ON BEACH*
Port O'Connor	Matagorda Island State Park	361-983-2215	*LEASHED DOGS ALLOWED ON BEACH*
Sabine Pass	Sea Rim State Park	409-971-2559	*LEASHED DOGS ALLOWED ON BEACH*
South Padre Island	Town Beach	800-767-2373	*LEASHED DOGS ALLOWED ON BEACH; UNLEASHED NORTH OF TOWN*

The dog-friendliest beaches on the Gulf of Mexico are in Texas.

DOGS ON PACIFIC OCEAN BEACHES

WASHINGTON

Dogs on leash are allowed in all Washington state parks but not in many swimming areas around Puget Sound. The uncrowded Pacific Coast beaches are some of the dog-friendliest in America - even Olympic National Park, which bans dogs from almost all of its 632,324 acres, opens some of its remote coastal beaches to dogs.

Inland:

Belfair	Belfair State Park	360-902-8844	*LEASHED DOGS ALLOWED ON BEACH BUT NOT IN SWIMMING AREAS*
	Twanoh State Park	360-902-8844	*LEASHED DOGS ALLOWED ON BEACH BUT NOT IN SWIMMING AREAS*
Bellingham	Larrbee State Park	360-902-8844	*LEASHED DOGS ALLOWED ON BEACH BUT NOT IN SWIMMING AREAS*
Blaine	Birch Bay State Park	360-902-8844	*LEASHED DOGS ALLOWED ON BEACH BUT NOT IN SWIMMING AREAS*
Blake Island	Blake Island State Park	360-902-8844	*LEASHED DOGS ALLOWED ON BEACH BUT NOT IN SWIMMING AREAS*
Bremerton	Illahee State Park	360-902-8844	*LEASHED DOGS ALLOWED ON BEACH BUT NOT IN SWIMMING AREAS*
Brinnon	Dosewallips State Park	360-902-8844	*LEASHED DOGS ALLOWED ON BEACH BUT NOT IN SWIMMING AREAS*
Burlington	Bay View State Park	360-902-8844	*LEASHED DOGS ALLOWED ON BEACH BUT NOT IN SWIMMING AREAS*
Coupeville	Fort Casey State Park	360-902-8844	*LEASHED DOGS ALLOWED ON BEACH BUT NOT IN SWIMMING AREAS*
	Fort Ebey State Park	360-902-8844	*LEASHED DOGS ALLOWED ON BEACH BUT NOT IN SWIMMING AREAS*
Des Moines	Saltwater State Park	360-902-8844	*LEASHED DOGS ALLOWED ON BEACH BUT NOT IN SWIMMING AREAS*
Federal Way	Dash Point State Park	360-902-8844	*LEASHED DOGS ALLOWED ON BEACH BUT NOT IN SWIMMING AREAS*
Freeland	South Whidbey Island State Park	360-902-8844	*LEASHED DOGS ALLOWED ON BEACH BUT NOT IN SWIMMING AREAS*

Gig Harbor	Kopachuck State Park	253-265-3606	*LEASHED DOGS ALLOWED ON BEACH BUT NOT IN SWIMMING AREAS*
Harstine Island	Jarrell Cove State Park	360-902-8844	*LEASHED DOGS ALLOWED ON BEACH BUT NOT IN SWIMMING AREAS*
Hope Island	Hope Island State Park	360-902-8844	NO DOGS ALLOWED IN PARK
Lopez Island	Spencer Spit State Park	360-902-8844	*LEASHED DOGS ALLOWED ON BEACH BUT NOT IN SWIMMING AREAS*
Marrowstone Island	Mystery Bay State Park	360-902-8844	*LEASHED DOGS ALLOWED ON BEACH BUT NOT IN SWIMMING AREAS*
Mukilteo	Mulkiteo State Park	360-902-8844	*LEASHED DOGS ALLOWED ON BEACH BUT NOT IN SWIMMING AREAS*
Oak Harbor	Deception Pass State Park	360-902-8844	*LEASHED DOGS ALLOWED ON BEACH BUT NOT IN SWIMMING AREAS*
	Joseph Whidbey State Park	360-902-8844	*LEASHED DOGS ALLOWED ON BEACH BUT NOT IN SWIMMING AREAS*
Olympia	Tolmic State Park	360-902-8844	*LEASHED DOGS ALLOWED ON BEACH BUT NOT IN SWIMMING AREAS*
Port Angeles	Clallam Bay Spit Beach County Park	360-417-2291	*LEASHED DOGS ALLOWED ON BEACH*
	Freshwater Bay	360-417-2291	*LEASHED DOGS ALLOWED ON BEACH*
	Pillar Point County Park	360-417-2291	*LEASHED DOGS ALLOWED ON BEACH*
	Salt Creek State Park	360-428-3441	*LEASHED DOGS ALLOWED ON BEACH*
Port Townsend	Fort Worden State Park	360-902-8844	*LEASHED DOGS ALLOWED ON BEACH BUT NOT IN SWIMMING AREAS*
Port Walow	Shine Tidelands State Park	360-902-8844	*LEASHED DOGS ALLOWED ON BEACH BUT NOT IN SWIMMING AREAS*
Poulsbo	Kitsap Memorial State Park	360-779-3205	*LEASHED DOGS ALLOWED ON BEACH BUT NOT IN SWIMMING AREAS*
Purdy	Penrose Point State Park	360-902-8844	*LEASHED DOGS ALLOWED ON BEACH BUT NOT IN SWIMMING AREAS*
Seattle	Alki Beach	206-296-8359	NO DOGS ALLOWED ON SEATTLE BEACHES
	Carkeek Park	206-296-8359	NO DOGS ALLOWED ON SEATTLE BEACHES
	Constellation Park	206-296-8359	NO DOGS ALLOWED ON SEATTLE BEACHES
	Des Moines Beach Park	206-296-8359	NO DOGS ALLOWED ON SEATTLE BEACHES
	Lincoln Park	206-296-8359	NO DOGS ALLOWED ON SEATTLE BEACHES
	Richmond Beach	206-296-8359	NO DOGS ALLOWED ON SEATTLE BEACHES
	Seahurst Park	206-296-8359	NO DOGS ALLOWED ON SEATTLE BEACHES
Sequim	Cline Spit Beach County Park	360-417-2291	*LEASHED DOGS ALLOWED ON BEACH*
	Dungeness Recreation Area	360-683-5847	*LEASHED DOGS ALLOWED ON BEACH*
	Panorama Vista Access	360-417-2291	*LEASHED DOGS ALLOWED ON BEACH*
	Port Williams County Park	360-417-2291	*LEASHED DOGS ALLOWED ON BEACH*
	Sequim Bay State Park	360-902-8844	*LEASHED DOGS ALLOWED ON BEACH BUT NOT IN SWIMMING AREAS*
Shelton	Potlatch State Park	360-902-8844	*LEASHED DOGS ALLOWED ON BEACH BUT NOT IN SWIMMING AREAS*

Silverdale	Scenic Beach State Park	360-902-8844	LEASHED DOGS ALLOWED ON BEACH BUT NOT IN SWIMMING AREAS
South Point	Fort Ward State Park	360-902-8844	LEASHED DOGS ALLOWED ON BEACH BUT NOT IN SWIMMING AREAS
Tacoma	Joemma Beach State Park	360-902-8844	LEASHED DOGS ALLOWED ON BEACH BUT NOT IN SWIMMING AREAS

Pacific Coast:

Forks	First Beach	360-374-2558	LEASHED DOGS ALLOWED ON BEACH
	Olympic National Park	360-565-3147	DOGS ARE ALLOWED ON THE BEACH FROM RIALTO BEACH NORTH TO ELLEN CREEK AND AT KALALOCH NORTH TO THE HOH RIVER
	Second Beach	360-374-2558	LEASHED DOGS ALLOWED ON BEACH
	Third Beach	360-374-2558	LEASHED DOGS ALLOWED ON BEACH
Hoquiam	Griffith-Priday Ocean State Park	360-902-8844	LEASHED DOGS ALLOWED ON BEACH BUT NOT IN SWIMMING AREAS
Ilwaco	Beerd's Hollow Beach	360-642-3145	LEASHED DOGS ALLOWED ON BEACH
	Fort Canby State Park	360-642-3070	LEASHED DOGS ALLOWED ON BEACH BUT NOT IN SWIMMING AREAS
Long Beach	10th Street Access	800-451-2542	LEASHED DOGS ALLOWED ON BEACH BUT NOT IN SWIMMING AREAS
	Bolsted Beach Access	800-451-2542	LEASHED DOGS ALLOWED ON BEACH BUT NOT IN SWIMMING AREAS
	Seaview Beach Access	800-451-2542	LEASHED DOGS ALLOWED ON BEACH BUT NOT IN SWIMMING AREAS
Ocean Park	Pacific Pines State Park	360-902-8844	LEASHED DOGS ALLOWED ON BEACH BUT NOT IN SWIMMING AREAS
Ocean Shores	Damon Point State Park	360-902-8844	LEASHED DOGS ALLOWED ON BEACH BUT NOT IN SWIMMING AREAS
	Ocean City State Park	360-902-8844	LEASHED DOGS ALLOWED ON BEACH BUT NOT IN SWIMMING AREAS
	Pacific Beach State Park	360-902-8844	LEASHED DOGS ALLOWED ON BEACH BUT NOT IN SWIMMING AREAS
	Town Beach	360-289-3331	LEASHED DOGS ALLOWED ON BEACH AND CAN RUN FREE ONCE YOU ARE PAST THE DUNES AND ON THE SAND
Oysterville	Leadbetter Point State Park	360-902-8844	LEASHED DOGS ALLOWED ON BEACH BUT NOT IN SWIMMING AREAS
	Oysterville Beach	360-902-8844	LEASHED DOGS ALLOWED ON BEACH BUT NOT IN SWIMMING AREAS
Westport	Grayland Beach State Park	360-902-8844	LEASHED DOGS ALLOWED ON BEACH BUT NOT IN SWIMMING AREAS
	Twin Harbors Beach State Park	360-902-8844	LEASHED DOGS ALLOWED ON BEACH BUT NOT IN SWIMMING AREAS
	Westport Light State Park	360-902-8844	LEASHED DOGS ALLOWED ON BEACH BUT NOT IN SWIMMING AREAS

OREGON

All of Oregon's beaches are public. You can step on every grain of Oregon sand for 400 miles and, in the rare exception of a ban due to nesting birds, your dog can be with you all the way.

North Coast:

Astoria	Fort Stevens State Park	503-861-1671	LEASHED DOGS ALLOWED ON BEACH
Cannon Beach	Arcadia Beach State Recreation Area	800-551-6949	LEASHED DOGS ALLOWED ON BEACH
	Ecola State Park	503-436-2844	LEASHED DOGS ALLOWED ON BEACH
	High Point State Recreation Area	800-551-6949	LEASHED DOGS ALLOWED ON BEACH
	Oswald West State Park	800-551-6949	LEASHED DOGS ALLOWED ON BEACH
	Tolovana Beach State Recreation Area	800-551-6949	LEASHED DOGS ALLOWED ON BEACH
Gearhart	Del Ray Beach State Recreational Area	800-551-6949	LEASHED DOGS ALLOWED ON BEACH
Manzanita	Nehalem Bay State Park	503-368-5154	LEASHED DOGS ALLOWED ON BEACH
Neskowin	Neskowin Beach State Recreation Area	800-551-6949	LEASHED DOGS ALLOWED ON BEACH
Pacific City	Bob Straub State Park	800-551-6949	LEASHED DOGS ALLOWED ON BEACH
Rockaway Beach	Manhattan Beach State Recreation Area	800-551-6949	LEASHED DOGS ALLOWED ON BEACH
Tillamook	Cape Meares State Park	800-551-6949	LEASHED DOGS ALLOWED ON BEACH
	Cape Lookout State Park	503-842-4981	LEASHED DOGS ALLOWED ON BEACH
	Oceanside Beach State Recreation Area	800-551-6949	LEASHED DOGS ALLOWED ON BEACH

Central Coast:

Depoe Bay	Depoe Bay State Park	800-551-6949	LEASHED DOGS ALLOWED ON BEACH
	Fogarty Creek State Park	800-551-6949	LEASHED DOGS ALLOWED ON BEACH
Lincoln City	D River State Recreation Area	800-551-6949	LEASHED DOGS ALLOWED ON BEACH
	Gleneden Beach State Recreation Area	800-551-6949	LEASHED DOGS ALLOWED ON BEACH
	Roads End Beach	541-994-3070	LEASHED DOGS ALLOWED ON BEACH
Newport	Agate Beach State Recreation Area	800-551-6949	LEASHED DOGS ALLOWED ON BEACH
	Beverly Beach State Park	541-265-9278	LEASHED DOGS ALLOWED ON BEACH
	Devils Punchbowl State Natural Area	800-551-6949	LEASHED DOGS ALLOWED ON BEACH
	Lost Creek State Park	800-551-6949	LEASHED DOGS ALLOWED ON BEACH
	Ona Beach State Park	800-551-6949	LEASHED DOGS ALLOWED ON BEACH
	Seal Rock State Recreation Area	800-551-6949	LEASHED DOGS ALLOWED ON BEACH
	South Beach State Park	541-867-7415	LEASHED DOGS ALLOWED ON BEACH
	Yaquina Bay State Park	800-551-6949	LEASHED DOGS ALLOWED ON BEACH

Waldport	Beachside Recreational Site	541-563-3220	*LEASHED DOGS ALLOWED ON BEACH*
	Driftwood Beach State Recreation Area	800-551-6949	*LEASHED DOGS ALLOWED ON BEACH*
	Governor Patterson State Park	800-551-6949	*LEASHED DOGS ALLOWED ON BEACH*
Yachats	Neptune State Scenic Viewpoint	800-551-6949	*LEASHED DOGS ALLOWED ON BEACH*
	Smelt Sands State Recreation Area	800-551-6949	*LEASHED DOGS ALLOWED ON BEACH*
	Stonefield Beach State Recreation Area	800-551-6949	*LEASHED DOGS ALLOWED ON BEACH*
	Yachats Ocean Road State Natural Site	800-551-6949	*LEASHED DOGS ALLOWED ON BEACH*

Southern Coast:

Oregon Dunes National Recreation Area		541-271-3611	*LEASHED DOGS ALLOWED ON BEACH*
Bandon	Bandon State Natural Area	800-551-6949	*LEASHED DOGS ALLOWED ON BEACH*
	Bullards Beach State Park	541-347-2209	*LEASHED DOGS ALLOWED ON BEACH*
	Face Rock State Scenic Viewpoint	800-551-6949	*LEASHED DOGS ALLOWED ON BEACH*
	Seven Devils State Recreation Area	800-551-6949	*LEASHED DOGS ALLOWED ON BEACH*
			LEASHED DOGS ALLOWED ON BEACH
			LEASHED DOGS ALLOWED ON BEACH
Brookings	Crissy Field State Recreation Area	800-551-6949	*LEASHED DOGS ALLOWED ON BEACH*
	Harris Beach State Park	541-469-2021	*LEASHED DOGS ALLOWED ON BEACH*
	McVay Rock State Recreation Area	800-551-6949	*LEASHED DOGS ALLOWED ON BEACH*
	Samuel H. Boardman State Scenic Corridor	800-551-6949	*LEASHED DOGS ALLOWED ON BEACH*
	Winchuck State Recreation Area	800-551-6949	*LEASHED DOGS ALLOWED ON BEACH*
Coos Bay	Cape Arago State Park	800-551-6949	*LEASHED DOGS ALLOWED ON BEACH*
	Shore Acres State Park	541-888-3732	*NO DOGS ALLOWED OUTSIDE VEHICLE*
	SunsetBay State Park	541-888-4902	*LEASHED DOGS ALLOWED ON BEACH*
Florence	Carl G. Washburne Memorial State Park	541-547-3416	*LEASHED DOGS ALLOWED ON BEACH*
	Devil's Elbow State Park	800-551-6949	*LEASHED DOGS ALLOWED ON BEACH*
	Muriel O. Ponsler State Scenic Viewpoint	800-551-6949	*LEASHED DOGS ALLOWED ON BEACH*
Gold Beach	Cape Sebastian State Scenic Corridor	800-551-6949	*LEASHED DOGS ALLOWED ON BEACH*
	Otter Point State Recreation Area	800-551-6949	*LEASHED DOGS ALLOWED ON BEACH*
	Pistol River State Scenic Viewpoint	800-551-6949	*LEASHED DOGS ALLOWED ON BEACH*
Port Orford	Cape Blanco State Park	541-332-6774	*LEASHED DOGS ALLOWED ON BEACH*
	Humburg Mountain State Park	541-332-6774	*LEASHED DOGS ALLOWED ON BEACH*
	Paradise Point State Recreation Area	800-551-6949	*LEASHED DOGS ALLOWED ON BEACH*

CALIFORNIA

Northern California is more friendly than Southern California. As the waters warm up heading south, the beaches become more restrictive. By the time you reach Los Angeles, don't expect to find any place to get your dog onto the sand. Beaches in the state can close to dogs with little warning due to nesting sites set up by the Snowy Plover, a small shorebird that is listed as a threatened species.

North Coast - Del Norte County:

Redwood National Park	Crescent Beach	707-464-1812	*LEASHED DOGS ALLOWED ON BEACH*
	Enderts Beach	707-464-1812	*LEASHED DOGS ALLOWED ON BEACH*
	Wilson Creek Beach	707-464-1812	NO DOGS ALLOWED ON BEACH
Crescent City	Garth Beach	707-457-3131	*LEASHED DOGS ALLOWED ON BEACH AND GRASS*
	Pebble Beach	707-457-3131	*LEASHED DOGS ALLOWED ON BEACH AND GRASS*
	South Beach	707-457-3131	*LEASHED DOGS ALLOWED ON BEACH AND GRASS*
Smith River	Clifford Kamph Memorial Park	707-464-7230	*LEASHED DOGS ALLOWED ON BEACH*
	Pelican State Beach	707-464-6100	*LEASHED DOGS ALLOWED ON BEACH*

North Coast - Humboldt County:

King Range National Conservation Area	Black Sands Beach	707-825-2300	*DOGS ALLOWED OFF-LEASH ON BEACH*
	Little Black Sands Beach	707-825-2300	*DOGS ALLOWED OFF-LEASH ON BEACH*
	Mattole River Beach	707-825-2300	*DOGS ALLOWED OFF-LEASH ON BEACH*
Arcata	Clam Beach County Park	707-445-7652	*DOGS ALLOWED OFF-LEASH ON BEACH*
	Mad River County Park	707-445-7651	*DOGS ALLOWED OFF-LEASH ON BEACH*
Eureka	Samoa Dunes Recreation Area	707-825-2300	*DOGS ALLOWED OFF-LEASH ON BEACH; MUST BE LEASHED ON TRAILS*
Ferndale	Centerville Beach County Park	800-346-3482	*DOGS ALLOWED ON BEACH; MUST BE LEASHED MARCH 1 TO SEPTEMBER 30*
	Crab County Park	800-346-3482	*DOGS ALLOWED ON BEACH; MUST BE LEASHED MARCH 1 TO SEPTEMBER 30*
Orick	Carruthers Cove Beach	707-825-2300	*DOGS ALLOWED ON BEACH*
	Gold Bluffs Beach	707-464-1812	NO DOGS ALLOWED ON BEACH
Trinidad	Agate Beach	707-677-1610	*LEASHED DOGS ALLOWED ON BEACH*
	Baker Beach	707-677-1610	*LEASHED DOGS ALLOWED ON BEACH*
	Big Lagoon County Park	800-346-3482	*LEASHED DOGS ALLOWED ON BEACH*
	College Cove	707-677-1610	*LEASHED DOGS ALLOWED ON BEACH*
	Indian Beach	707-677-1610	*LEASHED DOGS ALLOWED ON BEACH*
	Luffenholtz Beach	707-677-1610	*LEASHED DOGS ALLOWED ON BEACH*
	Moonstone Beach	707-677-1610	*LEASHED DOGS ALLOWED ON BEACH*
	Trinidad State Beach	707-677-1610	*LEASHED DOGS ALLOWED ON BEACH*

North Coast - Mendocino County:

Caspar	Caspar State Beach	707-937-5804	*LEASHED DOGS ALLOWED ON BEACH*
Fort Bragg	Glass Beach	707-961-6300	*LEASHED DOGS ALLOWED ON BEACH*
	MacKerricher State Park	707-964-9112	*LEASHED DOGS ALLOWED ON BEACH*
	Noyo Harbor Beach	707-961-6300	*LEASHED DOGS ALLOWED ON BEACH*
	Pudding Creek Beach	707-961-6300	*LEASHED DOGS ALLOWED ON BEACH*

Gualala	Gualala River Beach	707-834-3533	*DOGS ALLOWED ON BEACH*
	Gualala Point Regional Park	707-785-2377	*LEASHED DOGS ALLOWED ON BEACH*
Manchester	Manchester State Beach	707-882-2463	*LEASHED DOGS ALLOWED ON BEACH*
Mendocino	Mendocino Headlands State Park	707-937-5804	*LEASHED DOGS ALLOWED ON BEACH*
	Russian Gulch State Park	707-937-5804	*LEASHED DOGS ALLOWED ON BEACH*
	Van Damme State Park	707-937-5804	*LEASHED DOGS ALLOWED ON BEACH*
Point Arena	Bowling Ball Beach	707-884-3831	*LEASHED DOGS ALLOWED ON BEACH*
	Fish Rock Beach	707-884-3831	*LEASHED DOGS ALLOWED ON BEACH*
	Greenwood Creek State Beach	707-937-5804	*LEASHED DOGS ALLOWED ON BEACH*
	Schooner Gulch Beach	707-884-3831	*LEASHED DOGS ALLOWED ON BEACH*
Westport	Bear Harbor Beach	707-462-4705	*LEASHED DOGS ALLOWED ON BEACH*
	Jones Beach	707-462-4705	*LEASHED DOGS ALLOWED ON BEACH*
	Little Jackass Creek Beach	707-462-4705	*LEASHED DOGS ALLOWED ON BEACH*
	Needle Rock Beach	707-462-4705	*LEASHED DOGS ALLOWED ON BEACH*
	Seaside Creek Beach	707-462-4705	*LEASHED DOGS ALLOWED ON BEACH*
	Usal Beach	707-462-4705	*LEASHED DOGS ALLOWED ON BEACH*
	Wages Creek Beach	707-462-4705	*LEASHED DOGS ALLOWED ON BEACH*
	Westport-Union Landing State Beach	707-937-5804	*LEASHED DOGS ALLOWED ON BEACH*

North Coast - Sonoma County:

Bodega Bay	Arched Rock Beach	707-875-3483	*LEASHED DOGS ALLOWED ON BEACH*
	Bodega Dunes Beach	707-875-3866	NO DOGS ALLOWED ON BEACH
	Bodega Head	707-875-3866	NO DOGS ALLOWED ON BEACH
	Coleman Beach	707-875-3866	*LEASHED DOGS ALLOWED ON BEACH*
	Doran Beach Regional Park	707-875-3540	*LEASHED DOGS ALLOWED ON BEACH*
	Miwok Beach	707-875-3866	NO DOGS ALLOWED ON BEACH
	North Salmon Creek Beach	707-875-3866	NO DOGS ALLOWED ON BEACH
	South Salmon Creek Beach	707-875-3866	NO DOGS ALLOWED ON BEACH
Carmet	Carmet Beach	707-875-3483	*LEASHED DOGS ALLOWED ON BEACH*
	Portugese Beach	707-875-3483	*LEASHED DOGS ALLOWED ON BEACH*
	Schoolhouse Beach	707-875-3483	*LEASHED DOGS ALLOWED ON BEACH*
Jenner	Blind Beach	707-875-3483	*LEASHED DOGS ALLOWED ON BEACH*
	Goat Rock Beach	707-875-3483	NO DOGS ALLOWED ON BEACH
	Salt Point State Beach	707-847-3221	NO DOGS ALLOWED ON BEACH
	Stillwater Cove Regional Park	707-847-3245	*LEASHED DOGS ALLOWED ON BEACH*
Ocean View	Gleason Beach	707-875-3483	*LEASHED DOGS ALLOWED ON BEACH*
	Shell Beach	707-875-3483	*LEASHED DOGS ALLOWED ON BEACH*
	Wright's Beach	707-875-3483	*LEASHED DOGS ALLOWED ON BEACH*
Sea Ranch	Black Point Beach	707-785-2377	*LEASHED DOGS ALLOWED ON BEACH*
	Pebble Beach	707-785-2377	*LEASHED DOGS ALLOWED ON BEACH*
	Shell Beach	707-785-2377	*LEASHED DOGS ALLOWED ON BEACH*
	Stengel Beach	707-785-2377	*LEASHED DOGS ALLOWED ON BEACH*
	Walk-On Beach	707-785-2377	*LEASHED DOGS ALLOWED ON BEACH*

North Coast - Marin County:

Bolinas	Agate Beach	650-499-6387	DOGS ALLOWED ON BEACH UNDER VOICE CONTROL
	Bolinas Beach	650-499-6387	LEASHED DOGS ALLOWED ON BEACH
	RCA Beach	650-499-6387	LEASHED DOGS ALLOWED ON BEACH
Sausalito	Dunphy Park	415-289-4125	LEASHED DOGS ALLOWED ON BAY BEACH
	Marin Headlands	415-331-1540	LEASHED DOGS ALLOWED ON BEACH
	Rodeo Beach	415-331-1540	DOGS ALLOWED OFF LEASH FROM SHORELINE TO THE CREST OF THE DUNES
Stinson Beach	Dog Beach	415-868-0942	DOGS ALLOWED ON BEACH AT NORTH END OF STINSON BEACH
	Red Rock Beach	415-388-2070	NO DOGS ALLOWED ON BEACH
	Stinson Beach	415-388-2070	NO DOGS ALLOWED ON BEACH

North Coast - San Francisco County:

Golden Gate National Recreation Area	China Beach	415-561-4700	NO DOGS ALLOWED ON BEACH
	Crissy Field		LEASHED DOGS PERMITTED EXCEPT IN WILDLIFE PROTECTION AREAS; DOGS NOT PERMITTED ON LOTOS CREEK BOARDWALK
	Fort Funston		LEASHED DOGS ALLOWED EXCEPT IN WILDLIFE PROTECTION AREAS
	Lands End Beach		LEASHED DOGS ALLOWED ON BEACH
	Muir Beach		LEASHED DOGS ALLOWED IN DESIGNATED AREAS; DOGS NOT ALLOWED IN LAGOON OR REDWOOD CREEK
	Ocean Beach		LEASHED DOGS ALLOWED EXCEPT IN WILDLIFE PROTECTION AREAS
San Francisco	Baker Beach	650-556-8371	DOGS ALLOWED OFF LEASH ON BEACH

Central Coast - San Mateo County:

Daly City	Esplanade Beach	650-991-5101	DOGS ALLOWED OFF-LEASH ON BEACH
Half Moon Bay	Cowell Ranch Beach	650-726-8819	LEASHED DOGS ALLOWED ON BEACH
	Dunes Beach	650-726-8819	LEASHED DOGS ALLOWED ON BEACH
	El Granada Beach	650-726-8819	LEASHED DOGS ALLOWED ON BEACH
	Francis Beach	650-726-8819	NO DOGS ALLOWED ON BEACH
	Martin's Beach	650-726-4357	LEASHED DOGS ALLOWED ON BEACH
	Mirimar Beach	650-726-8819	LEASHED DOGS ALLOWED ON BEACH
	Pelican Point Beach	650-726-8819	LEASHED DOGS ALLOWED ON BEACH
	Venice Beach	650-726-8819	LEASHED DOGS ALLOWED ON BEACH
Montara	Gray Whale Cove State Beach	650-728-5336	LEASHED DOGS ALLOWED ON BEACH
	Montara State Beach	650-726-8819	LEASHED DOGS ALLOWED ON BEACH
Moss Beach	James V. Fitzgerald Marine Reserve	650-728-3584	NO DOGS ALLOWED ON BEACH
Pacifica	Pacifica State Beach	650-738-7381	LEASHED DOGS ALLOWED ON BEACH
	Rockaway Beach	650-738-7380	LEASHED DOGS ALLOWED ON BEACH
	Sharp Park Beach	650-738-7380	LEASHED DOGS ALLOWED ON BEACH
Pescadero	Bean Hollow State Beach	650-879-2170	LEASHED DOGS ALLOWED ON BEACH
	Gazos Creek Access	650-879-2170	LEASHED DOGS ALLOWED ON BEACH
	Pebble Beach	650-879-2170	LEASHED DOGS ALLOWED ON BEACH
	Pescadero State Beach	650-879-2170	LEASHED DOGS ALLOWED ON BEACH
	Pigeon Point Beach	650-879-2170	LEASHED DOGS ALLOWED ON BEACH

San Gregorio	Pomponio State Beach	650-879-2170	*LEASHED DOGS ALLOWED ON BEACH*
	San Gregorio State Beach	650-879-2170	*LEASHED DOGS ALLOWED ON BEACH*

Central Coast - Santa Cruz County:

Aptos	Lundborgh Beach	831-688-1467	*LEASHED DOGS ALLOWED ON BEACH*
	Manresa State Beach	831-761-1795	*LEASHED DOGS ALLOWED ON BEACH*
	Manresa Uplands	831-761-1795	*LEASHED DOGS ALLOWED ON BEACH*
	Rio Del Mar Beach	831-429-2850	*LEASHED DOGS ALLOWED ON BEACH*
	Seacliff State Beach	831-685-6500	*LEASHED DOGS ALLOWED ON BEACH; FURTHER SOUTH AT SEASCAPE DOGS CAN USUALLY RUN FREE*
Capitola	Capitola City Beach	831-475-7300	NO DOGS ALLOWED ON BEACH
	New Brighton State Beach	831-464-6330	LEASHED DOGS ALLOWED ON TRAILS ABOVE BEACH BUT NOT ON BEACH
Davenport	Ano Nuevo State Reserve	650-879-2025	NO DOGS ALLOWED ON BEACH
	Bonny Doon Beach	831-462-8333	*LEASHED DOGS ALLOWED ON BEACH*
	Davenport Beach	831-462-8333	*LEASHED DOGS ALLOWED ON BEACH*
	Davenport Landing Beach	831-462-8333	*LEASHED DOGS ALLOWED ON BEACH*
	Panther Beach	831-462-8333	*LEASHED DOGS ALLOWED ON BEACH*
	Scott Creek Beach	831-462-8333	*LEASHED DOGS ALLOWED ON BEACH*
	Yellowbank Beach	831-462-8333	*LEASHED DOGS ALLOWED ON BEACH*
Santa Cruz	Corcoran Lagoon Beach	831-420-6015	NO DOGS ALLOWED ON BEACH
	Cowell Beach	831-420-6015	NO DOGS ALLOWED ON BEACH
	Hooper Beach	831-420-6015	NO DOGS ALLOWED ON BEACH
	Key Beach	831-420-6015	NO DOGS ALLOWED ON BEACH
	Lighthouse Field State Beach	831-420-5670	*DOGS ALLOWED ON BEACH OFF-LEASH SUNRISE TO 10 AM AND 4 PM TO SUNSET*
	Lincoln Beach	831-420-6015	NO DOGS ALLOWED ON BEACH
	Main Beach	831-420-6015	NO DOGS ALLOWED ON BEACH OR BOARDWALK
	Mitchell's Cove	831-420-6015	*DOGS ALLOWED OFF-LEASH ON BEACH*
	Moran Lake Beach	831-462-8333	*LEASHED DOGS ALLOWED ON BEACH*
	Natural Bridges State Beach	831-423-4609	*LEASHED DOGS ALLOWED ON BEACH*
	Pleasure Point Beach	831-462-8333	NO DOGS ALLOWED ON BEACH
	Seabright Beach	831-429-2850	*DOGS ALLOWED ON BEACH*
	Steamer Lane	831-420-6015	NO DOGS ALLOWED ON BEACH
	Sunny Cove	831-420-6015	NO DOGS ALLOWED ON BEACH
	Twin Lakes State Beach	831-429-2850	*DOGS ALLOWED ON BEACH*
Watsonville	Sunset State Beach	831-763-7062	*LEASHED DOGS ALLOWED ON BEACH IN DESIGNATED AREAS*

Central Coast - Monterey County:

Big Sur	Andrew Molera State Park	831-667-2315	*LEASHED DOGS ALLOWED ON BEACH*
	Garrapata State Park	831-667-2315	NO DOGS ALLOWED ON BEACH
	Julia Pfeiffer Burns State Park	831-667-2315	NO DOGS ALLOWED ON BEACH
	Limekiln State Park	831-667-2403	*LEASHED DOGS ALLOWED ON BEACH*
	Pfeiffer Beach	831-667-2315	*LEASHED DOGS ALLOWED ON BEACH*
Carmel	Carmel City Beach	831-624-3543	*DOGS ALLOWED OFF-LEASH ON BEACH*
	Carmel River StateBeach	831-649-2836	*LEASHED DOGS ALLOWED ON BEACH*
	Point Lobos State Reserve	831-649-2836	NO DOGS ALLOWED ON BEACH
Marina	Marina State Beach	831-384-7695	*LEASHED DOGS ALLOWED ON BEACH*
Moss Landing	Moss Landing State Beach	831-649-2836	*LEASHED DOGS ALLOWED ON BEACH*
	Salinas River State Beach	831-649-2836	*LEASHED DOGS ALLOWED ON BEACH*
	Zmudowski State Beach	831-649-2836	*LEASHED DOGS ALLOWED ON BEACH*

Monterey	Macabee Beach	831-646-3866	LEASHED DOGS ALLOWED ON BEACH
	Monterey StateBeach	831-646-3866	LEASHED DOGS ALLOWED ON BEACH
	San Carlos Beach Park	831-646-3866	LEASHED DOGS ALLOWED ON BEACH
Pacific Grove	Asilomar State Beach	831-372-4076	LEASHED DOGS ALLOWED ON BEACH
	Lover's Point	831-648-3130	LEASHED DOGS ALLOWED ON BEACH
	Shoreline Park	831-648-3130	LEASHED DOGS ALLOWED ON BEACH
Pebble Beach	Fanshell Beach	831-646-3866	LEASHED DOGS ALLOWED ON BEACH
	Moss Beach	831-646-3866	LEASHED DOGS ALLOWED ON BEACH
	Spanish Bay	831-646-3866	LEASHED DOGS ALLOWED ON BEACH
Seaside	Sand Public Beach	831-394-3054	LEASHED DOGS ALLOWED ON BEACH

Central Coast - San Luis Obispo County:

Cambria	Moonstone State Beach	805-927-3624	LEASHED DOGS ALLOWED ON BEACH
Cayucos	Cayucos State Beach	805-781-5200	LEASHED DOGS ALLOWED ON BEACH
	Morrow Strand State Beach	805-772-2560	LEASHED DOGS ALLOWED ON BEACH IN DESIGNATED AREAS
Pismo Beach	Avila Beach	805-773-2208	LEASHED DOGS ALLOWED ON BEACH BEFORE 10 AM AND 5 PM
	Oceano Beach	805-773-2208	LEASHED DOGS ALLOWED ON BEACH
	Olde Port Beach	805-773-2208	LEASHED DOGS ALLOWED ON BEACH
	Pismo State Beach	805-489-2684	LEASHED DOGS ALLOWED ON BEACH
	Shell Beach	805-773-4382	LEASHED DOGS ALLOWED ON BEACH
San Simeon	San Simeon State Beach	805-927-2020	LEASHED DOGS ALLOWED ON BEACH
	W.R. Hearst Memorial State Beach	805-927-2020	LEASHED DOGS ALLOWED ON BEACH

Central Coast - Barbara County:

Carpinteria	Carpinteria City Beach	805-684-5405	NO DOGS ALLOWED ON BEACH
	Carpinteria State Beach	805-684-2811	NO DOGS ALLOWED ON BEACH
	Jellybowl Beach	805-684-5405	LEASHED DOGS ALLOWED ON BEACH
	Rincon Beach County Park	805-681-5650	LEASHED DOGS ALLOWED ON BEACH
	Rincon Point Beach	805-684-5405	NO DOGS ALLOWED ON BEACH
	Santa Claus Lane Beach	805-684-5405	NO DOGS ALLOWED ON BEACH
Goleta	El Capitan State Beach	805-968-1033	NO DOGS ALLOWED ON BEACH
	Gaviota State Park	805-968-1033	NO DOGS ALLOWED ON BEACH
	Goleta Beach County Park	805-967-1300	LEASHED DOGS ALLOWED ON BEACH
	Isla Vista Beach	805-967-1300	NO DOGS ALLOWED ON BEACH
	Refugio State Beach	805-968-1033	NO DOGS ALLOWED ON BEACH
Guadalupe	Rancho Guadalupe Dunes County Park	805-934-6123	LEASHED DOGS ALLOWED ON BEACH
Lompoc	Jalama Beach County Park	805-736-6316	LEASHED DOGS ALLOWED ON BEACH
	Ocean Beach County Park	805-934-6123	LEASHED DOGS ALLOWED ON BEACH
Santa Barbara	Arroyo Burro Beach County Park	805-687-3714	LEASHED DOGS ALLOWED ON BEACH
	Butterfly Beach	805-564-5418	NO DOGS ALLOWED ON BEACH
	East Beach	805-564-5418	NO DOGS ALLOWED ON BEACH
	Leadbetter Beach	805-564-5418	NO DOGS ALLOWED ON BEACH
	Mesa Lane Beach	805-564-5418	NO DOGS ALLOWED ON BEACH
	Thousand Steps Beach	805-564-5418	NO DOGS ALLOWED ON BEACH
	West Beach	805-564-5418	NO DOGS ALLOWED ON BEACH

Summerland	Lookout County Beach	805-969-1720	NO DOGS ALLOWED ON BEACH
	Summerland Beach	805-568-2461	*DOGS ALLOWED ON BEACH*

Central Coast - Ventura County:

Oxnard	Hollywood Beach	805-382-3007	*LEASHED DOGS ALLOWED ON BEACH BETWEEN 5 PM AND 9 AM*
	Mandalay County Park	805-654-3951	*LEASHED DOGS ALLOWED ON BEACH*
	McGrath State Beach	805-654-4744	NO DOGS ALLOWED ON BEACH
	Oxnard Beach Park	805-385-7950	*LEASHED DOGS ALLOWED ON BEACH*
	Silver Strand Beach	805-382-3007	*LEASHED DOGS ALLOWED ON BEACH BETWEEN 5 PM AND 9 AM*
Port Hueneme	Point Magu State Park	818-880-0350	*LEASHED DOGS ALLOWED ON BEACH*
Ventura	Channel Islands National Park	805-658-5700	NO DOGS ALLOWED ON ISLANDS
	Emma Wood State Beach	805-968-1033	*LEASHED DOGS ALLOWED ON BEACH*
	Faria Beach County Park	805-654-3951	*LEASHED DOGS ALLOWED ON BEACH*
	Hobson County Park	805-654-3951	*LEASHED DOGS ALLOWED ON BEACH*
	Marina Park	805-652-4550	*LEASHED DOGS ALLOWED ON BEACH*
	San Buenaventura State Beach	805-899-1400	NO DOGS ALLOWED ON BEACH
	Surfer's Point at Seaside	805-654-7800	*LEASHED DOGS ALLOWED ON BEACH*

Southern Coast - Los Angeles County:

Catalina Island	Avalon Bay Beach	310-305-9546	DOGS ALLOWED ON ISLAND BUT NOT ON BEACHES
	Ben Watson Beach	310-510-1520	DOGS ALLOWED ON ISLAND BUT NOT ON BEACHES
	Crescent Beach	310-510-1520	DOGS ALLOWED ON ISLAND BUT NOT ON BEACHES
	Descanso Beach	310-510-1520	DOGS ALLOWED ON ISLAND BUT NOT ON BEACHES
	Little Harbor Beach	310-510-1520	DOGS ALLOWED ON ISLAND BUT NOT ON BEACHES
	Pebbly Beach	310-510-1520	DOGS ALLOWED ON ISLAND BUT NOT ON BEACHES
Hermosa Beach	Hermosa Beach	310-372-2166	NO DOGS ALLOWED ON BEACH
Long Beach	Alamitos Bay Beach	562-570-3100	NO DOGS ALLOWED ON BEACH
	Belmont Shore Beach	562-570-3100 562-570-3215	*OFF-LEASH DOG ZONE BETWEEN ROYCROFT AND ARGONNE AVENUES* NO DOGS ALLOWED ON BEACH
Malibu	White Point County Park	310-457-9891 310-457-2525	NO DOGS ALLOWED ON BEACH NO DOGS ALLOWED ON BEACH
	Amarillo Beach	818-880-0350	NO DOGS ALLOWED ON BEACH
	Dan Blocker County Beach	818-880-0350	NO DOGS ALLOWED ON BEACH
	El Matador State Beach	818-880-0350	NO DOGS ALLOWED ON BEACH
	El Pescador State Beach	310-394-3261	NO DOGS ALLOWED ON BEACH
	La Piedra State Beach	818-880-0530	*LEASHED DOGS ALLOWED ON BEACH EXCEPT BETWEEN LIFEGUARD STAND 1 AN 3 BECAUSE OF TIDEPOOLS*
	Las Tunas County Beach	310-305-9546	NO DOGS ALLOWED ON BEACH
	Leo Carillo State Beach	310-305-9546	NO DOGS ALLOWED ON BEACH
	Malibu Lagoon County Beach	310-457-2511	NO DOGS ALLOWED ON BEACH
	Nicholas Canyon County Beach	310-457-2525	NO DOGS ALLOWED ON BEACH
	Paradise Cove	310-457-2525	NO DOGS ALLOWED ON BEACH
	Point Dume County Beach	310-372-2166	NO DOGS ALLOWED ON BEACH
	Surfrider Beach	310-372-2166	NO DOGS ALLOWED ON BEACH

Manhattan Beach	Manhattan County Beach	310-372-2166	NO DOGS ALLOWED ON BEACH
Marina del Rey	Marina Beach	310-344-3261	NO DOGS ALLOWED ON BEACH
Palos Verdes Estates	Abalone Cove Beach	310-377-0360	NO DOGS ALLOWED ON BEACH
	Malaga Cove Beach	310-372-2166	NO DOGS ALLOWED ON BEACH
	Royal Palms County Beach	310-372-2166	NO DOGS ALLOWED ON BEACH
Playa del Rey	Dockweiler State Beach	310-372-2166	NO DOGS ALLOWED ON BEACH
	Playa del Rey Beach	310-372-2166	NO DOGS ALLOWED ON BEACH
Redondo Beach	Redondo County Beach	310-372-2166	NO DOGS ALLOWED ON BEACH
	Torrance County Beach	310-372-2166	NO DOGS ALLOWED ON BEACH
San Pedro	Cabrillo City Beach	310-548-2914	NO DOGS ALLOWED ON BEACH
	White Point County Park	310-372-2166	NO DOGS ALLOWED ON BEACH
Santa Monica	Santa Monica State Beach	310-578-0478	NO DOGS ALLOWED ON BEACH
	Will Rogers State Beach	310-372-2166	NO DOGS ALLOWED ON BEACH
Venice	Venice City Beach	310-372-2166	

Southern Coast - Orange County:

Balboa	Balboa Beach	949-644-3309	NO DOGS ALLOWED ON BEACH
	Balboa Island	949-644-3309	NO DOGS ALLOWED ON BEACH
	West Jetty View Park	949-644-3309	NO DOGS ALLOWED ON BEACH
Capistrano Beach	Capistrano Beach	949-661-7013	NO DOGS ALLOWED ON BEACH
	Poche Beach	949-661-7013	NO DOGS ALLOWED ON BEACH
Corona del Mar	Corona del Mar State Beach	949-722-1611	*LEASHED DOGS ALLOWED ON BEACH BEFORE 9 AM AND AFTER 9 PM*
	Little Corona del Mar Beach	949-644-3044	*LEASHED DOGS ALLOWED ON BEACH*
Dana Point	Dana Point Harbor Beach	949-496-1094	NO DOGS ALLOWED ON BEACH
	Doheny State Beach	949-496-6171	NO DOGS ALLOWED ON BEACH
Huntington Beach	Bolsa Chica State Beach	714-846-3460	NO DOGS ALLOWED ON BEACH
	Huntington City Beach	714-536-5486	*DOGS ALLOWED ON BEACH AT "DOG BEACH" FOUND AT THE NORTHERNMOST POINT AT SEAPOINT AVENUE*
	Huntington State Beach	714-536-1454	NO DOGS ALLOWED ON BEACH
Laguna Beach	Brooks Beach	714-494-6572	*FROM JUNE 1 THROUGH SEPTEMBER 15 LEASHED DOGS ALLOWED ON BEACH ONLY BEFORE 8 AM AND AFTER 6 PM; LEASHED DOGS ALLOWED ON BEACH ANYTIME THE REST OF THE YEAR*
	Crystal Cove State Park	714-494-3539	NO DOGS ALLOWED ON BEACH
	Main Beach	714-497-0706	*FROM JUNE 1 THROUGH SEPTEMBER 15 LEASHED DOGS ALLOWED ON BEACH ONLY BEFORE 8 AM AND AFTER 6 PM; LEASHED DOGS ALLOWED ON BEACH ANYTIME THE REST OF THE YEAR*
	Victoria Beach	714-494-6572	*FROM JUNE 1 THROUGH SEPTEMBER 15 LEASHED DOGS ALLOWED ON BEACH ONLY BEFORE 8 AM AND AFTER 6 PM; LEASHED DOGS ALLOWED ON BEACH ANYTIME THE REST OF THE YEAR*

Newport Beach	Los Alenas Park	949-644-3044	NO DOGS ALLOWED ON BEACH
	Newport Beach Municipal Beach	949-644-3309	NO DOGS ALLOWED ON BEACH
	Santa Ana River County Beach	949-723-4511	NO DOGS ALLOWED ON BEACH
	West Newport Beach	949-644-3309	NO DOGS ALLOWED ON BEACH
San Clemente	Calafia Beach	949-361-8264	NO DOGS ALLOWED ON BEACH
	North Beach	949-361-8264	NO DOGS ALLOWED ON BEACH
	San Clemente City Beach	949-361-8264	NO DOGS ALLOWED ON BEACH
	San Clemente State Beach	949-492-0802	NO DOGS ALLOWED ON BEACH
	San Onofre State Beach	949-492-4872	NO DOGS ALLOWED ON BEACH
Seal Beach	Seal Beach	310-430-2527	NO DOGS ALLOWED ON BEACH
South Laguna	Aliso Beach County Park	949-497-0706	*FROM JUNE 1 THROUGH SEPTEMBER 15 LEASHED DOGS ALLOWED ON BEACH ONLY BEFORE 8 AM AND AFTER 6 PM; LEASHED DOGS ALLOWED ON BEACH ANYTIME THE REST OF THE YEAR*
	Camel Point Beach	949-661-7013	*FROM JUNE 1 THROUGH SEPTEMBER 15 LEASHED DOGS ALLOWED ON BEACH ONLY BEFORE 8 AM AND AFTER 6 PM; LEASHED DOGS ALLOWED ON BEACH ANYTIME THE REST OF THE YEAR*
	Salt Creek Beach Park	949-661-7013	NO DOGS ALLOWED ON BEACH
	1,000 Steps Beach	949-661-7013	*FROM JUNE 1 THROUGH SEPTEMBER 15 LEASHED DOGS ALLOWED ON BEACH ONLY BEFORE 8 AM AND AFTER 6 PM; LEASHED DOGS ALLOWED ON BEACH ANYTIME THE REST OF THE YEAR*
Sunset Beach	Sunset Beach	949-509-6683	NO DOGS ALLOWED ON BEACH
Surfside	Surfside Beach	310-430-2613	NO DOGS ALLOWED ON BEACH

Southern Coast - San Diego County:

Cardiff	Cardiff State Beach	760-753-5091	*LEASHED DOGS ALLOWED ON BEACH FROM SOUTH END OF SAN ELIJO LAGOON TO SOLANA*
	San Elijo State Beach	760-753-5091	*LEASHED DOGS ALLOWED ON BEACH FROM SWAMI'S BEACH TO SAN ELIJO LAGOON MOUTH*
Carlsbad	Carlsbad State Beach	760-438-3143	NO DOGS ALLOWED ON BEACH
	South Carlsbad State Beach	760-438-2675	NO DOGS ALLOWED ON BEACH
Coronado	Coronado Beach		*DOGS ALLOWED ON BEACH ONLY THROUGH A NARROW CORRIDOR FROM OCEAN BOULEVARD ALONG THE FENCE AT NORTH ISLAND NAVAL AIR STATION GATE 5*
Del Mar	Del Mar City Beach	858-755-1556	NO DOGS ALLOWED ON BEACH
	North Beach	858-755-1556	*ROM VIA DE LA VALLE TO 27TH STREET DOGS ALLOWED ON BEACH UNDER VOICE CONTROL FROM SEPTEMBER 15 TO JUNE 15; ALLOWED LEASHED ON BEACH OTHERWISE*

Encinitas	Beacons Beach	760-633-2750	NO DOGS ALLOWED ON BEACH
	Boneyard Beach	760-633-2750	NO DOGS ALLOWED ON BEACH
	D Street Beach	760-633-2750	NO DOGS ALLOWED ON BEACH
	Encinitas Beach	760-633-2750	NO DOGS ALLOWED ON BEACH
	Moonlight Beach	760-633-2750	NO DOGS ALLOWED ON BEACH
	Stone Steps Beach	760-633-2750	NO DOGS ALLOWED ON BEACH
	Swami's	760-633-2750	NO DOGS ALLOWED ON BEACH
Imperial Beach	Imperial Beach	619-423-8328	*LEASHED DOGS ALLOWED SOUTH OF IMPERIAL BEACH BOULEVARD AND NOT ALLOWED NORTH OF IMPERIAL BEACH BOULEVARD*
	Silver Strand State Beach	619-435-5184	NO DOGS ALLOWED ON BEACH
La Jolla	Black's Beach	619-221-8899	NO DOGS ALLOWED ON BEACH
	Marine Street Beach	619-221-8899	*LEASHED DOGS ALLOWED ON BEACH BEFORE 9 AM AND AFTER 6 PM*
	Windansea Beach	619-221-8899	*LEASHED DOGS ALLOWED ON BEACH BEFORE 9 AM AND AFTER 6 PM*
Mission Beach	Mission Beach	619-221-8899	*LEASHED DOGS ALLOWED ON BEACH BEFORE 9 AM AND AFTER 6 PM*
Oceanside	Buccaneer Beach	760-435-4018	NO DOGS ALLOWED ON BEACH
	Oceanside City Beach	760-435-4018	NO DOGS ALLOWED ON BEACH
Pacific Beach	Pacific Beach	619-221-8899	*LEASHED DOGS ALLOWED ON BEACH BEFORE 9 AM AND AFTER 6 PM*
	Tourmaline Surfing Park	619-221-8899	*LEASHED DOGS ALLOWED ON BEACH BEFORE 9 AM AND AFTER 6 PM*
San Diego	Ocean Beach	619-221-8899	*LEASHED DOGS ALLOWED ON BEACH BEFORE 9 AM AND AFTER 6 PM; DOGS ALLOWED OFF-LEASH NORTH OF THE BICYCLE PATH THAT TERMINATES ON THE NORTH EDGE OF THE VOLTAIRE STREET PARKING LOT*
Solana Beach	Delmar Shores Beach Park	858-755-1569	NO DOGS ALLOWED ON BEACH
	Fletcher Cove Beach Park	858-755-1569	NO DOGS ALLOWED ON BEACH
	Seascape Surf Beach Park	858-755-1569	NO DOGS ALLOWED ON BEACH
	Tide Beach Park	858-755-1569	NO DOGS ALLOWED ON BEACH

Your dog will find more chances to wrestle a piece of driftwood to the sand on Northern California beaches than in Southern California.

DOGS ON GREAT LAKES BEACHES

LAKE SUPERIOR

Possessing the largest surface area of any freshwater lake in the world, there is enough water in Lake Superior to easily fill the other four Great Lakes to overflowing. Lake Superior is known for its cold water and rugged shoreline but there are some sandy beaches scattered across its 300 or so miles of southern shores. Other beaches are more of the cobble variety. Most of the shoreline is sparsely populated and that bodes well for finding a dog-friendly beach.

Michigan:

Pictured Rocks National Lakeshore		906-387-2607	*AT GRAND MARAIS, LEASHED DOGS ALLOWED ON BEACH FROM TWELVEMILE BEACH CAMPGROUND TO AU SABLE LIGHTHOUSE; AT MUNISING, DOGS ALLOWED ON BEACH AT MINERS BEACH EXCEPT ON LAKESHORE TRAIL AT EAST END OF BEACH; DOGS ALLOWED ON SAND POINT UNTIL TRAIL BEGINS TO CLIMB CLIFFS*
Big Bay	Burns Landing Beach	906-225-8150	*DOGS ALLOWED ON BEACH*
Brimley	Brimley State Park	906-482-0278	NO DOGS ALLOWED ON BEACH
Copper Harbor	Keweenaw Point	800-338-7982	*DOGS ALLOWED ON BEACH*
Eagle Harbor	Great Sand Bay	800-338-7982	NO DOGS ALLOWED ON BEACH
Eagle River	Five Mile Point	800-338-7982	*DOGS ALLOWED ON BEACH*
Grand Marais	Woodland Park	906-494-2381	*LEASHED DOGS ALLOWED ON BEACH*
Hancock	F.J. McLain State Park	906-482-0278	NO DOGS ALLOWED ON BEACH
Marquette	McCartys Cove	906-228-0460	NO DOGS ALLOWED ON BEACH
	South Beach	906-228-0460	NO DOGS ALLOWED ON BEACH
	Tourist Park	906-228-0460	NO DOGS ALLOWED ON BEACH
Munising	Grand Island National Recreation Area	906-387-3700	*LEASHED DOGS ALLOWED ON BEACH*
Paradise	Whitefish Point	906-492-3219	*DOGS ALLOWED ON REMOTE BEACHES FROM POINT ON WEST, ACCESSED BY UNDEVELOPED ROADS*
Toivola	Agate Beach	800-338-7982	*DOGS ALLOWED ON BEACH*

Wisconsin:

Ashland	Bayview Park	800-284-9484	*LEASHED DOGS ALLOWED ON BEACH*
	Kreher Beach	800-284-9484	*LEASHED DOGS ALLOWED ON BEACH*
	Maslowski Beach	800-284-9484	*LEASHED DOGS ALLOWED ON BEACH*
Bayfield	Broad Street Beach	800-447-4094	*DOGS ALLOWED ON BEACH*
Superior	Barker's Island	715-392-2773	NO DOGS ALLOWED ON BEACH

Minnesota:

Duluth	Park Point Beach	218-723-3337	*LEASHED DOGS ALLOWED ON BEACH*

LAKE MICHIGAN

Dogs will have to admire the spectacular dunes and sandy beaches of the eastern shore of Lake Michigan mostly from the car as dogs are not allowed on Michigan state beaches and most county and town beaches. In-season, the metropolises of Indiana, Illinois and Wisconsin are even more restrictive. Your best bets to dip into Lake Michigan, the only Great Lake totally within the United States, are the national lakeshores and the state parks of Wisconsin's Door County.

Michigan - Upper Peninsula:

Cedar River	J.W. Wells State Park	906-863-9747	NO DOGS ALLOWED ON BEACH
Escanaba	Fuller Park	906-789-7862	*LEASHED DOGS ALLOWED ON BEACH*
	Ludington Park	906-786-4141	*LEASHED DOGS ALLOWED ON BEACH*
Garden Corners	Fayette Historic State Park	906-644-2603	NO DOGS ALLOWED ON BEACH
Gladstone	VanCleve Park	906-786-9234	*DOGS ALLOWED ON CAMPGROUND AND PARK BEACHES BUT NOT IN SWIMMING BEACH*
Manistique	Town Beach	906-341-5010	*LEASHED DOGS ALLOWED ON BEACH*
St. Ignace	Lake Michigan Sand Dunes	906-643-8717	*DOGS ALLOWED ON BEACH*

Michigan - Northwest:

Sleeping Bear Dunes National Lakeshore		231-326-5134	*DOGS ALLOWED ON BEACH EXCEPT ON PLATTE POINTE BEACH, NORTH MANTIOU ISLAND, SOUTH MANITOU ISLAND AND D.H. DAY CAMPGROUND BEACH*
Acme	Acme Township Beach	231-938-1350	NO DOGS ALLOWED ON BEACH
	Bayside Beach	231-938-1350	NO DOGS ALLOWED ON BEACH
	Dock Street Beach	231-938-1350	*LEASHED DOGS ALLOWED ON BEACH*
	Tony Gilroy Township Park	231-938-1350	NO DOGS ALLOWED ON BEACH
Beaver Island	Beaver Island Public Beach	231-448-2205	*LEASHED DOGS ALLOWED ON BEACH*
	Bill Wagner Memorial Campground Beach	231-448-2205	*LEASHED DOGS ALLOWED ON BEACH*
	Harbor Beach	231-448-2205	*LEASHED DOGS ALLOWED ON BEACH*
	Iron Ore Beach	231-448-2205	*LEASHED DOGS ALLOWED ON BEACH*

Charlevoix	Fisherman's Island State Park	231-547-6641	NO DOGS ALLOWED ON BEACH
	Lake Michigan Beach	231-547-2101	*DOGS ALLOWED ON BEACH*
	Mt. McSauba Beach	231-547-2101	*DOGS ALLOWED ON BEACH*
	Peninsula Municipal Park Beach	231-547-2101	*DOGS ALLOWED ON BEACH*
Eastport	Barnes Park	231-599-2712	NO DOGS ALLOWED ON BEACH
Empire	Empire Beach	231-271-9895	NO DOGS ALLOWED ON BEACH
	Esch Road Beach	231-271-9895	NO DOGS ALLOWED ON BEACH
Glen Arbor	Glen Arbor Municipal Beach	231-271-9895	NO DOGS ALLOWED ON BEACH
Harbor Springs	Thorne Swift Nature Preserve	231-526-7999	NO DOGS ALLOWED ON BEACH
	Zoll Street Beach	231-526-7999	*DOGS ALLOWED ON BEACH*
	Zorn Park	231-526-7999	NO DOGS ALLOWED ON BEACH
Leland	Leland Municipal Beach	231-271-9895	NO DOGS ALLOWED ON BEACH
Mackinaw City	Cecil Bay Beach	231-436-5574	*DOGS ALLOWED ON BEACH*
	Wilderness State Park	231-436-5381	NO DOGS ALLOWED ON BEACH
Northport	Leelanau State Park	231-922-5270	NO DOGS ALLOWED ON BEACH
	Northport Beach	231-271-9895	NO DOGS ALLOWED ON BEACH
	Peterson Park	231-271-9895	NO DOGS ALLOWED ON BEACH
Old Mission	Haserot Beach	231-223-7322	*LEASHED DOGS ALLOWED ON BEACH*
	Old Mission Lighthouse Park Beach	231-223-7897	*LEASHED DOGS ALLOWED ON BEACH*
Petoskey	Magnus City Beach	231-347-4150	*DOGS ALLOWED IN PLAY AREAS BUT NOT IN SWIMMING AREAS*
	Petoskey State Park	231-347-2311	NO DOGS ALLOWED ON BEACH
Suttons Bay	Suttons Bay Municipal Beach	231-271-5077	NO DOGS ALLOWED ON BEACH
Traverse City	Bowers Harbor Beach	231-922-4480	*LEASHED DOGS ALLOWED ON BEACH BUT NOT IN DESIGNATED SWIMMING AREAS*
	Bryant Park	231-922-4480	*LEASHED DOGS ALLOWED ON BEACH BUT NOT IN DESIGNATED SWIMMING AREAS*
	Clinch Park Beach	231-922-4903	*LEASHED DOGS ALLOWED ON BEACH BUT NOT IN DESIGNATED SWIMMING AREAS*
	East Bay Park Beach	231-922-4480	*LEASHED DOGS ALLOWED ON BEACH BUT NOT IN DESIGNATED SWIMMING AREAS*
	Traverse City State Park	231-922-5270	NO DOGS ALLOWED ON BEACH
	West End Beach	231-922-4480	*LEASHED DOGS ALLOWED ON BEACH BUT NOT IN DESIGNATED SWIMMING AREAS* NO DOGS ALLOWED ON BEACH
Yuba	Sayler Park	231-938-1350	NO DOGS ALLOWED ON BEACH

Michigan - Central West:

Arcadia	Arcadia Park	877-626-4783	NO DOGS ALLOWED ON BEACH
Elberta	Elberta Bluffs	231-352-7251	NO DOGS ALLOWED ON BEACH
Grand Haven	Grand Haven	616-842-3210	*NO DOGS ALLOWED ON BEACH BETWEEN THE SWIMMING BUOYS BETWEEN MEMORIAL DAY AND LABOR DAY; LEASHED DOGS ALLOWED ANYTIME SOUTH OF SOUTHERLY BUOY*
	Grand Haven State Park	616-798-3711	NO DOGS ALLOWED ON BEACH
	Kirk Park	616-646-8117	*DOGS ALLOWED ON BEACH OCTOBER 1 TO MAY 1*
	North Beach Park	616-646-8117	*DOGS ALLOWED ON BEACH OCTOBER 1 TO MAY 1*
Holland	Riley Beach	616-355-1300	NO DOGS ALLOWED ON BEACH
Ludington	Buttersville Beach	877-420-6618	*DOGS ALLOWED ON BEACH*
	Loomis Street Boat Launch	877-420-6618	*DOGS ALLOWED ON SMALL BEACH ON EITHER SIDE OF LAUNCH*
	Ludington State Park	231-843-8671	NO DOGS ALLOWED ON BEACH
	Stearns Park Beach	877-420-6618	NO DOGS ALLOWED IN PARK OR ON BEACH
Manistee	Fifth Avenue Beach	231-723-2575	*LEASHED DOGS ALLOWED ON BEACH*
	First Street Beach	231-723-2575	*LEASHED DOGS ALLOWED ON BEACH*
	Lake Michigan Recreation Area	231-723-2211	*LEASHED DOGS ALLOWED ON BEACH EXCEPT IN DESIGNATED RECREATION AREAS*
	Orchard Beach State Park	231-723-7422	NO DOGS ALLOWED ON BEACH
Montague	Medbury Park-North Side	231-893-4585	*DOGS ALLOWED ON BEACH*
	Meinert County Park	231-894-4881	*DOGS ALLOWED ON BEACH*
	White Lake Channel	231-893-4585	*DOGS ALLOWED ON BEACH*
Muskegon	Kruse Park	231-724-6704	*DOGS ALLOWED ON BEACH*
		231-724-6704	*DOGS ALLOWED ON SOUTH END OF BEACH AT WEST END OF SHERMAN AVENUE*
North Muskegon	Muskegon State Park	231-744-3480	NO DOGS ALLOWED ON BEACH
Norton Shores	P.J. Hoffmaster State Park	231-798-3711	NO DOGS ALLOWED ON BEACH
Pentwater	Charles Mears State Park	231-869-2051	NO DOGS ALLOWED ON BEACH
Whitehall	Duck Lake Channel Beach	231-893-4585	*DOGS ALLOWED ON BEACH*
	Whitehall River Lighthouse Museum Beach	231-744-3480	*DOGS ALLOWED ON BEACH*

Michigan - Southwest:

Benton Harbor	Jean Klock Park	616-983-7111	NO DOGS ALLOWED ON BEACH
	Rocky Gap Park	616-983-7111	NO DOGS ALLOWED ON BEACH
Bridgman	Weko Beach	616-465-3406	NO DOGS ALLOWED ON BEACH
Covert	Covert Township Park	269-764-1421	NO DOGS ALLOWED ON BEACH
Hagar Shores	Roadside Park	616-925-6301	*DOGS ALLOWED ON BEACH*

Holland	Holland State Park	616-399-9390	NO DOGS ALLOWED ON BEACH
	Tunnel Park	800-506-1299	NO DOGS ALLOWED ON BEACH
New Buffalo	Township & City Beaches	269-469-1011	NO DOGS ALLOWED ON BEACH
Saugatuck	Oval Beach Recreation Area	616-867-1418	NO DOGS ALLOWED ON BEACH
	Saugatuck Dunes State Park	616-637-2788	NO DOGS ALLOWED ON BEACH
Sawyer	Warren Dunes State Park	616-426-4013	NO DOGS ALLOWED ON BEACH BUT CAN GO ON TRAILS
South Haven	Dyckman Park Beach	269-637-0700	NO DOGS ALLOWED ON BEACH
	North Beach	269-637-0700	NO DOGS ALLOWED ON BEACH
	Oak Street Beach	269-637-0700	NO DOGS ALLOWED ON BEACH
	Packard Beach	269-637-0700	NO DOGS ALLOWED ON BEACH
	South Beach	269-637-0700	NO DOGS ALLOWED ON BEACH
	Van Buren State Park	616-637-2788	NO DOGS ALLOWED ON BEACH
St. Joseph	Lions Beach	616-983-6325	NO DOGS ALLOWED ON BEACH
	Silver Beach	616-983-6325	NO DOGS ALLOWED ON BEACH BUT CAN GO ON SIDEWALKS AND PIER
	Tiscornia Park	616-983-6325	NO DOGS ALLOWED ON BEACH
Stevensville	Glenlord Beach	616-429-1802	NO DOGS ALLOWED ON BEACH
	Grand Mere State Park	616-426-4013	NO DOGS ALLOWED ON BEACH
	Township Beach	616-429-1802	NO DOGS ALLOWED ON BEACH
Union Pier	Chikaming Township Beach	616-395-1525	NO DOGS ALLOWED ON BEACH
	Lake Minchigan Beach	616-395-1525	NO DOGS ALLOWED ON BEACH

Indiana:

Indiana Dunes National Lakeshore	219-926-7561	*DURING THE SUMMER LEASHED DOGS ALLOWED ON THE EASTERNMOST BEACHES - MT. BALDY AND CENTRAL AVENUE; AFTER SEPTEMBER 30 OTHER BEACHES OPEN TO DOGS*
Chesterton	Indiana Dunes State Park	219-926-1952	NO DOGS ALLOWED IN THE SWIMMING AREAS
Gary	Lake Street	219-885-7407	NO DOGS ALLOWED IN THE SWIMMING AREAS
	Marquette Park	219-885-7407	NO DOGS ALLOWED IN THE SWIMMING AREAS
	Wells Street	219-885-7407	NO DOGS ALLOWED IN THE SWIMMING AREAS
Michigan City	Washington Park	219-873-1506	NO DOGS ALLOWED ON BEACH OR PARK
Whiting	Whihala Beach County Park	219-659-7700	NO DOGS ALLOWED ON BEACH OR PARK

Illinois:

Beach Park	North Marina	847-746-1770	NO DOGS ALLOWED ON BEACH
	North Point	847-746-1770	NO DOGS ALLOWED ON BEACH
Chicago	City Beaches	312-742-3647	NO DOGS ALLOWED ON CHICAGO BEACHES
	Belmont Beach	312-742-3647	*THIS IS NOT AN OFFICIAL CHICAGO BEACH SO DOGS ARE ALLOWED ON THIS SMALL BEACH IN A FENCED AREA*

Evanston	Clark Street Beach	847-492-7082	NO DOGS ALLOWED ON BEACH
	Dog Beach	847-492-7082	*LICENSED AND VACCINATED DOGS ALLOWED ON THIS BEACH AT CHURCH STREET BUT A BEACH TOKEN IS REQUIRED FOR NON-RESIDENTS FROM MAY TO OCTOBER WHICH COSTS $80-$100*
	Lighthouse Beach	847-492-7082	NO DOGS ALLOWED ON BEACH
Lake Bluff	Sunrise Beach	847-283-0850	*DOGS ALLOWED IN SEASON WITH A BEACH PASS*
Lake Forest	Lake Forest Beach	847-615-4207	NO DOGS ALLOWED ON BEACH
Waukegan	Waukegan Municipal Beach	847-336-1044	NO DOGS ALLOWED ON BEACH
Wilmette	Gillson Park	847-256-9660	*NO DOGS ALLOWED IN PARK BUT CAN GO ON BEACH AT THE SOUTHERN TIP OF THE PARK BETWEEN THE PIER AND HARBOR MOUTH; NON-RESIDENT TOKEN REQUIRED IN SEASON AT COST OF $150*
Winnetka	Elder Beach	847-501-2040	*DOGS ARE ALLOWED ON BEACH SOUTH OF ELDER LANE ONLY; TOKENS REQUIRED IN-SEASON*
	Maple Beach	847-501-2040	NO DOGS ALLOWED ON BEACH
	Tower Beach	847-501-2040	NO DOGS ALLOWED ON BEACH
Zion	Illinois Beach State Park	847-662-4828	NO DOGS ALLOWED ON THE BEACH OR NATURE PRESERVE; CAN BE IN CAMPGROUND, PICNIC AREA AND ON TRAILS HOWEVER

Wisconsin - Southeast:

Cleveland	Hika Park	920-693-8256	NO DOGS ALLOWED ON BEACH
Kenosha	Alford Park	262-653-4080	NO DOGS ALLOWED ON BEACH
	Eichelman Beach	262-653-4080	NO DOGS ALLOWED ON BEACH
	Pennoyer Park	262-653-4080	NO DOGS ALLOWED ON BEACH
	Simmons Island Park	262-653-4080	NO DOGS ALLOWED ON BEACH
	Southport Park	262-653-4080	NO DOGS ALLOWED ON BEACH
Manitowoc	Red Arrow Park	920-683-4530	NO DOGS ALLOWED ON BEACH
Milwaukee	Bender Beach	414-257-6100	NO DOGS ALLOWED ON BEACH
	Bradford Beach	414-257-6100	NO DOGS ALLOWED ON BEACH
	Doctor's Park Beach	414-257-6100	NO DOGS ALLOWED ON BEACH
	Grant Beach	414-257-6100	NO DOGS ALLOWED ON BEACH
	McKinley Beach	414-257-6100	NO DOGS ALLOWED ON BEACH
	South Shore Beach	414-257-6100	NO DOGS ALLOWED ON BEACH
Racine	North Beach	262-636-9101	NO DOGS ALLOWED ON BEACH
Sheboygan	Kohler-Andrae State Park	920-451-4080	*NO DOGS ALLOWED ON SWIMMING BEACH BUT DOGS ARE ALLOWED ON THE BEACH AREA NORTH OF THE PARK NATURE CENTER*
	Sheboygan Lakefront	920-459-3366	NO DOGS ALLOWED ON BEACH
Two Rivers	Neshotah Beach	920-793-5592	NO DOGS ALLOWED ON BEACH
	Point Beach State Forest	920-794-7480	*LEASHED DOGS ALLOWED ON BEACH*

Wisconsin - Northeast:

Algoma	Crescent Beach	920-487-5203	NO DOGS ALLOWED ON BEACH OR ANY ALGOMA PARKS
Baileys Harbor	Anclam Park	920-839-2366	*LEASHED DOGS ALLOWED ON BEACH*
	Baileys Harbor County Park	920-839-2366	*LEASHED DOGS ALLOWED ON BEACH*
Egg Harbor	Egg Harbor Beach	920-743-6141	*LEASHED DOGS ALLOWED ON BEACH*
	Murphy Park	920-743-6141	*LEASHED DOGS ALLOWED ON BEACH*
Ellison Bay	Ellison Bay Beach	920-743-4456	*LEASHED DOGS ALLOWED ON BEACH*
	Newport State Park	920-854-2500	*DOGS CAN USE THE BEACH AT THE NORTH BEACH AT THE END OF EUROPE BAY ROAD. MUST BE LEASHED ON THE BEACH BUT CAN GO OFF LEASH IN WATER*
Ephraim	Ephraim Village Beach	920-854-5501	NO DOGS ALLOWED ON BEACH
Fish Creek	Fish Creek Beach	920-743-4456	*LEASHED DOGS ALLOWED ON BEACH*
	Nicolet Bay Beach	920-743-4456	*LEASHED DOGS ALLOWED ON BEACH*
	Peninsula State Park	920-868-3258	NO DOGS ALLOWED ON BEACH
Jacksonport	Lakeside Park	920-823-2314	NO DOGS ALLOWED ON BEACH
	Whitefish Dunes State Park	920-823-2400	*DOGS ALLOWED ON BEACH*
Sister Bay	Sister Bay Park	920-854-4118	*LEASHED DOGS ALLOWED ON BEACH*
Sturgeon Bay	Otumba Park	920-743-6246	NO DOGS ALLOWED ON BEACH
	Sunset Park	920-743-6246	NO DOGS ALLOWED ON BEACH
Washington	Gislason Public Beach	920-847-2522	*LEASHED DOGS ALLOWED ON BEACH*
	Percy Johnson Memorial County Park	920-847-2522	*LEASHED DOGS ALLOWED ON BEACH*
	Rock Island State Park	920-847-2235	NO DOGS ALLOWED ON BEACH
	Schoolhouse Beach	920-847-2522	*LEASHED DOGS ALLOWED ON BEACH*
	Sand Dune Beach	920-847-2522	*LEASHED DOGS ALLOWED ON BEACH*

LAKE HURON

Lake Huron features 3,827 miles of shoreline, characterized by shallow water and many sandy beaches. None of this will matter much to your dog, however, since the Lake Huron beaches in Michigan are mostly closed to him.

Michigan:

Alpena	Bay View Park	989-354-4181	NO DOGS ALLOWED ON BEACH
	Blair Street Park	989-354-4181	NO DOGS ALLOWED ON BEACH
	Mich-E-Kewis Beach	989-354-4181	NO DOGS ALLOWED ON BEACH
	Starlight Beach	989-354-4181	NO DOGS ALLOWED ON BEACH
	Thompson Park	989-354-4181	NO DOGS ALLOWED ON BEACH
Bay City	Bay City State Park	989-684-3020	NO DOGS ALLOWED ON BEACH
Caseville	Albert E. Sleepe State Park	989-856-4411	NO DOGS ALLOWED ON BEACH
Cheboygan	Cheboygan State Park	231-627-2811	NO DOGS ALLOWED ON BEACH

East Tawas	East Tawas City Park	800-558-2927	NO DOGS ALLOWED ON BEACH
	Tawas Point State Park	989-362-5041	NO DOGS ALLOWED ON BEACH
Harrisville	Harrisville State Park	989-724-5126	NO DOGS ALLOWED ON BEACH
Lakeport	Lakeport State Park	810-327-6224	NO DOGS ALLOWED ON BEACH
Lexington	Burtchville Township Park	810-359-2262	NO DOGS ALLOWED ON BEACH OR BREAKWALL
	Jeddo Road Beach	810-359-2262	NO DOGS ALLOWED ON BEACH OR BREAKWALL
	Keewahdin Road Beach	810-359-2262	NO DOGS ALLOWED ON BEACH OR BREAKWALL
	Krafft Road Beach	810-359-2262	NO DOGS ALLOWED ON BEACH OR BREAKWALL
	Metcalf Road Beach	810-359-2262	NO DOGS ALLOWED ON BEACH OR BREAKWALL
Macinac Island	Island Beaches	800-454-5227	*LEASHED DOGS ALLOWED ON ISLAND*
Mackinaw City	Mackinaw City Beach	800-666-0160	NO DOGS ALLOWED ON BEACH
Oscada	Oscada Beach	800-235-4625	NO DOGS ALLOWED ON BEACH
Port Austin	Port Crescent State Park	989-738-8863	NO DOGS ALLOWED ON BEACH
Port Huron	Lakeside Beach	810-739-7322	NO DOGS ALLOWED ON BEACH
	Lighthouse Park	810-984-9760	NO DOGS ALLOWED ON BEACH
Rogers City	P.H. Hoeft State Park	989-734-2543	NO DOGS ALLOWED ON BEACH
St. Ignace	Kiwanis Beach	906-643-8717	NO DOGS ALLOWED ON BEACH
Tawas	Tawas City Park	800-558-2927	NO DOGS ALLOWED ON BEACH

LAKE ERIE

Although its shores are the most densely populated of any of the Great Lakes, there is plenty of opportunity for a dog to explore Lake Erie. The smallest of the five lakes, Erie waters average only about 62 feet in depth and warm rapidly in the summer for happy dog paddling.

New York:

Blasdell	Woodlawn Beach State Park	716-826-1930	*NO DOGS ALLOWED ON BEACH DURING SUMMER OPERATING HOURS*
Brockton	Lake Erie State Park	716-792-9214	*LEASHED DOGS ALLOWED ON BEACH BUT NOT IN BATHING AREAS*
Dunkirk	Dunkirk Beach	716-366-3262	NO DOGS ALLOWED ON BEACH
	Point Gratiot Park	716-366-3262	*LEASHED DOGS ALLOWED ON BEACH EXCEPT DURING SUMMER FROM 12-6 IN LIFEGUARDED AREAS*
Evans	Bennett Beach	716-947-0970	NO DOGS ALLOWED ON BEACH
	Evans Town Park Beach	716-947-0970	NO DOGS ALLOWED ON BEACH
	Lake Erie Beach	716-947-0970	NO DOGS ALLOWED ON BEACH
	Wendt Beach	716-947-5660	NO DOGS ALLOWED ON BEACH

Irving	Evangola State Park	716-549-1802	*LEASHED DOGS ALLOWED ON BEACH BUT NOT IN BATHING AREAS*
Silver Creek	George Borrello Park	716-934-3240	*LEASHED DOGS ALLOWED ON BEACH*
Sunset Bay	Town Beach	716-934-3240	*LEASHED DOGS ALLOWED ON BEACH*
Westfield	Barcelona Beach	716-326-9243	*DOGS ALLOWED ON BEACH*

Pennsylvania:

Erie	Presque Isle State Park	814-833-7424	*DOGS ARE NOT ALLOWED IN SWIMMING AREAS, WHICH ARE THE SUPERVISED BEACHES*

Ohio:

Ashtabula	Walnut Beach	440-993-7164	*LEASHED DOGS ALLOWED ON BEACH*
Cleveland	Cleveland Lakefront Park	216-881-8141	NO DOGS ALLOWED ON BEACH
	Edgewater Park	216-881-8141	NO DOGS ALLOWED ON BEACH
	Euclid Beach	216-881-8141	NO DOGS ALLOWED ON BEACH
	Huntington Reserve	216-351-6300	NO DOGS ALLOWED ON BEACH
	Villa Angela	216-881-8141	NO DOGS ALLOWED ON BEACH
Fairport Harbor	Lakefront Park	440-639-9972	NO DOGS ALLOWED ON BEACH
Geneva	Geneva State Park	440-466-8400	NO DOGS ALLOWED ON BEACH
Huron	Lakefront Park	419-433-8487	*DOGS ALLOWED ON BEACH*
	Nickel Plate Beach	419-433-7244	*DOGS ALLOWED ON BEACH*
Lorain	Lakeside Landing	440-458-5121	*LEASHED DOGS ALLOWED ON BEACH*
Marblehead	East Harbor State Park	419-734-4424	*LEASHED DOGS ALLOWED ON DESIGNATED PARTS OF BEACH*
Mentor	Headlands Beach State Park	216-881-8141	NO DOGS ALLOWED ON BEACH
Oak Harbor	Crane Creek State Park	419-836-7758	NO DOGS ALLOWED ON BEACH
Oregon	Maumee Bay Park	419-836-7758	NO DOGS ALLOWED ON BEACH
Port Clinton	City Beach	419-732-2206	*LEASHED DOGS ALLOWED ON MAIN BEACH; EAST AND WEST SIDES DOGS MAY RUN FREE AND IN THE WATER*
Put-in-Bay	Kelleys Island State Park	419-797-4530	NO DOGS ALLOWED ON BEACH
	South Bass Island State Park	419-797-4530	NO DOGS ALLOWED ON BEACH
Vermilion	Main Street Beach	440-967-4477	*LEASHED DOGS ALLOWED ON BEACH*

Michigan:

Luna Pier	City Beach	734-242-3366	NO DOGS ALLOWED ON BEACH
Sterling	Sterling State Park	734-289-2715	NO DOGS ALLOWED ON BEACH

LAKE ONTARIO

Not many people have settled most of the hundreds of miles of shoreline of the south side of Lake Ontario in New York. There aren't many beaches and not many bans on dogs - as long as they don't try to swim with the humans.

New York:

Fair Haven	Fair Haven Beach State Park	315-947-5205	*LEASHED DOGS ALLOWED ON BEACH BUT NOT IN BATHING AREAS*
Hamlin	Hamlin Beach State Park	585-964-2462	*LEASHED DOGS ALLOWED ON BEACH BUT NOT IN BATHING AREAS*
Henderson	Southwick Beach State Park	315-846-5338	*LEASHED DOGS ALLOWED ON BEACH BUT NOT IN BATHING AREAS*
Pulaski	Selkirk Shores State Park	315-298-5737	*LEASHED DOGS ALLOWED ON BEACH BUT NOT IN BATHING AREAS*
Rochester	Ontario Beach Park	716-256-4950	NO DOGS ALLOWED ON BEACH OR IN PARK
Sackets Harbor	Westcott Beach State Park	315-646-2239	*LEASHED DOGS ALLOWED ON BEACH BUT NOT IN BATHING AREAS*
Sandy Creek	Sandy Island Beach	315-349-3451	NO DOGS ALLOWED ON BEACH
Texas	Mexico Point State Park	315-963-8216	*LEASHED DOGS ALLOWED ON BEACH BUT NOT IN BATHING AREAS*
Wilson	Wilson-Tuscarora State Park	716-751-6361	*LEASHED DOGS ALLOWED ON BEACH BUT NOT BOARDWALK*

Tips For Taking Your Dog To The Beach

🐾 The majority of dogs can swim and love it, but dogs entering the water for the first time should be tested; never throw a dog into the water. Start in shallow water and call your dog's name - or try to coax him in with a treat or toy. Always keep your dog within reach.

🐾 Another way to introduce your dog to the water is with a dog that already swims and is friendly with your dog. Let your dog follow his friend.

🐾 If your dog begins to doggie paddle with his front legs only, lift his hind legs and help him float. He should quickly catch on and will keep his back end up.

🐾 Swimming is a great form of exercise, but don't let your dog overdo it. He will be using new muscles and may tire quickly.

🐾 Be careful of strong tides that are hazardous for even the best swimmers.

🐾 Cool ocean water is tempting to your dog. Do not allow him to drink too much sea water. Salt in the water will make him sick. Salt and other minerals found in the ocean can damage your dog's coat so regular bathing is essential.

🐾 Check with a lifeguard for daily water conditions - dogs are easy targets for jellyfish and sea lice.

🐾 Dogs can get sunburned, especially short-haired dogs and ones with pink skin and white hair. Limit your dog's exposure when the sun is strong and apply sunblock to his ears and nose 30 minutes before going outside.

🐾 If your dog is out of shape, don't encourage him to run on the sand, which is strenuous exercise and a dog that is out of shape can easily pull a tendon or ligament.

A Dog Paddlers Guide to Keeping the Open Side Up
by Eren Howell
Owner of Dog Paddling Adventures

As a lifelong paddler and wilderness guide in Ontario, Canada, I was faced with a choice when my wife Kathryn and I got Jessie as a pup in 2000... either find a cheap dog sitter, or introduce Jessie to my passion and profession, the canoe. Really there was no choice, and since that day there have been too many amazing memories to name, to go along with a few bloopers for good measure!

Before thinking about taking your pup for a paddle, there are a few things you can do before hand to help make your experience a more positive one. First, a lifejacket may seem obvious for you to wear (as it should be), but it is also an important piece of equipment for Fido as well. It provides a huge margin of safety and security in case of a tip, emergency, or simply a long swim after a stick. It is also very helpful in the boat because of the large handle on its back which helps to control your pup while in the boat, as well as to help him in if he falls/jumps overboard. Lastly, when it is wet, it actually helps to keep your pup cool on a hot day by trapping moisture and keeping the sun away from him.

Another thing to remember is that a tired dog is a good dog, and a walk before you get into the boat is probably the best thing that you can do to ensure a good day for both of you. Although canoeing is great exercise for you, don't forget that your pup has been watching you pack up at home with excitement, sat patiently for a long car ride, and is in a new and exciting place. To then ask her to sit still like a good dog for an hour in the boat may be too much to ask. Let her roam off leash for a while and explore the shoreline, go for a nice long swim, or play fetch before trying to get out on the water.

When your first experience begins and you put your boat in the water, trying to convince your pup that jumping into this awkward vessel is a good thing is actually easier than one might expect. I have found over the years that 90% of the time your pooch will trust you and hop right in, especially if your have a couple of choice treats to offer him as an enticement. Generally, you should get the dog in first and then you can join her while your canoe partner stabilizes the canoe at the shoreline.

At this point it makes the most sense to take a few minutes to hang out, because Fido will want to explore all the corners of the canoe, and you should let him. A few practice ins and outs to let your pup realize it is quite easy sometimes helps the more anxious pups out as well. Now that everybody is familiar and cozy, you can launch you ship!

When canoeing with your dog, there are a few basic principles about paddling in general that will make your experience much more enjoyable (re: dry!). A low centre of gravity is a good thing. All of our boats are outfitted with kneepads on the hull floor in front of each seat, but a folded extra towel will work just fine. By keeping your bum on the seat and your knees on the ground, you have created three points of contact with your boat and are now as locked into your canoe as is possible without straps. This has increased the stability of your boat in an enormous way, and the first time your pup jumps onto the gunwales (the top 'rails' along the canoe), you will notice the difference. This stable position may become uncomfortable for your knees and/or ankles after awhile, so take calm moments to rest up and sit fully on the seat and stretch out your legs. This is also a perfect time to pass around some ju-jubes.

While on the water, there seem to be a couple of spots in the canoe which dogs tend to prefer hanging out in. Many dogs (our Jessie included) seem to enjoy riding in the bow (front) of the canoe. This area of the boat is quite narrow, but your pup may enjoy being close to the bow paddler, and even having her backside resting in between or on your legs. The other common space is right in front of the stern (rear) paddler, this time either on a soft clothes pack, or on the floor between your legs. Either one is good, but if your dog is big (80lbs+), the bow may become too crowded. As well, if your pup is this large and sitting up high on the packs, it will affect your stability. The floor is the best place for a large dog, at least until you become more comfortable.

Once you get out on the water, things generally begin to fall into place. The canoe might seem to your dog as a great big convertible, and she may want to lean over and take a few sips of water before simply enjoying the view. Make your first leg of the journey a reasonably short one, depending on the weather and your puppy's performance, perhaps no more than one hour. And for the first while until you are completely comfortable in the boat together it is also a good idea to stay reasonably close to shore, within a one minute paddle or so. If you were to experience a capsize (uncommon, but a paddling reality just the same) a one minute paddle becomes a 10 minute swim while towing the boat with you're your clothes on. Hopefully you have chosen to paddle with another boat, and they can retrieve your loose gear, paddles, and other waterproof floatables.

One of the final 'rules' of going dog paddling is this: 95% of all dumps occur within 5 feet of shore. This can happen because of two simple occurrences. One, the human element becomes careless and looses focus, and ends up wet right at the mucky shoreline. Either that, or the puppy factor becomes too excited about the prospect of running in the bush, peeing, and chasing squirrels, and clumsily jumps out and takes the relaxed paddler with them. Either way, be aware of this possibility as your journey comes to an end, and you will have fewer funny stories to tell, and more dry car rides home.

Kathryn, Eren, Kailey and Jessie Howell own and operate Dog Paddling Adventures where they bring people together who share a mutual interest in the wilderness and their pets. Their paddling, hiking and winter adventures allow for any dog lover to enjoy the outdoors (whether a beginner or experienced), while at the same time enjoying a bonding experience that is truly unique. Share the beauty of Ontario's finest lakes, riverways and provincial parks by contacting them at dogpaddlingadventures.com.

Index...

towns and cities appear in italics

featured parks with descriptions are in bold

UNITED STATES

Arizona

Canyon de Chelly National Monument	30
Catalina State Park	**113**
Encanto Park	**173**
Glen Canyon National Recreation Area	28
Grand Canyon National Park	26, **115**
Kaibib National Forest	**115**
Organ Pipe Cactus National Monument	32
Petrified Forest National Park	30, **111**
Phoenix	173
Saguaro National Park	30
South Mountain Park	**173**
Tucson Mountain Park	**114**

Arkansas

Hot Springs National Park	28, **95**

California

17-Mile Drive	**127**
Alabama Hills	**122**
Balboa Park	**177**
Big Sur	**129**
Carmel-by-the-Sea	**128**
Converse Basin	**120**
Death Valley National Park	121
Emerald Bay	**126**
Golden Gate Park	**178**
Golden Gate National Recreation Area	26, **178-179**
Griffith Park	**164**
Joshua Tree National Park	29
Lake Earl State Wildlife Area	**131**
Lassen Volcanic National Park	31
Lava Beds National Monument	33
Los Angeles	164
✓**Mission Trails Regional Park**	177
✓**Mt. Tallac**	**125**
Mt. Whitney	**121**
Nelder Grove	**119**
Pinnacles National Monument	33
Point Reyes National Seashore	22
Redding	**189-190**
Redwood National and State Parks	31, 130
San Diego	177
San Francisco	178
Santa Monica National Recreation Area	31, **164**
Sequoia & Kings Canyon National Park	28
Shasta Lake National Recreation Area	**190**
Smith River National Recreation Area	**131**
Tahoe Rim Trail	**123**
Tallac Historic Site	**125**
Whiskeytown National Recreation Area	30
Yosemite National Park	27, **118**

Colorado

Black Canyon of the Gunnison National Park	33, **104**
Boulder	102
Cherry Creek State Park	**159**
✓**City Park**	**159**
Curecanti National Recreation Area	29
Denver	159
Dinosaur National Monument	32
Grand Mesa National Forest	104
Great Sand Dunes National Monument	32
✓**Gunnison National Forest**	**104**
Mesa Verde National Park	31
✓**Pikes Peak**	**103**
Rocky Mountain National Park	27
Steamboat Springs	**191**
✓**Uncompahgre National Forest**	**104**

Delaware

Cape Henlopen State Park	**73**
Trap Pond State Park	**73**

District of Columbia

National Mall	**183**
Rock Creek Park	28, **183**

Florida

Amelia Earhart Park	**165**
Apalachicola National Forest	**79**
Canaveral National Seashore	29
Everglades National Park	29
Gulf Islands National Seashore	26
Miami	165
Oleta River State Park	**165**
St. Andrews State Park	**78**
Wakulla Springs State Park	**78**

Georgia

Atlanta	150
Grant Park	**150**
Chattahoochee River National Recreation Area	27, **150**
Chickamauga & Chattanooga National Military Park	30

Idaho

Craters of the Moon National Monument	33
✓**Hells Canyon National Recreation Area**	**108**
Ketchum	187
Lake Coeur d'Alene	**107**

Illinois

Chicago	154
✓**Grant Park**	**154**
✓**Ned Brown Preserve**	**154**

Indiana

✓**Indiana Dunes National Lakeshore**	28, **154**

Kentucky

Mammoth Cave National Park	28, **86**
Daniel Boone National Forest	**88**
Cumberland Gap National Historic Park	29, **139**

Louisiana
Audubon Park   169
Fontainebleau State Park   169
New Orleans   169

Maine
Acadia National Park   27, 48-49
Bar Harbor Shore Path   49
Baxter State Park   59
Camden Hills State Park   50
Quoddy Head State Park   50

Maryland
Antietam National Battlefield   143
Assateague Island National Seashore   72
Assateague Island State Park   72
Baltimore   151
Catoctin Mountain Park   31, 84-85
Chesapeake & Ohio National Historic Park   27, 138
Druid Hill Park   151
Gunpowder Falls State Park   151
Harpers Ferry National Historic Park   32, 142-143

Massachusetts
Blue Hill Reservation   152
Boston   152
Boston Common   152
Cape Cod National Seashore   26, 60
Martha's Vineyard   61
Mt. Greylock State Reservation   59
Nantucket Island   61
Walden Pond State Reservation   152

Michigan
Belle Isle Park   160
Detroit   160
Pictured Rocks National Lakeshore   31, 92
Sleeping Bear Dunes National Lakeshore   29, 93
Waterloo State Recreation Area   160

Minnesota
Fort Snelling State Park   167
Loring Park   167
Minneapolis   167
Voyageurs National Park   32

Mississippi
DeSoto National Forest   80
Gulf Islands National Seashore   26
Vicksburg National Military Park   29

Missouri
Forest Park   175
Kansas City   162
Loose Park   162
Mark Twain National Forest   96
Route 66 State Park   175
St. Louis   175
Weston Bend State Park   162

Montana
Gallatin National Forest   106
Glacier National Park   28
Little Bighorn Battlefield National Memorial   31

Nebraska
Scotts Bluff National Monument   33
Toadstool Geological Park   101

Nevada
Lake Mead National Recreation Area   26
Las Vegas   163
Mount Rose Wilderness   126
Prey Meadows/Skunk Harbor   124
Red Rock Canyon National Conservation Area   163
Sunset Park   163
Tahoe Rim Trail   123
Valley of Fire State Park   163
Winnemucca Lake   124

New Hampshire
Crawford Notch State Park   51
Franconia Notch State Park   52
Mount Washington   53

New Jersey
Delaware Water Gap National Recreation Area 26, 67
Gateway National Recreation Area: Sandy Hook 26, 69
Island Beach State Park   69
Morristown National Historic Park   32, 144
Sunset Beach   70
Wharton State Forest   70-71

New Mexico
Bandelier National Monument   32
Carlsbad Caverns National Park   31
White Sands National Monument   31, 112

New York
Adirondack Park   56
Burroughs Range   63
Central Park   170
Devil's Path   63-64
Fire Island National Seashore   30
Gateway National Recreation Area: Riis Park   26
Harriman Park   170
Kaaterskill Falls   64
Lake George   56-57
Lake Placid   58
Minnewaska State Park Preserve   66
New York City   170
Niagara Falls State Park   89-91
North-South Lake   65
Saratoga National Historic Park   33, 145

North Carolina

Blue Ridge Parkway	26, 81-82
Cape Hatteras National Seashore	27, 76
Cape Lookout National Seashore	30
Fort Raleigh National Historic Site	76
Guilford Courthouse National Military Park	30, 141
Jockey's Ridge State Park	77
Wright Brothers National Memorial	77

North Dakota

Theodore Roosevelt National Park	31

Ohio

Cincinnati	155
Cleveland	156
Columbus	157
Cuyahoga Valley National Park	27, 156
Eden Park	155
Edgewater Park	156
Goodale Park	157
Hocking Hills State Park	157
Mount Airy Forest	155

Oklahoma

Chickasaw National Recreation Area	28

Oregon

Crater Lake National Park	31
Hells Canyon National Recreation Area	108
Jacksonville	186
Rogue River National Forest	186

Pennsylvania

Delaware Water Gap National Recreation Area	26, 31
Fairmount Park	172
French Creek State Park	172
Gettysburg National Military Park	28, 140
Hartwood Acres	174
Medal of Honor Grove	147
Philadelphia	172
Pinnacle	147
Pittsburgh	174
Presque Isle State Park	91-92
Ricketts Glen State Park	68
Schenley Park	174
Valley Forge National Historic Park	29, 146-147
World's End State Park	68

Rhode Island

Cliff Walk	62

South Carolina

Battery/White Point Gardens	153
Charleston	153
Congaree Swamp National Monument	33
Cowpens National Battlefield	33
Hunting Island State Park	153
Kings Mountain National Military Park	32, 141

South Dakota

Badlands National Park	29
Centennial Trail	100
Custer State Park	98-99
Jewel Cave National Monument	33
Mickelson Trail	100
Mount Rushmore National Monument	28, 97
Spearfish Canyon	99-100
Wind Cave National Park	30, 99

Tennessee

Big South Fork National Recreation Area	29, 87
Chickamauga & Chattanooga National Military Park	30
Fort Donelson National Battlefield	32
Great Smoky Mountains National Park	26
Pickett State Park	87

Texas

Amistad National Recreation Area	29
Big Bend National Park	32
Brazos Bend State Park	161
Dallas	158
Fort Richardson State Historical Park	158
Guadalupe Mountains National Park	33
Houston	161
Lake Meredith National Recreation Area	29
Padre Island National Seashore	30
Sam Houston Park	161
White Rock Lake Park	158

Utah

Antelope Island State Park	176
Arches National Park	30
Bryce National Park	29
Cedar Breaks National Monument	30
Canyonlands National Park	32
Capitol Reef National Park	30
Colorado Riverway Recreation Area	188-189
Coral Pink Sand Dunes State Park	116-117
Dead Horse Point State Park	188
Dixie National Forest	116
Goblin Valley State Park	117
Liberty Park	176
Zion National Park	28

Vermont

Camel's Hump State Park	54
Smuggler's Notch	55
Stowe Recreation Path	55

Virginia

Back Bay National Wildlife Refuge	75
Blue Ridge Parkway	26, 81-82
Colonial National Historic Park	27
First Landing State Park	74
Fredericksburg & Spotsylvania National Military Park	31
Harpers Ferry National Historic Park	32, 142-143
Manassas National Battlefield	30
Petersburg National Battlefield	33
Shenandoah National Park	81

Washington

Mount Rainier National Park	29
✓Mount Si	180
North Cascades National Park	31
Olympic National Park	27
Olympic Peninsula	132
Ross Lake National Recreation Area	133
San Juan Island National Historic Park	32
Seattle	180
Seward Park	180

West Virginia

Spruce Knob-Seneca Rocks National Recreation Area	83
Harpers Ferry National Historic Park	32, 142-143

Wisconsin

Apostle Islands National Lakeshore	33
✓Granville Dog Park	166
Kettle Moraine State Forest	166
Milwaukee	166

Wyoming

Devil's Tower National Monument	31, 97
Grand Teton National Park	27
✓Flaming Gorge National Recreation Area	105
✓Yellowstone National Park	27, 105

CANADA

Alberta

Banff National Park	109
Fish Creek Provincial Park	134
Kananaskis Country	135
Jasper National Park	110
Nose Hill Park	134
Waterton National Park	134

British Columbia

✓Bodega Ridge	135
✓Cypress Provincial Park	182
East Sooke Provincial Park	135
Mount Robson Park	134
Ocean Boulevard - Victoria	135
Roche Cove Provincial Park	135
Starratt Wildlife Sanctuary	134
Stanley Park	182
Vancouver	182

Manitoba

✓Assinboine Park	184
Whiteshell Provincial Park	184
Winnipeg	184

New Brunswick

Bouctouche Eco-Heritage Trail System	45
Fundy National Park	44
Kouchibouguac National Park	44-45
Sugarloaf Provincial Park	47

Nova Scotia

Cape Breton Highlands National Park	42-43
Cape Chignecto Provincial Park	43
Cape Split	43

Ontario

Bronte Creek Provincial Park	181
✓High Park	181
✓Queen Victoria Park	89-91
Toronto	181

Prince Edward Island

Prince Edward Island National Park	45
North Cape	45

Quebec

Chemin de la Presqu'île	168
Forillon National Park	47
Gaspésie National Park	47
Gatineau Park	171
Mont-Royal Park	168
Montreal	168
Ottawa	171
Parliament Hill	171
Percé	47

Did we miss your favorite place to hike with your dog?

Let us know at www.hikewithyourdog.com and we'll share it with our readers.

You can order additional copies of
THE CANINE HIKER'S BIBLE
directly from the publisher

Send orders to:

THE CANINE HIKER'S BIBLE
PO BOX 467-X
MONTCHANIN DE 19710

Please enclose $19.95 for each book plus $3.00 for Shipping & Handling ($4.00 to Canada)

Name: _____

Address: _____

City/State/Zip: _____

Cruden Bay Books
PO Box 467
Montchanin, DE 19710
Phone: 302-999-8843
Fax: 302-326-0400
E-mail: crubay@earthlink.net
www.hikewithyourdog.com

Want to order THE CANINE HIKER'S BIBLE for your organization?
Quantity discounts available.